DATE DUE

May 13, 2010	
MAY 0 4 2011	
JUN 29 2011	
APR 2 0 2017	

WOMEN OF VALOR

WOMEN OF VALOR

The Rochambelles on the WWII Front

Ellen Hampton

First published in 2006 by
PALGRAVE MACMILLAN™
175 Fifth Avenue, New York, N.Y. 10010 and
Houndmills, Basingstoke, Hampshire, England RG21 6XS.
Companies and representatives throughout the world.

PALGRAVE MACMILLAN is the global academic imprint of the Palgrave
Macmillan division of St. Martin's Press, LLC and of Palgrave Macmillan
Ltd. Macmillan® is a registered trademark in the United States, United
Kingdom and other countries. Palgrave is a registered trademark in the
European Union and other countries.

ISBN-13: 978-1-4039-7143-2
ISBN-10: 1-4039-7143-9

Library of Congress Cataloging-in-Publication Data

Hampton, Ellen.
    Women of valor : the Rochambelles on the WWII front / Ellen Hampton.
       p.   cm.
    Includes bibliographical references and index.
    ISBN 1-4039-7143-9
    1. United States. Army. Rochambeau Group.   2. World War,
1939–1945—Participation, Female.   3. World War, 1939–1945—
Regimental histories—United States.   4. World War, 1939–1945—Medical
care—Europe, Western.   5. United States. Army—Medical personnel—
Biography.   6. United States. Army—Transport of sick and wounded.
I. Title.
D807.U6H36   2006
940.54'753—dc22
                                                                      2006043162

All photographs, except where indicated, are used with permission of the
Mémorial du Maréchal Leclerc de Hauteclocque et de la Libération de Paris-
Musée Jean Moulin and the City of Paris.

A catalogue record of the book is available from the British Library.

Design by Letra Libre

First edition: September 2006

10 9 8 7 6 5 4 3 2 1

Printed in the United States of America

*This book is dedicated to my dear uncles,
who brought home from World War II
stories to last a lifetime:*

*John H. Meyer †, Col.,
4th Infantry Division, 12th regiment,*

and

*Robert I. Gilbert, Lt.,
2nd Infantry Division, 38th Regiment.*

Contents

Acknowledgments

Many Rochambelles gave much of their time and opened up their personal archives in order to bring this story to light. Jacqueline ("Jacotte") Fournier, the eldest of the group, spent many hours remembering the tiniest details of her life as an ambulance driver sixty years ago. It wasn't easy, and it is a measure of her patience that it wasn't until nearly the end that she threw up her hands: "Ellen, you squeeze me like a lemon!" Jacqueline and her sister Suzanne were of invaluable assistance, as were Jacqueline's memoirs. Rosette Trinquet Peschaud and Marie-Thérèse Pezet Tarkoy also were kind enough to let me read and use material from letters they wrote home during the war. They answered far too many questions, and Rosette patiently explained the jokes in Toto's Rules when they were less than clear to me. Raymonde Jeanmougin took time out from her busy days at the Maison de la 2e DB to find books, dossiers, and phone numbers, and also to recount her own experiences. Danièle Heintz Clément and her husband Jacques were delightful hosts on several occasions, and Danièle's well-thought-out perspectives on the war experience were particularly helpful. Edith Schaller Vézy, a monument to energy and verve, provided stories, along with permission to use material from her memoir, which were vital to this book. Many thanks also are due Arlette Hautefeuille Ratard, Madeleine Collomb Bessières, Anne Hastings, Janine Bocquentin Barral, Christiane Petit, Laure de Breteuil, and Michette de Steinheil. I am grateful to the volunteers and staff of the Mémorial du Maréchal Leclerc de Hauteclocque et de la Libération de Paris, particularly Charles Pegelu de Rovin, whose patience and knowledge were unending. Any mistakes in the book are my own and despite their great assistance.

I also would like to thank my agent, Robert Shepard, whose unflagging support and enthusiasm for the Rochambelles has been an inspiration, and my editor at Palgrave Macmillan, Alessandra Bastagli, whose clear vision greatly improved the story's shape.

Many friends and family members have been steadfast in their certainty that the story of the Rochambelles would see the light of publication, and I appreciate their faith! I also would like to thank those whose comments and suggestions on the manuscript were most helpful: Christine Toomey, Nancy L. Green, Patricia Leroy, Charles Trueheart. Last but far from least, I would like to thank my husband and children for the time and energy they also gave to this project.

The Rochambelles

Florence Conrad (1886–1966). American. Served as a nurse in WWI; as an ambulance driver, cantine organizer, and mail transporter in 1939–40; and organized the Rochambeau Group in New York in 1943. Appointed major in the Free French Army and led the Rochambelles until August 1944.

Suzanne Torrès (1908–1977). French. Served as an ambulance driver in 1939–40, joined the Rochambeau Group in September 1943, and was appointed lieutenant in the Free French Army. Led the group until the German surrender, on May 8, 1945.

*Joined the group
in New York
in spring 1943
(the "archi-pures")*

Jacqueline Fournier (1910–). French. Served as an ambulance driver through the war, returning to civilian life in June 1945.

Germaine de Bray. French. Left the group in December 1943 to join the Free French organization in Algiers.

Laure de Breteuil (1924–). French. Worked in hospital at Rabat, Morocco, married a French soldier there, and remained behind when the Rochambeau Group moved on.

Elizabeth de Breteuil (1903–1962). French. Helped Florence Conrad get the group accepted into the Free French Army. Left the group in December 1943 to join the Free French organization in Algiers.

Anne de Bourbon-Parme (1923–). French. Left in December 1943 to join the Free French organization in Algiers.

Anne Ebrard Hastings (1924–). French, married to an American. Served as an ambulance driver through the German surrender in 1945.

Marianne Glaser (?–1971). Austrian. Trained as an ambulance driver, but served as a translator for the U.S. Army from landing in France in August 1944 until wounded in Paris later that month.

Jacqueline Lambert de Guise (?–1996). French. Served as a nurse until November 1944, then switched to ambulance driving, and continued on to Indochina.

Hélène Fabre. French. Served as a nurse through to the German surrender in May 1945.

Marie-Louise "You" Courou-Mangin (1917–2000). French. Married a French officer in Rabat in March 1944; left the group in August 1944 because of pregnancy.

Ena Bratianu (?–1995). Romanian. Served as a nurse through the end of the war.

Yvonne Barbier (1896–1987). French. Served as a nurse through the end of the war.

*Joined the group
in Morocco
(the "Moroccans")*

Raymonde Jeanmougin Brindjonc (1922–). French. Served as an ambulance driver through the European campaign.

Christiane Petit (1919–). French. Served as an ambulance driver through the German surrender.

Rosette Trinquet (1920–). French. Served as an ambulance driver through the German surrender and continued on to Indochina.

Arlette Hautefeuille (1919–). French. Served as an ambulance driver through September 1944. Married a French officer in Paris in August 1944 and quit because of pregnancy.

Madeleine Collomb (1917–). French. Served as an ambulance driver through the German surrender and continued on to Indochina.

Lucie Deplancke (?–1985). French. Served as an ambulance driver through November, and then returned to the group for Indochina.

Zizon Sicco (?–1974). French. Served as an ambulance driver through the German surrender.

Edith Schaller (1910–). French. Served as an ambulance driver through the German surrender and continued on to Indochina.

Michette de Steinheil (1920–). French. Served as an ambulance driver through the German surrender.

Anne-Marie Davion (1911–1984). French. Served as an ambulance driver through the German surrender.

Marguerite Benicourt Marchandeau (1920–). French. Served as an ambulance driver through November 1944.

Denise Colin (?–1980). French. Served as an ambulance driver through January 1945; left due to illness.

Crapette Demay (?–1987). French. Served as an ambulance driver through the German surrender and continued on to Indochina.

Kyra de Widstedt, Paulette Baudin, Antoinette Berger, Lucienne Berthelet, Liliane Walter, Biquette Ragache and **Geneviève Roland** also joined the group in Morocco and served through the European campaign. Paule Debelle and Yvonne Negre joined in Morocco, served through Europe, and continued on to Indochina.

*Joined the group
in England,
July 1944*

Polly Wordsmith (?–1965). American. Left the group in August 1944, severely wounded in the first week after landing in France.

Micheline Grimprel (1918–?). French. Disappeared in August 1944 in Normandy.

Ghislaine Bechmann. French. Served through the European campaign.

Christiane Portalier. French. Left the group in Normandy.

*Joined the group
in France*

Danièle Heintz (1922–). French. Joined the group outside Paris and served through the European campaign.

Marie-Thérèse Pezet (1913–). French. Joined the group in Paris and served through the European campaign.

Janine Bocquentin (1923–). French. Applied to the group in Paris, worked at Val de Grace hospital there until called to join the group in Lorraine, October 1944. Served through the European campaign and continued on to Indochina.

Michelle "Plumeau" Mirande (?–1989). French. Served through the European campaign and continued on to Indochina.

Tony Rostand (?–2001). French. Served through the European campaign.

Suzanne Evrard, Berthe Brunet, Nicole Mangini, Amicie Berne, Jeanne Challier, Hélène Langé, Geneviève Vaudoyer, and Yvette Verge also joined the group in France and served through the European campaign.

WOMEN OF VALOR

Introduction

Women in an armored division! General Leclerc had never heard of such a thing. But there was the offer: if he wanted 19 brand-new Dodge ambulances for his fledgling division, he would have to take the women drivers with them. The women had been organized in New York months before by a wealthy American widow, Florence Conrad. She had brought the ambulances and drivers to Morocco in October 1943 by U.S. military transport, and there she was at the other end of the telephone line, insisting that the women's ambulance group join Leclerc's Second Armored Division. In a moment of surprised silence, Leclerc calculated. Ambulances driven by women were better than no ambulances at all. He probably figured the women would cut and run at the first firefight, and then he could replace them with proper male drivers. He relented. He told Conrad that the women could join the division if they could get through the rigorous training there in Morocco.

Accepting women into an armored division was an iconoclastic move on Leclerc's part, but it fit perfectly in the context of his military strategy. Leclerc had a way of doing the unexpected, the audacious, the foolhardy—and making it look brilliant. Women certainly were unexpected in an armored division in 1943. At that time, women in France could not vote and had no more property rights than minors. They were not full-fledged citizens. Yet neither were they strangers to war.

Women have always been in the rocket's red glare, French women perhaps even more than those of other nations. Napoleon's *Grande Armée* counted scores of women working as food and goods suppliers, laundresses and prostitutes, as well as fighting soldiers, one of whom was decorated for bravery by Napoleon himself. Women stood fast at Austerlitz, retreated across the Berezina, and surely cried at Waterloo. The *Grande Armée*, which was the prototype of the modern army, also invented the ambulance, using horse-drawn wagons and removable stretchers.

The American Civil War saw service by an estimated six to seven hundred little-known women, many of them disguised as men, as well as those who served as food suppliers and nurses.[1] After the turn of the century, the U.S. Army and Navy established the Nurse Corps, a women's unit, and with the First World War, the navy, Marine Corps and Coast Guard recruited women auxiliaries. Auxiliaries could replace male workers in various support jobs, but would not have military status, and thus not have military pay or benefits. The army and navy eventually allowed women to join officially as nurses, and many worked in Belgium, Italy and England during World War I. By 1918, more than 30,000 women had served in the U.S. military.

Ambulance driving perhaps first took on a certain cachet in World War I. Both men and women volunteers—with the American Field Service, the Norton-Harjes group, and the American Red Cross—included many well-known writers who had physical exemptions from military service but wanted to see the war (Hemingway and Dos Passos, for example). Ivy League colleges and prep schools also raised money to buy ambulances and recruited drivers from their campuses, and society women from New York, London, and Paris vied to outdo each other with relief efforts and aid organizations. For example, some 25,000 American women went to France to work in the social services association founded in badly damaged Picardy by Anne Tracy Morgan, sister of banker J.P. Morgan Jr. Because the war had a static front, combat was localized and usually could be avoided. The risk of women volunteers being killed by shelling or shooting was reduced.

By World War II, the idea of women joining the war effort was promoted in the United States, and the number of participants grew to tenfold the number of those in World War I. Much of the female participation was on the civilian home front, as women filled positions vacated by men departing to become soldiers. Before the end of the war, 350,000 American women also served in the military, most of them in the United States but as nurses, communications workers and dieticians overseas as well. In June 1943, Congress agreed to incorporate the U.S. women's army auxiliary into the regular army, with pay and benefits, and coordination of command was one of the main arguments for doing so. The World War II Women's Auxiliary Corps (WAC) members, however, were forbidden to serve in combat areas. Many of them came under fire, and some ended up on the front lines, but none of them served regularly in combat units. Even the Army Nurse Corps, a women's group whose members did accompany invading combat forces on beachheads in Tunisia, Normandy, and Anzio, normally was assigned to hospitals behind the lines.

Today, women in the American armed forces are restricted from assignment to infantry, armored, or ground artillery battalions in an attempt to remove them from the risk of combat. Because recent wars have tended to urban terrain and guerrilla tactics, even support and maintenance units have ended up under intense fire, rendering the restriction fairly meaningless. Army officers quoted in the *Washington Post* in May 2005 said that they got around the policy by declaring women soldiers "attached in support of" a forbidden unit rather than "assigned" to it.[2] In 1943, General Leclerc pulled a similar end run around U.S. Army officials who refused to let the Rochambelles onto a military transport ship. "They're not women, they're ambulance drivers!" he snapped, and they were allowed to board with the rest of their division.

The Rochambelles weren't the only French women who joined the Second World War. Because France was occupied, participating in the armed forces of liberation required leaving the country, and some 3,500 women managed to do so and join the French auxiliary forces abroad. Thousands of others stayed home and braved great danger by working with the Resistance and the Maquis, groups who worked undercover in society or lived secretly in the brush (the maquis) to carry out guerrilla raids. Other women joined the medical corps of the French First Army, and served in the invasion of Italy and in the south of France as doctors, nurses and ambulance drivers. The army women's auxiliary counted 18,300 members in 1945. But the Rochambelles were the only women's group constituted as such and assigned to a combat unit on the European front. That is where they broke through a barrier and landed in a position of historical significance.

The Rochambelles did not join the Second Division to change the role of women in the military, or to upset preconceived ideas about women in combat. They did not describe themselves as early feminists or militants for women's rights. They joined the army because they wanted to help restore France to independence. They were young, idealistic, and they acted on patriotic instinct. At the same time, their generation was raised to be modest and discreet, not to trumpet their achievements. Almost to a woman, when asked about their war experiences, the Rochambelles insisted that they had done nothing the least bit interesting, and denied that they had anything to say that anyone would want to hear. Only three of the fifty-one women who eventually served in the group in Europe published a memoir.

Thus their story has been overlooked, swept aside in the flood of memoirs from the 2 million Allied men who served in the war. In terms of historical narrative, World War II was monopolized by men until recently, when several memoirs by U.S. Army nurses have been published. The women's memories of war are markedly different from the men's. First, as noncombatants, the Rochambelles were not distracted by having to fight the war itself. Their stories are not about strategy and armament, except for what it often did to the human body. Second, as women, they noticed and reported on aspects of the war that the men did not. They concerned themselves with relationships within the division and the relationship of their group to other division units. They also interacted more with the civilian population than did the soldiers. Civilians learned long ago to fear groups of men in uniform; women in uniform did not present the same threat.

The Rochambelles also were the forerunners of women in combat, and it is important to understand their experiences as a base line for what followed. The values and expectations of that "Greatest Generation" may have been different from those of young people today, but women soldiers in Iraq, for example, have faced many of the same problems and prejudices that were on the horizon sixty years ago. Not only have women soldiers fought in combat situations in Iraq, but they have had a second front in Washington with Congress debating whether they are strong enough to represent their country at war. As recently as the 2006 Defense Authorization Bill, a House Armed Services Committee amendment attempted to further restrict women's roles in the armed forces. French military women have faced their own bureaucratic battles, but in 1998 the government opened the door to women in all military posts except on navy submarines and in some special forces units. There is no interdiction against women in combat positions, and their deployment is decided by unit commanders rather than by the National Assembly.

The Rochambelles occupied an unusual situation in a war that was unique in history, and with a little bit of luck, will remain so. They were a minuscule part of the enormous Allied war machine assembled in the face of Adolf Hitler's 1940 invasion of Poland, Denmark, Norway, the Netherlands, Belgium, and eventually, France. The French army on its eastern front was quickly overrun and Paris was occupied by the Nazis on June 14, 1940. World War I hero Marshal Philippe Pétain took over the French government and bargained for a shared occupation of the country between the

Nazis and what became known as the Vichy government, because it set up in the spa town of Vichy. The surrender and occupation led thousands of French to try to escape the country, fleeing to French colonial territories in North Africa, or to England, or to North and South America. From their four corners of the world, these expatriates were gathered by General Charles de Gaulle to form the Free French, initially an opposition political group based in London, and then a provisional government-in-exile based in Algiers. The Free French established a military wing under then-Colonel Leclerc in 1942 which eventually was equipped by and attached to the U.S. Army as the French Second Armored Division. That is where the young women who became known as the Rochambelles landed and began their military careers.

The French Second Armored Division became home to soldiers from all over the world, including Germans come to fight against the Nazis. It was as varied a group as could be, and women were part of the complexity of the division. The liberation of Europe was not carried out single-handedly by the Americans, but by the British, Poles, Canadians, Australians, and the French as well. The American contribution was decisive and its leadership extraordinary, but America did not act alone.

After the war, during which the women had a certain freedom and great responsibility, many of the Rochambelles had trouble adjusting to civilian life. Some turned to work, some to family. All of them considered serving in the war the greatest gift they could have had; it laid a foundation of lifelong friendship among the women, and also with the male veterans, even those they met years later at Second Division reunions. The Rochambelles say they speak a language among themselves that defies outsider understanding. They share the bond of many veterans—that of having lived through the worst, and having done it well.

Rochambelle Anne Hastings summed up the experience: "War is something that you can't quite describe. It's bad and horrible but there were strong and good moments. It's a mixed bag." And afterwards, were colors a little flat, conversation a little trivial? Not for her. "I didn't find life dull at all after that, but it would have been difficult to find anything as exciting, except having babies."

Most of the Rochambelles were single, some were married, two had left their husbands, and one was a lesbian. In other words, they were an ordinary sample of women. What was extraordinary was their response to the times in which they lived: the chaos of the war opened a space for action that previously had been closed to women. It suddenly was possible to participate in changing the course of history, and they all felt very strongly that they should do so. Setting aside their personal comfort and security was the first, and perhaps most difficult, sacrifice. Once they were on their way, and once in the midst of war, they did what had to be done.

I first met the Rochambelles when Rosette Trinquet Peschaud, Raymonde Jeanmougin, and Jacqueline Fournier came to speak to the Paris chapter of the Daughters of the American Revolution, and their talk left me astounded. Like General Leclerc, I had never heard of women in a World War II armored division. I definitely had never heard of women on the front lines of World War II in Europe, and I had heard plenty of stories about the war. Two of my uncles served there, and their tales of combat and glory were regular family fare. But women weren't in those stories. Women waited at home, often for the worst.

The Rochambelles waited only for an opportunity. They stepped forward when their country needed them, overcame numerous obstacles to do so, and stood firm in the face of danger and adversity. We can all hope to find ourselves in their story.

CHAPTER ONE

A New York Exile

The idea of summer in the woods of Michigan, staying in a cabin on Cedar Lake, greatly appealed to Jacqueline Fournier. A fresh lake breeze and a simple way of living would be a fine alternative to the sophistication and culture that were her habits in Paris. She packed her water-skis and summer clothes, and boarded the luxury French Line flagship *Normandie* at Le Havre, unaware that she was stepping into a five-year exile. Like the rest of the world in that spring of 1939, Jacqueline did not see the shadow of hardship that lay ahead, or the twists in the path that eventually would lead her back home.

She was twenty-nine years old and single, with blue eyes, short, dark brown hair, and a quiet and serious manner. She had been working as secretary to a Paris-based writer, Jean Pellenc, for seven years. His wife was American, and in May 1939, they asked if she would join them for a four-month vacation in the States to help care for their three-year-old son. They were going to spend the summer at Cedar Lake and then visit Pittsburgh. Jacqueline had sailed the Adriatic and the Aegean; she had visited England and Switzerland, but crossing the Atlantic was a voyage of a larger order. That was further afield than she had ever been, and she was thrilled at the idea.

They docked in New York harbor after six days at sea. Skyscrapers! She had never seen them before. They seemed to tilt for a day or two after she got off the ship. They took a train to Detroit, and a car was waiting there to take them to Cedar Lake. She spent the summer swimming and playing tennis; the boat turned out to be not powerful enough to pull a skier. The family had given her a car to use, and she drove into a nearby town for an occasional milkshake. So much was new. The drugstore, the five-and-ten. Hamburgers. Cafeterias. The wooden cabin in Michigan was the antithesis of the elegant Paris apartment where she grew up, where meals were formal, education was strict and classical, and she and her two younger sisters were looked after by an English nanny. Even as a grown woman with a job, Jacqueline was tied to the rather rigid structure of bourgeois family life. But in the woods of Michigan, everything was easy, and she felt free and relaxed. It was as pleasant a summer as she could imagine.

The idyll was shattered in early September, with the news that France and Britain had declared war on Germany. Summer was over. They packed up and drove to Pittsburgh, where Madame Pellenc's family had a home. There was no question of going back to France, even if they could find trans-Atlantic transport, which had disappeared into the breach of the war. They would be stuck on the American side of the Atlantic for quite a while. None of them dreamed it would be five years.

The Pellencs offered lodging and support for as long as she liked, but Jacqueline felt that she should strike out on her own. She went to New York and took a room at a women's hotel on Madison Avenue, stayed for two weeks, and then found lodgings with a French family that had emigrated to the States before the war. In November, she found a job in the military mission of the French consulate, buying explosives and chemicals. She didn't know anything about the materiel, but at least it was work, and if the salary was low, she had enough to eat. Missing music, she started scrimping and saving her meager pay—based on the weakened franc—to buy a radio. She had looked at different models, and had her eye on one with a wooden cabinet, which she thought would have a nicer sound. On Christmas Eve, 1939, she went to the store and bought it, took it home, and set it next to the chimney to find the following morning, a Christmas gift to herself. It was a small, cold Christmas, but at least she could finally listen to the world. She waited until the after-Christmas sales to buy a winter coat. She had arrived with no warm clothes, and it was already below freezing.

In the spring of 1940, she and a Swiss office-mate called Ellen Gautier rented an apartment together, "furnished" with a sad couch and two twin beds, but a large empty living room that suited them perfectly. Their first move was to rent a baby-grand piano and put it in the center. They struck a deal: the first one home from work got an hour, not a minute more, on the piano, and then it was the other's turn. They had musician friends as well and got together to play as often as possible. Around Jacqueline, music was always in the air.

"I liked my life there," she said. She walked and walked the streets of the city, discovering it bit by bit. She ice-skated at Rockefeller Center and played tennis at a friend's apartment-house courts. She and Ellen met a fellow who took them water-skiing and horseback-riding. Sports and music kept her from missing her family too much, or feeling too alone in the big city. "I loved New York. I still have it under my soles," she said years later.

The Nazis invaded France in May 1940, and with the French surrender in June, the consulate in New York closed. Jacqueline had "government official" stamped on her passport because of her work there, and needed a civilian visa in order to find another job. It wasn't easy. She had to go to Montreal to apply for entry into the U.S. as a civilian. She managed to accomplish that by October 1940, and through friends, found work at Roger & Gallet, the cosmetics company. But back in New York at last, Jacqueline discovered that the French were now being treated as "enemy aliens" because of the Nazi occupation of their country and the Vichy government's collaboration. French friends with pleasure boats suddenly had their licenses confiscated; American friends in the U.S. military suddenly could no longer see them. Not only were the French in exile, they found themselves isolated socially and treated with mistrust.

The reports from France were bleak. She had no more news of her family, and could only imagine their suffering. In fact, her father's export business had been closed by the Nazis, leaving the family with no income. Her maternal grandfather, who had lived through the German occupation of France in 1870, and had lost both his sons in the First World War, now lost his family home in Herblay to Nazi occupation. Going to collect his sons' portraits and military medals from the house, he collapsed suddenly and died. Jacqueline's sister Suzanne said he died of chagrin, that he simply could not face a third round of tragedy. Many in France felt the same way. The devastation of the First World War was not yet in the past, but an enduring sorrow in every village, in nearly every family. The rapidity of the French surrender in 1940 was in large part due to this legacy of loss.

Jacqueline would not hear of her grandfather's death until four years later. Once the Nazis occupied France, she was cut off from her family. Through a friend in Lyon, they managed to send her a Red Cross postcard, limited to twelve words and censored by the Nazi authorities. It arrived in New York in August 1943, fourteen months after it was mailed. Jacqueline's reply on the back of the same card, again limited to twelve words, took eighteen months more to get back to Paris. In the end, she got there before it did.

In November 1942, the Allies invaded North Africa, the first step in staging an assault on the European continent. In response, the Nazis took over all of France, eliminating the previous demarcation line that had left the south of the country relatively undisturbed by the occupation. Now the fig leaf of Vichy's autonomy was removed, and the entire nation was being pressured to produce for the German war effort. Conditions slid from bad to worse, and there was nothing to be done about it from the other side of the Atlantic. Jacqueline began to feel trapped and helpless, far from those she loved, cut off from contact. Trying to overcome the feeling of despair, she searched for a way to contribute to the war effort. She had no training as a nurse, and did not want to spend three years in nursing school. She thought of learning to drive an ambulance, as many young women had done in the First World War. She signed up for a First Aid course, and then a U.S. Army Motor Mechanics' course. She was allowed to take the classes and learn the skills, but as a French citizen, she was barred from working with U.S. troops in military installations.

In *The New York Times*, Jacqueline read a few lines about a Colonel Leclerc, whose skeletal column of soldiers had wrested much of the French African empire over to the cause of the Free French, the political and military arm of those who opposed the Vichy collaboration and fought for an independent government. As the Allied campaign continued to roust the Germans from North Africa and the former French empire cast off its Vichy chains, the possibility of liberating France began to seem within reach.

Jacqueline was determined to be an active part of the cause. She wrote a letter to General Marie Béthouard, chief of the Free French mission in Washington, stating that she wished to serve as an ambulance driver in the Free French army. She carefully avoided saying she was a qualified and experienced bilingual secretary, looking to avoid the trap of office work. Nonetheless, Jacqueline received a response from his office saying that any volunteers would have to be men. Time and again, she hit nothing but brick walls, as the newspapers piled up in her apartment and another winter set in.

And then, like a bolt from the blue, a dynamic woman named Florence Conrad called her on the telephone. Conrad was organizing a women's ambulance corps to help the Free French. Was Jacqueline interested?

⤜⟶═◉◖═⟵⤛

Florence Conrad made a strong impression on everyone she met. She was tall, imposing, strong-willed, and attractive. She had been widowed twice and had a surfeit of both money and energy. She was American, and though she had been raised in France since childhood, she retained a strong American accent when speaking French. Her accent threw people off balance, and that, in turn, helped Conrad get what she wanted. Conrad was an artist of persuasion, a master of verbal combat.

She also had seen real combat. Conrad had married at age nineteen and had a daughter, but was widowed early. When the First World War began, she went to work as an army nurse, serving three kilometers behind the front at Saint Quentin. She was not alone; the war had interrupted France's *Belle Epoque*, and many French women of the upper classes devoted their energies to support services. Conrad was among the 25,000 American women who joined them, serving in France as ambulance drivers, nurses, and social workers.

"We were all young women of a time and a world of insouciance and gaiety," Conrad wrote in 1942. "We had relegated our riding skirts, our tennis rackets and evening gowns to the back of closets that wouldn't be reopened until after victory. Immaculate poplin blouses, hard on the skin, had replaced silks and muslins. We put our good will to the service of the doctors who battled death for the existence of young men wounded while fighting, our dancing and sporting partners themselves perhaps wounded as well, and cared for by still-inexperienced nurses like us."[1]

After the war, she married again and was widowed again. But her second husband, Henry Rosenfeld, left her wealthy. In the 1930s, the widowed Conrad lived in a mansion in Paris and led a very social life, until the next war awakened her sense of duty. She didn't wait for the hostilities to begin. From the declaration of war in September 1939 to the German invasion of May 1940—a period of tension and uncertainty that became known as the Phony War—Conrad was a whirlwind of action.

She had a car, a rare enough possession in Depression-era France, and a deep sense of the value of France's cultural treasures. Conrad badgered friends among the conservators at the Louvre until they agreed that she could help move precious artworks to safety, in case Paris was bombed. She was assigned to lead a convoy of trucks to a chateau in the countryside, carrying no less than the Venus de Milo and the Winged Victory of Samothrace.

The convoy departed smoothly and all was proceeding apace when, on the outskirts of Paris, Conrad spotted a line of army artillery trucks heading toward the city. The army had the right of way on all roads, but she was afraid that if the Louvre trucks were forced to the side, they would slide into the drainage ditch and the statues would be broken. She also knew that explaining to army drivers that art should take precedence over artillery would be a waste of breath. So she "lost control" of her car and came to a halt in front of the army column, which abruptly ground to a halt, and the Louvre trucks kept going forward. She played the incompetent woman driver the soldiers expected to see, and did not manage to get her car back in gear until after the Louvre trucks were safely by. "In war, as in love, anything goes," she noted.[2]

In that long pause between September 1939 and May 1940, the French believed their Maginot Line of eastern defenses would hold against the Germans. The army was installed along the line, ready to defend the nation, but no invasion came, and autumn turned to winter, winter to spring. An idle army is a depressed army, and Conrad found in the soldiers' lack of occupation an opportunity to get involved. She got permission from a friend at the Préfecture of Paris to drive to the restricted zone in the east, and went from general to general until she found one who allowed her to set up a canteen where off-duty soldiers could gather. She chose Etain as its location, as it was closest to the front, and wrote a check for 10,000 francs to get it going. She said she made her money back in a month. By December, an army general invited her to lunch to find out why her canteen worked so well and the army-run centers did not. As usual, Conrad wasted no words. Men didn't know how to look after men, she told the officer. The soldiers needed mothers, sisters, and friends to listen to them. Boredom was their biggest enemy of the moment: waiting for the worst to happen was more agonizing than living through it.

The general said the army wanted to avoid letting private efforts get in the way of the war as they had in World War I. The canteen would have to become part of the army system in order to continue, but Conrad would have a free hand to set up others and operate them as she liked. She opened another canteen at Verdun for Christmas, and then at Charny, calling in friends to help run them. One friend, Georgette Bentley Mott, arrived from Biarritz driving an ambulance full of gifts for the soldiers. Conrad learned that the soldiers were freezing at night because of a lack of blankets, that pneumonia had already killed several of them before the war had even started. She sent Mott to Paris with a blank check and told her to buy as many blankets as she could. When Mott questioned whether Conrad should spend her own money, Conrad replied that she was taking a page from Saint Theresa: "Do immediately what needs to be done, and find the means later."[3]

Conrad and her friends opened their sixth and last canteen at Aumetz, just across the Belgian border, in the spring. Shortly afterward, Conrad was named "godmother" to an army regiment—complete with a red, white, and blue ribbon and medal—and given the honorary rank of corporal by the new regimental commander and her old friend, Captain Gustave Gounouilhou, in civilian life the owner of the *Petite Gironde* newspaper in Bordeaux. The ceremony happened to take place square on the Maginot Line, northeast of Etain. Conrad laughed out loud when she realized it.

On May 3, 1940, an army doctor asked if Conrad could take care of the local Aumetz clinic when the offensive began, because he would be working on the front lines. She and her friend Françoise Verhille, who had helped set up the string of canteens, drove up there and spent the following nights with one ear cocked for the sound of artillery. It came soon enough. Conrad awoke on the night of May 11 to the doctor's wife pounding on her door with news that the long-awaited invasion had begun. She made sure her car, and those of her friends, had full tanks of gas, and then ran to the clinic.

The first soldier was carried in by his comrades, his intestines spilling out. She gave him a shot of morphine so that he would die peacefully, and then she went outside. She tripped over a body, a young man who'd been shot through the eye. There, in the chilling night, she felt the echo of the damage and destruction she had lived through twenty-five years before. Once again, eastern France would be soaked with the blood of a generation of young men. On the eve of the Debacle, as the French collapse came to be called, Florence Conrad knew she would see hell twice in a lifetime.

In the first night of fighting alone, 900 wounded arrived at the hospital in Sedan. Conrad decided that driving an ambulance would be more useful than assisting in a clinic, but the one ambulance at her disposal, a rattletrap Renault with no shock absorbers, starter, or brakes, wasn't going to go far. She sent Françoise Verhille to Paris with a blank check to buy another ambulance, meanwhile persuading the Defense Ministry and the newly organized Service Automobile Féminine Française, or S.A.F.F, to approve her addition to the corps. The Citroën car factory agreed to furnish some more ambulances, and Conrad was named liaison for ambulance services.[4] There were other ambulance groups, including the Assistance Sanitaire Automobile, with 180 women drivers and nurses working along the Maginot Line until June 1940, and several private individual efforts. During this hectic opening episode of the war in France, individuals wanted to help, and the army attempted to fit them into an official structure, but it was all happening far too quickly. The Germans were pouring across the Maginot Line as though it were made of sand rather than stone. On May 20 Saint Quentin fell, and on the following day Péronne was taken. In the first two weeks of the war, the S.A.F.F. lost six ambulances: three without trace, a fourth taken prisoner, a fifth blown up by a mine, and the sixth bombed in a convoy just behind Conrad and Verhille.

"I suppose we should be afraid," Verhille said flatly.

"Afraid of what?" Conrad asked. "Afraid to leave this dirty world, as rotten as it is? We've had more than our share of good times. Women like us don't want to die of old age, so why not here and now?"[5]

By early June, they were moving the wounded from treatment centers along the front to hospitals westward, as bombing and artillery attacks reached further into France. On the evening of June 11, the doctors left as well, and Conrad and Verhille worked through the night, the wounded coming in like a rising tide. In the morning they packed the ambulance full and left for Bar-le-Duc. From June 11 until June 19, when France surrendered to the Germans, just about everyone got up from the east and tried to get to the west. Soldiers struggled under the weight of seventy-pound packs on their backs, farmers drove livestock ahead of them, women brought babies into the world on wagons by the roadside, and children were separated from their families and lost. There was no food and no water. Conrad drove soldiers when she could, when the ambulance wasn't full of wounded. The retreat was a Boschian scene of panic and despair, the shuffling columns moving west one day, south another, chased by stories of German atrocities.

Conrad tried to cross the Moselle River westward but the bridge had been blown out. She drove her ambulance along the river and fell straight into a German roadblock. She surrendered immediately and showed her U.S. passport. The officer in charge told a soldier to accompany her to the nearest post. He got in, and she drove to the post, where the soldier got out, telling her to wait there. "What an idiot! Naturally I was not going to 'wait there,'"she wrote.[6] She took off into the deepening dusk, driving north along the river, hoping the bridge at Charmes was still intact. She found it, and started across, but halfway there she screamed and slammed on the brakes. The bridge had been blown out in the middle. German soldiers came running.

The Germans made her drive west to Dompaire, to a prisoners' camp. She was so tired when she arrived that she crawled onto a stretcher in the back of her ambulance and slept through the night. In the morning she found 20,000 French prisoners in the camp, plus two ambulances from her unit. She went to see the camp commander, and showed her U.S. passport again. She was free to leave: the Americans were not yet belligerents in the war. The commander allowed her to take some wounded prisoners to the hospital at Thaon, where the nuns showed her to a room and she slept straight through for twenty-four hours. She was exhausted.

But she wasn't going to give up. Conrad got an *Ausweis*, or official pass, from the German authorities to run the ambulance between Etain and Paris, transporting wounded French soldiers. She drove across Paris the night the surrender was signed, and there was not a French soul on the streets. She saw only four German guards.[7]

Back home in the chic Passy neighborhood of the 16th arrondissement, Conrad was unable to rest. She saw long lines of people outside the Red Cross offices: no one knew the fate of their relatives in the army. Were they still alive? Had they been taken prisoner? She had an idea, and drove east with it. She called on the German command staff and asked if she could collect mail from the prisoners. She designed a simple card that had no more than the address of the camp, a simple message: "Ma chérie, Je suis en bonne santé. Je t'embrasse. (My dear, I am in good health. I send a kiss.)" And the prisoner's signature. She began at Lunéville, where among the prisoners she found her honorary regimental commander Gustave Gounouilhou. She later would help him escape occupied France. She then visited camps at Baccarat and Sarrebourg. The prisoners could write nothing else, she had promised the German officials, otherwise the cards would all have to be read by a censor, and it would take weeks. The point was to let families know as soon as possible that their men were alive.

Returning to Paris with lists of prisoners and 100,000 cards in the ambulance, she panicked: how was she going to send them? The banks were closed, and she couldn't get 100,000 francs to buy stamps. She thought of the Red Cross, and the Office of Prisoners of War. Finally the American Red Cross took charge of distributing the cards, and Conrad worked with the director of the National Archives on a form for the soldiers to fill out with their personal and family information. In all, Conrad visited seventy prisoner-of-war camps and hospitals that summer, and brought back 100,000 pieces of mail each time. She took dried sausages and canned food with her to distribute to the prisoners, bringing the last twenty cans of American soup from the gourmet food store Hédiard at Place Madeleine. By the end of the summer, the Germans had put in place a formal system of communication, and she was no longer needed. She went back to Paris.

In September 1940, a friend at the U.S. embassy called with a warning. The Gestapo was spreading a rumor that she had carried weapons in her ambulance. She brushed it off. Then an army contact called and asked if she would help in sorting out wounded soldiers who could be released from hospitals from those who needed a longer stay. The Germans wanted to release them all where they were, and the French wanted to get the serious cases to Val de Grace Hospital in Paris. As an American, Conrad had room to move where the French did not. She went. While she was in Reims, Jeanne Krug of the champagne family came to ask for help. She had taken in 300 babies during the retreat but had trouble finding milk for them all. She said the cows were giving bad milk because of the chaos, and she could not find condensed milk. Conrad called the Civil Aid Services in Paris, who took charge of the babies' milk. Conrad took prisoner after prisoner from eastern hospitals to Paris, driving a thousand kilometers every few days.

In November 1940 she went south to Vichy, where government officials had retreated to maintain a French state during the German occupation. Conrad wanted to organize her financial affairs between France and the United States. She visited some old friends and had tea with Madame Pétain, wife of the marshal who was now head of government. The following month, on one of her runs to the prisoners' camps, she saw the men barefoot in the snow. She went back to Madame Pétain for help, and a committee was organized to make wooden clogs for them. Conrad also visited a British women's prison camp in Besançon. The women were sleeping on a concrete floor covered with a little straw, with no heating and few blankets. There were five toilets for 7,000 people. When they arrived, the camp was filthy and lice-infested. The women of Besançon had come and provided them with cleaning materials, but the prisoners were still freezing. Conrad promised to try to help. She took the visit as a personal warning as well: if the United States entered the war, she would be interned in similar quarters. For a woman of Conrad's energy, being sidelined from the action would be punishment even more difficult to endure than the tough conditions of a prisoner-of-war camp.

In early 1941, a French general with whom she was friendly asked her to go to the States and inform the Americans about the situation in France. But when she visited Marshal Philippe Pétain, the aging Vichy leader, he tried to dissuade her, denying the implications of "collaboration" with the Nazis. He preferred to think of it as a "barter system," he told her. Conrad believed that Pétain was wrong, and packed her bags for New York. "It took all of my courage to leave," she wrote.[8]

The expatriate French she found in New York had become bitterly divided into two camps: those who supported General Henri Giraud and his First Army and those loyal to General Charles de Gaulle and his Free French Forces. Giraud and his group represented conservative, traditional, Catholic France, while the Gaullists considered themselves the vanguard of a more inclusive future. The Lorraine Cross with two horizontal bars, symbol of the Gaullists, was viewed with outright hostility by the Giraud group. From 1940 to 1943 inter-French squabbling served as background static in the exile community, with each group vying for international recognition as the official Vichy opposition.

Conrad didn't pay much attention to the fuss. She knew that any gathering of the French would result in cultural fission, a search for differences between one another rather than the finding of common ground. With the Allied victory in North Africa in May 1943, Conrad sensed a larger battle in the offing. Naturally, she wanted to help, and she had both an idea and the connections to make it happen. Conrad decided to organize an ambulance corps, and to have it trained, equipped and prepared for duty when the battle to liberate France would begin. That wasn't all: Conrad wanted women to drive the ambulances, because that would free up the men for fighting. She remembered what her friend the general had said about keeping volunteer efforts from getting in the way of the war. If the women were part of the army, they would not be treated as meddling civilians. The greatest difficulty, she understood perfectly, would be getting a women's ambulance corps attached to an army. Conrad embraced the challenge, and the chance to contribute to her dearest cause: the liberation of France.

She started by asking for money from wealthy friends. Donating funds to buy ambulances was very much in fashion in New York at the time, and civic associations, high school clubs, and citizenship groups all were participating in the effort. Conrad soon had enough money to buy nineteen brand-new Dodge model WC 54 1.5-ton, four-wheel-drive ambulances. Built by the Wayne Society of Richmond, Indiana, and assembled on a Dodge chassis, they had no armor plating, no weapons, a double-clutch gearshift, and a top speed of eighty-five kilometers per hour.[9] Conrad then began recruiting drivers, spreading the word among friends and posting advertisements in the French departments of local universities.

From Bryn Mawr College came Germaine de Bray, a professor of French. From the Parsons School of Design came Laure de Breteuil and Anne de Bourbon-Parme, both eighteen-year-old art students. Laure's mother, Elisabeth de Breteuil, also signed up, partly to keep an eye on the two young women.

"All the boys around us were leaving for the army, the Americans to the American army, the French to England or Canada," Laure de Breteuil said in an interview. "It was natural. I was not going to just sit there and wait for things to happen." But the War Department had other ideas about women joining the war effort, and the Free French military leaders weren't supportive, either. "They weren't interested, and why should they be?" Laure said. Conrad and Elisabeth de Breteuil went several times to Washington to try to persuade Free French army officials that their project had merit.

Anne Ebrard Hastings was working on a doctorate in government at Harvard University at the time. She was born in Paris in 1915, and married an American, Wendell Hastings, in France in September 1940. They moved to Cambridge, Massachusetts, and when the United States entered the war, Wendell Hastings went into the Office of Secret Services (OSS), the forerunner of the CIA. Anne wanted to do something, but what? "I thought, one becomes a nurse," she said. "That's what happened to the other generation."

She took a nurses' training course, and then her husband saw Conrad's notice recruiting ambulance drivers for the Free French. He suggested she get a driver's license and see if she could join. "I thought I'd like the adventure, and I thought it'd be awful to stay in the States cozily, doing nothing. Before [the war] I loved mountain-climbing, rock-climbing really, the harder the better," she said. "I wanted to prove myself, and see if I would be afraid." She also was motivated by her family history. Her father had died in a German prison camp during the First World War.

Lulu Arpels, of the Van Cleef & Arpels jewelry family, and Marianne Glaser, an Austrian who was desperate for news of her adult daughter in France, signed up with Conrad's team. Jacqueline Lambert de Guise, a great beauty, and Hélène Fabre, heiress to a shipbuilding fortune, also joined, as did Marie-Louise (nicknamed "You" from childhood) Courou-Mangin, and several others. Jacqueline Fournier, finally escaping her secretarial destiny, signed on and became known as "Jacotte," to distinguish her from the other Jacqueline.

The women began ambulance training at the old World's Fair grounds in Flushing, Queens. Training included mechanics' courses, stripping down engines, repairing small breakdowns, and changing tires. They also took army-run medical training in first aid, which involved bandaging, giving shots, and taking temperatures, and they worked as volunteers in New York hospitals to broaden their medical knowledge. All the training was well thought-out and useful, and contributed to turning them into short-term health professionals.

The mechanics part was somewhat less successful. Laure de Breteuil was not the only one to be intimidated by the exercise of changing a truck tire. "I looked at one of the wheels and said 'If I have to change that damn thing I'll never be able to,'" she explained. "That's when I decided to be more on the nursing side of things." The women mastered cleaning out carburetor jets, which frequently jammed up and stalled the engine, replacing spark plugs and removing fan belts.

Conrad kept recruiting, signing up a dozen Americans, among them Leonora Lindsley, who had lived in Paris with her journalist parents before the war. Together, the women went to Saks Fifth Avenue and Brooks Brothers to order their gear: long underwear, a dress uniform, fatigues, a pale blue mechanics' jumpsuit they took to calling "the evening gown," and a heavy trenchcoat.

Conrad was as tireless in organizing her new corps as she had been in France in 1940, and in the Great War twenty-five years earlier, when she was a young nurse. But now she was fifty-seven years old, and conscious of the difference in age from her new charges, most of whom were in their early twenties. She knew she needed a younger subordinate officer to run the squad while she oversaw their duties and served as liaison with U.S. and French military authorities. A friend thought she knew the ideal candidate.

⊷⇒◯⊂⊷

Suzanne Rosambert Torrès was thirty-five years old, a smart, no-nonsense lawyer, born and raised in Paris, but fluent in English because her mother was American. She was separated from her husband, a well-known Paris lawyer and World War I veteran named Henri Torrès. When the new war was declared, Henri left France for New York, but Suzanne went straight to the eastern front, helping run one of the volunteer ambulance services and acting as liaison between the volunteers and the military command. She was devastated by the surrender, and when she heard Charles de Gaulle's June 18, 1940 speech urging the French to fight on from abroad, she was determined to do exactly that. But first she had to find a way out of the country. Meeting up with like-minded friends, she traveled to Bordeaux, and then looked for a route to the French colonies in North Africa.

They needed an airplane, and Torrès soon encountered none other than Antoine de Saint-Exupéry, the famed pilot and author of *The Little Prince*. Saint-Exupéry wasn't encouraging: his plane was not in good shape, he said, and the trip was dangerous. But Torrès brought a lawyer's powers of persuasion to every argument, a quality that had served her before and would serve her many times in the battles ahead. She convinced the legendary pilot and they got under way, stopping outside Perpignan, where the rest of the French air fleet had taken refuge. Some of the French pilots were ready to take the planes to the relative safety of North Africa, and joined Saint-Exupéry in flight. At the droning of the engines, Torrès fell into an exhausted sleep. Saint-Exupéry seemed annoyed that she could rest so deeply under such extreme conditions, and woke her several times to warn her of imminent danger. His fears notwithstanding, they landed at Oran, and went on to Algiers.[10]

With the Vichy authorities in Algiers enforcing Nazi dictates, the handful of Free French sympathizers found themselves in an atmosphere of conspiracy and intrigue, and nowhere was safe for very long. Torrès moved to Morocco and then Marseilles and then on to Spain, where she caught a ship to Brazil. She stayed with family in São Paulo for nine months, and then in February 1942 moved to New York. By then, the United States had joined the war, the number of de Gaulle followers was growing, and Torrès hoped she could find transport from New York to rejoin the Free French in North Africa.

In the meantime, Torrès found a job working in an art gallery in the afternoons and helping at the anti-Vichy *France Forever* newsletter offices in the morning. She said later that she felt like a wasp stuck in a jar, hitting against the glass. Then Gustave Gounouilhou, friend of both Conrad and Torrès, invited her to a cocktail reception at Conrad's home. Torrès did not want to go. She didn't know Conrad and had begun to hate the frivolity of the New York social scene. Fortunately, for once Torrès wasn't the only persuasive one. Gounouilhou insisted. As soon as she got inside the door, Conrad grabbed Torrès, sat her down on a couch, and began telling her about the group of women ambulance drivers she was organizing. She wanted Torrès to help run it. Torrès took one look at Conrad, with her halo of curly white hair, thick eyeglasses and intense manner, and dismissed everything she said as the obsession of a society dilettante. The woman could not be serious. Torrès left the party as soon as she could, without even saying goodbye.[11]

Still, the seed was planted. The idea that she could run a women's ambulance squad seemed far-fetched. It couldn't possibly work. Torrès called Gounouilhou. He was completely confident that if Florence Conrad intended to organize an ambulance squad, it would happen. Then Torrès started to complain that the other thirteen French recruits belonged to Giraud camp, while she was devotedly Gaullist. She couldn't possibly work with them. Florence Conrad raised a skeptical eyebrow to her objections and continued visiting her regularly at the art gallery.

By July 1943, however, as the war deepened and France suffered ever more under the Nazis, cracks in the French exile community began to heal. At the end of summer Torrès felt perhaps she could work with Conrad's squad, and worried that she was too late, that the group had been outfitted and was ready to go. She ran to Conrad's office suite to find the group packing, each of them trying to cram uniforms, boots, sleeping bags and cantines into army-style duffel bags. But Conrad knew her woman. She had ordered a complete uniform for Torrès, confident that she would come through in the end.

"It did not take me long to understand that for her, 'No' was not an answer and that she did not loosen her powerful jaw from her chosen prey,"

Torrès wrote.[12] It was the beginning of a friendship that would last for the rest of their lives, even though their relationship was never easy or smooth. They were strong personalities, strangers to compromise, and perhaps too much alike, but they both understood and embraced the mission that united them.

Before Torrès could swallow the news that she was already part of the group, her childhood friend Lulu Arpels jumped up and introduced her as "Toto," when no one had ever called her that before. It stuck, as a nom de guerre, and long after the war as well.

The group needed a name as well. Jacotte said they wanted a French name that would be easily recognized by Americans, but the obvious one, Lafayette, had been taken by the World War I aviation aces of the Escadrille Lafayette. The Comte de Rochambeau, Jean-Baptiste de Vimeur, who led French infantry troops to Yorktown in 1781 and helped win the American Revolution, was the second-best-known name. The women ambulance drivers would be called the Rochambeau Group.

As the group became officially recognized as part of the Free French forces, a result of hard lobbying by Conrad and Elisabeth de Breteuil, the dozen American women in it were refused permission by the State Department to serve under French command. They were deeply disappointed to be left behind. Leonora Lindsley signed up with the American Red Cross instead, and met up with the French near the end of the European campaign. Conrad got a personal exemption, and the fourteen remaining French members of the group prepared for departure. Commensurate with their positions in the group, Conrad sewed four stripes on her uniform, for major, and Torrès sewed on two stripes for lieutenant. Neither of them had permission from any military authority to do so. They promoted themselves, and kept their stripes all through the war.

The Rochambeau Group left Pennsylvania Station in early September 1943, fifteen women in smart khaki uniforms and overloaded duffel bags traveling by train to Washington, D.C., where they were met by French military officials. They spent two weeks in the women's quarters at Camp Patrick Henry, Virginia, where they started learning to march and encountered their first PX, or post exchange. There they acquired some GI-issue olive-drab fatigues for everyday work. Then they were taken to the Virginia coast and left on the quay with 6,000 American soldiers and a group of fifteen Women's Army Corps (WAC) members. All were waiting to board the

Pasteur, a French passenger liner given over to British command for war transport. It was a long wait. Red Cross volunteers served coffee and a jazz band played to entertain the troops. When the band learned there were French among them, they struck up "La Madelon" and "Sambre et Meuse," two old French standards. "It was so unexpected and so touching that we wanted to go thank them," Jacotte wrote.[13] But the crowd started moving toward the gangplanks. It was time to board.

Laure de Breteuil had a sudden twinge of doubt. "When we boarded the transport ship I said, 'What the hell am I doing here? We're a bunch of fools.'" Jacotte also had wrestled with doubt. Could she hold up under pressure? Was she too sensitive for this work? Before they left New York she had spent a night awake, pacing the floor, staring out the window, holding her conscience and her fortitude up for raw examination. "Would I have the necessary courage, the surface calm? Would I do what needed to be done, would my nerves be truly solid? And if I broke down? What shame, what contempt I would endure, having presumed to have strength, and be unable to face it! I would be crushed. . . . By the time dawn crept in, I had decided: if ever I was to be afraid, let it be that night and never again. With the grace of God, I would make it."[14]

On board the *Pasteur*, the men were given hammocks strung around the different decks, and slept in eight-hour shifts. For the women, several small cabins had been assembled into a dormitory with thirty bunks, from ceiling to floor, stacked so close together the women slid into them on their backs and could not turn over once in. They were ordered to wear their lifejackets at all times, and once a day they had an evacuation drill in case of attack. It was claustrophobic even for those who didn't know the meaning of the word. Jacotte exercised every day by climbing the stairs between the decks, and Toto found some bridge-playing officers on the upper deck. There was nothing to do, but the weather was calm and clear. The ship changed direction every seven minutes; Jacotte heard that it took a submarine seven minutes to fix a position and launch a torpedo.

Neither the women nor the men had any idea where they were going. One soldier thought maybe the women would be better informed, and asked Jacotte surreptitiously if she knew their destination. Eleven days later, they found out. A crowd had gathered on the quay to watch them disembark. They were in Casablanca.

CHAPTER TWO

Desert Transitions

An old Berber fishing port spun by cinema into a world capital of romance, the town was named Dar el-Beïda by the Arabs in the 1770s, translated by a Spanish shipping company into Casablanca. It is the largest city in Morocco, renowned for its Art Deco architecture, revered for its grandiose Hassan II Mosque, yet Casablanca will always be haunted by Humphrey Bogart and Ingrid Bergman. The film was released in 1943, and at the very moment Hollywood was celebrating its newest studio fiction, the Rochambeau Group was on the hard cold ground of reality, camping in an empty school in Casablanca. Things were not looking romantic in the least.

Morocco would be the beginning of a great many changes for those already in the Rochambeau Group, and for the dozen women who would join the group there. It was where all of them would shed their civilian identities and become soldiers, where they would learn to override their instinct for the individual and act as an entity. It also was where the women of the Rochambeau Group became known as "Rochambelles," a sobriquet that went beyond beauty to a hint of belonging, in their case, to the Second Armored Division. Changes were afoot in many and unimaginable ways.

Except for three or four among them who had friends or relatives in Casablanca, the women stayed at the school, sleeping on straw pallets in a first-floor classroom. Dinner was an unidentifiable murky soup, then lentils or split peas, and sometimes an orange. They had managed to cross the Atlantic, no small feat in wartime, but they had no assignment; they belonged to no one's army as yet. Still, they were in good spirits. When Jacotte saw the morning raising of the French flag outside the school, her heart soared. She was on the right track at last.

Around 9 o'clock on their first morning there, Anne Hastings stuck her head out of her sleeping bag and picked up an imaginary telephone from an imaginary nightstand, and ordered herself a luxury room-service breakfast: "Scrambled eggs and bacon, fruit juice, pancakes with maple syrup, toast and marmalade, cereal with cream and a large of pot of coffee," she said, "and make it snappy!" They all burst out laughing. There wasn't going to be any breakfast and probably not any lunch either. Conrad and Toto had gone to Algiers to find an army unit for the Rochambeau Group, and the women's mission was to wait at the school. Murky soup and lentils were delivered every evening by the Free French army.

With nothing better to do, they toured Casablanca. It was Jacotte's first time in Morocco and the first visit to the African continent for most of the women. Morocco had become a French protectorate by treaty in 1912, with a Moroccan sultan and French military governor ruling in tandem. It was, and though independent since 1956, remains, largely French-speaking in the cities. It also was full of French and other Europeans who had fled the Nazi occupation. Women walking around the city in a military uniform caused no reaction from the locals, but they nonetheless avoided the medina, the old Arab labyrinth of market stalls and houses, if they were alone.

One day, Anne and Jacqueline hitchhiked to Rabat, the nation's capital sixty kilometers north, and said it was easy, that all the traffic was military. Jacotte and Hélène decided to go as well, although neither of them would ever have considered hitchhiking in the past. For a solid hour, not one vehicle passed. They were about to give up when a Jeep stopped and a general got out and asked where they were going. They told him and he apologized, he wasn't going that far. They were both blushing with embarrassment and apologizing as he drove off, feeling as though they'd somehow been caught at risqué behavior. Then a Red Cross staff car picked them up, and offered to bring them back to Casablanca that afternoon. Jacotte and Hélène walked the ancient stone ramparts along the coast and sipped mint tea, savoring the freedom of being in new territory.

The women had met some U.S. Army officers on the ship over, and were invited by them to dine at their mess hall from time to time. The men were happy to socialize with Jacotte and Lulu Arpels and the other English-speaking women, and the women were pleased to avoid the murky soup and lentils. But after one dinner, Jacotte awoke with a fever and diarrhea, a serious case of food poisoning. Three days later she was still sick, and so weak she could hardly walk. Some of her dinner partners also had fallen ill with food poisoning, but none as severely as she. Lulu came to the school with a pony cart and took her to the friends' house where she'd been staying, a

room with a real bed and sheets, and called one of the officers, a major-doc-
tor in a U.S. medical battalion. He brought medicine, and after three or
four days she felt better. The major took her out for walks and bicycle rides
to build her strength back up, and found her a family home with an extra
room to stay in while she recovered. She stayed a week or so, and then one
of the women came to get her in an ambulance, as the group had been
moved to Rabat while Jacotte was recovering.

Conrad and Toto had found a job for the Rochambeau Group, a plum
assignment with the Free French forces. Conrad had gone to see Free
French General Marie-Pierre Koenig, whom she knew from her work in
the early part of the war. Koenig became a hero in his own right in June
1942, when he led his French troops, outnumbered and surrounded by
German and Italian armies, to safety at Bir Hakeim (Libya). Now Koenig
was in Algiers, organizing the North Africa veterans into an army fit to invade the European continent. Conrad described their unit and equipment
and asked for an assignment. Koenig said he could try the Fifth Division,
part of General Jean-Marie de Lattre de Tassigny's First Army, or the Second Division, being assembled under General Leclerc. Conrad didn't hesitate. She wanted to serve under Leclerc.

Leclerc was forty-one years old in 1943, a career Army officer who had
built a solid reputation in the North Africa campaigns across Chad, Libya,
and Tunisia. He had been twice captured and had twice escaped the Germans in the French Debacle of June 1940, and then slipped into Africa to
bring Cameroon to the Free French side as early as August 1940. From
abroad, de Gaulle appointed him military commander of Chad territory,
and he spent the next three years quilting together an army from the remains of French colonial troops, Foreign Legionnaires, Republican veterans of the Spanish Civil War, and civilian escapees from Vichy France. With
the Allied victory in 1943 in Tunisia, North Africa became a staging ground
for an assault on the European mainland.

De Gaulle decided that Leclerc's troops would form an armored division based on the American model, with four regiments of tanks and artillery, one antitank company, one light artillery company, one transport
squadron, two engineering companies, two heavy mechanics companies and
one medical battalion. The newly formed Second Armored Division,
known in French as the 2e DB (Deuxième Division Blindée), would be
equipped, supplied and attached to the U.S. Army.

Leclerc was the nom de guerre of Philippe de Hauteclocque, taken to protect his wife and five of their six children, who remained at their Picardy chateau during the Nazi occupation (his eldest son joined the division). Leclerc was a natural leader, the kind of officer who demanded as much from himself as from his troops, who was visible at the front lines, seeming to be everywhere at once, pointing the way forward with his ever-present walking stick. He didn't smoke, didn't drink, and was so thin the soldiers wondered if he even ate. He had a fearsome temper and a modicum of patience, and was so respected that to this day his memory can bring tears to the eyes of gray-haired veterans. "There are certainly differences between General Leclerc and the good Lord above, but I would have trouble naming them," one veteran who worked closely with him quipped. Leclerc was also fiercely independent. When asked the secret of his success in 1943, he snapped: "The absence of the telephone and the distance from all superior authority."[1]

Leclerc did not bother with verbosity, and the comments he did make tended to sting. In an October 1943 speech to his officers in Morocco, Leclerc laid out the political scene as he saw it: "Before 1939, one part of the leadership class brought the country to the abyss into which it has fallen. Since 1940, another part has missed the opportunity of reinforcement from the Empire, thus directly or indirectly assisting Germany's game. When tomorrow you meet a notable, you can always ask yourself if he was an incompetent before 1940, or a coward since."[2]

Leclerc, naturally, had his enemies. The elder General Henri Giraud was quoted as saying, with a sneer, "For me, General Leclerc will always remain Captain de Hauteclocque." Some veteran army officers refused to serve under him because of his young age. Those who did, however, did so with absolute loyalty. And Conrad, with her unerring instinct for people, wanted the Rochambeau Group in Leclerc's division. "He had been victorious everywhere, he was terrific," Jacotte said in an interview. "He already had a sort of halo by that time."

2nd Armored Division insignia

Still, it was a gamble. The Fifth Division was slated to invade Italy, while plans for the Second Armored Division were vague and ill defined. If the Rochambeau Group went with the Second Division and it was not assigned to duty in Europe, they would be stuck. "We didn't know if he would take us from Morocco or anywhere," Jacotte said. "We were afraid we wouldn't get to go."

With Conrad and Toto in his office, Koenig called Leclerc. Leclerc thought he had misheard. Women? In an armored division? Never heard of it. Leclerc said he'd take the ambulances, but he did not want any women drivers. Conrad said he couldn't have the ambulances without the drivers. Leclerc balked. Women in his division! Conrad held firm. Leclerc relented, temporarily. He would see how the women did in training and maneuvers in North Africa. If they held up, he would accept them in the division. "Florence pulled off a master coup," Jacotte recalled. "For her, nothing was impossible. It was a waste of time to tell her no."

Leclerc did not want women in the division because he feared they would cause dissension and rivalry between the men soldiers, according to Guy Chauliac, a colonial troops doctor who joined Leclerc in 1940 in Chad. Chauliac, a lieutenant at the time, commanded the Thirteenth Medical Battalion's Third Company. The medical battalion counted some 450 members, 104 of whom were doctors, divided into three companies. Ambulance drivers were split among the three companies: the Rochambeau Group in one; a group of male British Quakers, conscientious objectors, in another, and some Navy auxiliary members (including eight or nine women called "Marinettes") in a third.

"We thought the women were going to cause trouble," Chauliac said in an interview. "When you put 300 men with 10 women, there will be trouble. There was hostility towards them on the part of the brass. Leclerc was afraid they would complicate things." Other male members of the medical battalion were less concerned. François Jacob was a twenty-year-old Parisian with two years of medical school behind him in 1940, when he left France to join the Gaullist forces. He got on a ship sailing to try to liberate Dakar with members of the rough-hewn Foreign Legion, and there were a few women volunteer nurses aboard. The Legionnaires got a little too interested in the women, and the captain had to post a sentinel with a bayonet outside their door. The attack on Dakar failed, but so did the Legionnaires. Three years later Jacob was working in the division hospital at Rabat as an auxiliary doctor. "By the time the Rochambelles arrived, things had become a little more civilized," Jacob recalled.

Jacob said the military command may have been opposed to women in the division, but the doctors by and large didn't mind. "We were sort of happy to see some women," he said in an interview. And the doctors soon asked for a regular group of six nurses to be assigned to the hospital instead of to drive ambulances. The women had made themselves not only useful, but necessary.

Conrad promised Leclerc that the women would not be trouble, and she sat on them like a mother hen to make sure they weren't. Conrad enforced a strict formality of military manners, requiring snappy salutes to superior officers and correct uniform appearance, as well as the proper use of rank in verbal address. The women, like all civilians new to the military, had to learn the ranking code of stripes, stars, and epaulets, and which color beret signified which unit (red for Spahis, black for the 501st Tank Regiment). Conrad would not allow the women to socialize with enlisted men—only with officers—and then only under supervision.

The Rochambeau Group was assigned to the medical battalion's First Company, and found their commander, Captain Charles Ceccaldi, even more exacting than Conrad. Ceccaldi, whom Toto nicknamed "The Corsican" for his family origins, sat in wait for the women to step out of line. Ceccaldi was not pleased to have landed the women's group in his company, and was tougher on them than on the men.

The Rochambeau Group moved onto a houseboat at the formerly chic Nautical Club on the Bou Regreg River at Rabat, their ambulances lined up neatly on the quay. The houseboat had one sink, holes in the floor, and rats in the hull. It was neither clean nor comfortable, but the women looked back on their time there with fondness. Jacotte used to gaze at the harbor leading to the Atlantic Ocean and at the Moroccans, with their measured pace and white robes against the cerulean sky, and gauge the distance from New York, with its bustle and hurry and gray steel and brownstone. She had changed continents, shifted latitudes, and most of all, entered a whole new mental landscape.

Obey. Follow. Obey. Military life, for an independent, intellectually gifted woman such as Jacotte, wasn't easy. No one told her anything: information was compartmentalized and guarded, given out only in tiny meaningless bits. She had to get used to doing what she was told without asking questions, and it went against her grain. "Obedience, then: do what you're told to do, and don't ask why." She faked it until she could do it without flinching.

Not everyone in the group was able to adjust, and at the end of 1943 some of the women left. Elisabeth de Breteuil, Anne de Bourbon-Parme, and Germaine de Bray went to Algiers to work for the Free French government, convinced that the Rochambeau Group would never leave North Africa. Their departure brought the group's ranks down to eleven, plus Conrad and Toto. They were Jacotte's best friends from New York, and they tried to persuade her to join them, but she refused, holding tight to the idea that she would be of some use in liberating France if she stayed. She missed their company, but Laure de Breteuil stayed behind to work at the military hospital in Rabat, and they became good friends despite their difference in ages. At eighteen, Laure was the youngest of the Rochambeau Group, and Jacotte, at thirty-three, one of the oldest. Both came from families of culture and wealth, both had had their cozily assured futures hijacked by the war, and both women were enjoying it thoroughly. Laure was as tiny as Jacotte, with an elfin smile and gravelly, Lauren Bacall voice.

Laure was among the six women assigned to nursing duty at the hospital run by the Thirteenth Medical Battalion when they arrived. The hospital was installed in the former music conservatory, with segregated wards for black and white patients. It was support work with few supplies, no more than a few bedsheets reserved for the most feverish of patients. "Changing" a bed meant shaking out a straw pallet.

"It only had the name 'hospital,'" Laure said. They treated victims of car accidents, people with malaria and other illnesses, and then men started arriving in bad shape from prison camps in Spain. (Many of the French who escaped over the Pyrénées were imprisoned in Spain for as long as six months before being released to Morocco.) Laure's passion was art, but the army needed nurses, not artists. She was transferred at one point to the hospital's sterilization service, where they used fuel stoves that reeked when they worked and blew up when they didn't. "They used to call me the witch. I'd come out black in the face and screaming," she said. But the stoves also provided hot water for the British Quakers' tea, and in exchange, they helped her with the sterilizing. And she preferred the sterilization service to the venereal disease ward, where Ceccaldi sent Hélène Fabre, one of the younger and more innocent of the group.

Along with nurses, the Rochambeau Group had brought some basic medical supplies from the States, such as thermometers, pencils and charts, cotton, gauze, bandages, and compresses. Their contribution to the hospital was badly needed.

"The result was positive," Jacotte wrote in her memoirs. "Florence won the first round: the doctors, after one week, had to admit that our presence was not as nefarious as they had wanted to believe." Nonetheless, when Laure had a friend in Tangiers send a package of syringes and thermometers to the hospital, Ceccaldi lectured her angrily for having gone outside military procedures of procurement.

At this point, there were not enough women to provide a team of two drivers for each of the nineteen ambulances. Conrad began spreading the word among French families living in Morocco that the group was looking for more members, and sending her drivers to transport recovering soldiers to family homes instead of the hospital: it was good driving practice for the women, and an effective way to look for new recruits.

Toto went as far as Algiers looking for candidates, and ran into Antoine de Saint-Exupéry again there, shortly before his fatal last flight. She had trouble finding candidates for the group because the Auxiliaires Féminines de l'Armée de Terre (the unfortunately named A.F.A.T.), or women's auxiliary army corps, also was recruiting. The women's auxiliaries took support jobs, often secretarial, and were not given military status. They were civilians hired by the army, and were not likely to see any fighting. Being an ambulance driver would pose much more risk.

When Toto returned from Algiers, she found Raymonde Jeanmougin Brindjonc waiting for her on the houseboat. Raymonde was married. Her husband was working in England as an airplane mechanic with the Free French, and their five-month-old baby had fallen ill and died in July. She then signed up for the army nursing squad in Algiers, and had gotten orders to join General de Lattre's First Army, ready to depart for Italy, but she refused to go: she was a de Gaulle supporter and she wanted to go with Leclerc. Her shocked colonel explained that in the army one did not choose one's assignment, and sent her home. She cried for ten days, sure that she had ruined her chances of helping with the war, and then got new orders. She was afraid to open them, but when she did, they were for Leclerc's division, the Thirteenth Medical Battalion. She got on a train that took five days to get from Algiers to Rabat, the only woman on a train full of soldiers. She walked five or six kilometers to Temara, where the division was bivouacked south of Rabat, only to be told that the medical battalion was in the city. A sympathetic soldier gave her a ride back in his Jeep, and she finally found the houseboat.

Raymonde, by her own account, was shy but stubborn. She was twenty-one years old, with enormous blue eyes and a cloud of dark hair, soft-spoken and self-effacing. When Toto arrived, Raymonde said simply that she had been transferred to the Rochambeau Group. Toto, irritable as ever, told her she could go back where she came from, because the Rochambeau Group picked its own recruits. Raymonde recounted her travels to get to the houseboat and said she wasn't going anywhere. Toto relented. They ended up being ambulance partners and friends. Raymonde developed great respect for Toto and didn't mind her blasts of fury. "She was terrific," Raymonde said. Her temper was natural and not an affectation or manipulation. "She was not afraid of anything. She was commanding, intelligent, she argued with everyone, she was always at ease."

Toto was not universally loved, however. Others described her as difficult, ambitious and petty. Laure de Breteuil, who, along with her mother, was a target of Toto's disdain, said she had nothing to say about Toto. In her memoir, Toto wrote that Elisabeth de Breteuil had had her army overcoat lined with mink, which Laure termed "pure fiction." While in Rabat, Laure married a cousin who had also joined the division, Jean de Breteuil. She chose to stay in Rabat with him when the Rochambeau Group moved on. "Suzanne Torrès was so glad to get rid of me," Laure said. She found a job in the social services branch of the army, teaching new recruits to drive. "It was terrifying. Some of those girls didn't know left from right." Later she became pregnant and took maternity leave from the army. She and her husband lived in a hotel in Rabat that had been requisitioned by the U.S. military.

More recruits from Morocco, having heard about the women's unit, started coming in, curious to see if they could join. They were of varying ages and backgrounds, and were in Morocco for different reasons, but they had in common a certain boredom with their current horizons, and a strong desire to help with the war effort.

Christiane Petit's father, a French army colonel who had been in charge of Port Lyautey (now Kénitra), when Allied troops landed there in 1942, met Florence Conrad in February 1944 and suggested that his daughter sign up. She had a driver's license, if no medical training, and she was eager to join the war effort. She was twenty-four years old, the eldest of nine children, and tired of working in a women's support center at Meknès. Jacotte and "You" Courou-Mangin went to pick her up two days later. As the daughter of an army officer, Christiane did not feel as uncomfortable in a military setting as did some of the other women. She knew many of the younger division officers; they had been students at the St. Cyr military academy when her father taught there. "We learned to dance together," she recalled. Christiane, a devout Catholic, was so intensely spiritual that Toto called her "the Mystic." In her clear blue eyes was an unwavering religious passion, and she got down on her knees every night on the houseboat to pray.

Rosette Trinquet had moved to Morocco with her parents in 1938, at the age of eighteen, and got her driver's license in 1940. In Morocco she drove a pickup truck that ran on "*gazogène*," gas produced by burning charcoal. She noted that at her age, she wouldn't have been allowed to take a train from Paris to Rouen unchaperoned, but her parents thought it would be fine for her to drive an ambulance in the war. Circumstances were introducing contradictions into previously indelible lines of social etiquette. Nonetheless, Rosette, whose long legs and blonde good looks attracted many an admirer, needed little more defense than her blunt manner, steely nerves and sense of humor. Rosette also had the gift of certainty, and stepped as sure-footedly into the war as she did everything else.

If Rosette's parents did not see the risk in driving an ambulance, Captain Jacques Guerin did. He fell for "You" Courou-Mangin the first time he saw her, talking on the telephone at the houseboat. Her decisive, confident manner and statuesque elegance impressed him deeply. Captain Guerin had fought across Africa with Leclerc, but his first personal campaign of the war was to get "You" to agree to marry him. After the two had taken a day trip to Marrakesh, he succeeded, and on March 2, 1944 they were married by the division chaplain. They held a reception afterwards on the houseboat with the Rochambeau Group and some division officers.

Jacques would have carried her across the gangway, but at nearly six feet, she stood ten inches taller than he did. She called him her "little man,"and they began a long and happy marriage in separate living quarters. They took opportunities for private time when they could, and "You"got pregnant right away, but miscarried, and kept driving ambulances. Guerin later said he wanted to get "You" pregnant to get her out of the ambulance corps; he thought it was going to be too dangerous.

On the contrary, Captain Georges Ratard suggested that his girlfriend join the Rochambeau Group, and taught her how to drive so that she could.

Ratard had met Arlette Hautefeuille, a twenty-three-year-old with a sporty stride and an open face, when he rented a room from her family in Rabat. They became friends, though Ratard was an intellectual, fascinated by Latin and Greek, and Arlette was ever active, preferably outdoors. Arlette signed up with enthusiasm and her parents' approval. "I hated the Germans and I could not fight," she said. Driving would at least be a contribution to the war. First, Ratard asked her to marry him, she accepted, and they agreed to wait until he had news of his family in Brittany, with whom he had not had contact for more than a year. Arlette moved onto the houseboat in the Bou Regreg.

Arlette already had experienced the war in her hometown of Calais, in 1940, when screaming Stuka bombers struck in nightly raids, sending the family to sleep in the coal cellar for safety. They had two cats, both of whom would dive for the cellar two minutes before the air raid siren would sound. Arlette's mother put a mattress in the cellar, and every night they carried down a bucket, some toilet paper and a bottle of water to drink. Arlette remembered spending her twentieth birthday in the dark of the cellar. Ever after, she slept with her shutters open at night and avoided closed spaces.

Arlette's father had served in the First World War, and took away with him a virulent hatred for Germans. A reserve officer in the army, he was captured in the 1940 surrender and escaped, making his way to Morocco, where his mother and brother lived. Arlette's mother was left alone in France with no income. The army stopped paying her husband's salary at the surrender, saying there was no evidence that he was alive, and the bank refused to allow a withdrawal from their savings account without her husband's signature. As a woman, she had no legal right to their money. Broke and hungry in a German-occupied town, Arlette and her mother did what only desperate women would do: they got on their bicycles and pedaled south, direction Marseille, a thousand kilometers away through German-held territory. They were caught and escaped several times, and eventually reached Marseille and the boat to Morocco. Arlette remembered standing on the quay crying, not from fear or relief or fatigue, but from hunger.

The women from Morocco had not suffered the German invasion and occupation, but nor had they entirely escaped the war up to that point. The year before, when the Allies invaded her hometown of Safi (Morocco), Madeleine Collomb went to help at the hospital and found herself assisting a surgeon who was amputating a young man's damaged leg. The electricity failed in the middle of the operation, and Madeleine ran home and got two lanterns so that they could continue.

"After the first operation, I left the room and sat down on the ground outside; I nearly passed out," Madeleine said in an interview. "The doctor came and tapped me on the knee and said, 'Come on, there's another one.'" They worked through the night, and she got used to the blood.

Madeleine was born in 1917 in Morocco to French parents; her father worked in the civil administration at Safi. While the Vichy French government was still in power in Morocco, she had taken a Red Cross emergency care course and was told that if "anything" happened, she should go to the hospital. "We knew something was going to happen," she said.

As a young woman, Madeleine sailed her own boat, rode horses, drove, and enjoyed sports. After the Allies took over, she had to request permission from the U.S. Army to go sailing in the bay off of Safi. She was given permission, and she and her family became friends with a couple of French-speaking American officers. Madeleine's first idea of helping in the war effort was to fly a plane, but her father wouldn't let her. When she heard about the women's ambulance group, she thought her father would nix that idea as well, but to her surprise, he didn't say no. "He thought they'd never take me," she said. He was wrong.

Conrad and Toto also were weeding out recruits they didn't believe would hold up in the war, such as a young blonde who jumped on a chair and screamed every time she saw a mouse on the houseboat, which unfortunately was often. Toto much preferred Lucie Deplancke's attitude: a rat started running across the clothesline she was hanging clothes on, and both of them stopped suddenly when they saw each other. Lucie, without missing a beat, snapped at the rat: "So, are you going or am I hanging?"[3]

Lucie was a native Parisian who had been running a clothing boutique in Rabat. She was witty, high-spirited, and unabashed by military authority: if there was fun to be had, Lucie would find it and carry everyone along with her, laughing joyfully. She had been married to a young aviator, but the marriage had ended over Lucie's affair with a ballet dancer.

At five-foot-two, Zizon Sicco inherited the uniform and equipment of a departed recruit who was nearly six feet tall. She also was given a left boot size seven and a right boot size eight, while she wore a size six. What Zizon wore, didn't wear, and had to wear would be her personal demon throughout the war. She went into Rabat and had some suede boots made to fit her, and got the uniform tailored. An avid de Gaulle supporter, she had moved to Morocco with her parents at the occupation, and they had opened their house to Allied and Free French soldiers who needed a place to stay.

The night she was accepted into the Rochambeau Group she had a dream rooted in her childhood worship of Joan of Arc. "I dreamed that Charles VII was waiting for me, but I was looking fruitlessly for a suit of armor and a standard on the black market, since those articles did not appear on my ration card." Was she prepared to go to war? It was a question many of the women were asking themselves. She crossed the gangplank to go live on the houseboat feeling that she was walking into a new life. "I left behind my past as a civilian to enter into an adventure that transformed me with happiness."[4]

Zizon was tiny, but tough. She'd been driving for twelve years and had completed a cross-desert road race, but Toto nonetheless sent her out with an army monitor to check her skills. She thought she had done well, but when they got back, the monitor told Toto that Zizon needed a lot more lessons, and winked at her before she could protest. The next day he explained that if they went out driving they didn't have to spend the day taking apart the motor and cleaning every piece of it. She considered it a valuable lesson in military ways.

Zizon was invited to dinner one night with Conrad and conservative leader General Giraud, and wore a Lorraine Cross insignia, the symbol of the upstart Free French, despite Conrad's rebuke that it would offend Giraud. Instead of being offended, Giraud placed her by his side at dinner and wanted to hear all about the French in Morocco. Breaches were closing in the coalescing effort to oust the common enemy.

Recruits continued to arrive at the houseboat. The tragic loss of her young husband in an airplane accident had left Edith Schaller adrift and devastated, and she decided to go to nursing school to try to move on. When the war began in 1939, she left her native Alsace to join her brother, who was living in Marrakesh. She got a job in social services at the Casablanca Air Base and then, because she was fluent in English as well as German and French, she was hired by the American officer's club at Marrakesh to organize social activities. She was bored with the job, tired of Coca-Cola and sandwiches, and particularly annoyed at having to entice young, married women to attend the American dances without their husbands. She heard about the Rochambeau Group in early 1943, quit her job, and went straight to the houseboat. She stood on the deck in a brightly colored dress in the midst of busy women wearing olive-green fatigues, and felt like she was entering another world. She was thirty-four years old, with neither husband nor child to define her path, and going to war might at least offer an outlet for all the fury and despair she had stored up since her husband's death.

Michette de Steinheil had grown up in Rabat, daughter of a French military officer who, with impeccable timing, retired from the Vichy-led forces one week before the Allied invasion of Morocco. She was twenty-four years old and separated from her husband when her brother told her about the women's ambulance corps. He had met a Rochambelle, Anne-Marie Bonnel Davion, and thought Michette would fit in with the group. Michette was delighted to find a way to contribute to the war effort, and also put some distance between herself and her wandering husband, a baron who was ten years older than she when she married him at age nineteen. Anne-Marie also was separated from her husband, and had moved to Morocco to stay with relatives, who, it turned out, were good friends of Toto's. Anne-Marie and Michette liked each other immediately, and became ambulance partners for the duration of the war. Their fellow drivers (and more than a few veterans) still talk about how stunningly pretty the two of them were, with their sparkling eyes and disarming smiles. They left a trail of wistful hearts in the wake of their ambulance.

For some of the recruits, the route to Morocco had been a hazardous and rugged hike across the Pyrénées Mountains dividing France from Spain. Marguerite Marchandeau had been active in the Resistance, and when the secrecy of her cell was broken by the Gestapo, she and her boyfriend fled to the Pyrénées and the relative safety of Spain. She hiked for twenty-four hours, wearing espadrilles in the snow, to get across the border.[5] After a brief stay in Spain, they were sent to Morocco with other French exiles, and there, they joined the Second Division. Denise Colin and her husband André also had sneaked across the Pyrénées, on Christmas Eve of 1942, and lived clandestinely in Barcelona until they were able to reach Casablanca in July 1943. Both of them joined the Free French there, and Denise, a fourth-year medical student, was assigned to the Thirteenth Medical Battalion as an ambulance driver (François Jacob, with two years' less schooling, was named an assistant doctor). André, a chemical engineer, was attached to the baking unit, underscoring the French belief in Napoleon's dictum, that an army marches on its stomach.

Meanwhile, Lulu had fallen seriously ill with typhus and had to be hospitalized. Convinced that she had caught it from the rats on the houseboat, she refused to return to it upon her recovery. Instead, she left Rabat and the Rochambeau Group to join the Free French headquarters in Algiers.

In all, twenty-two women signed on in Morocco, bringing the total to thirty-two, including Conrad and Toto. At this point a division in the group was clear. There were the "Archi-Pures," or those who had created the group in New York, and the "Moroccans," who had signed on in Morocco. Within the "Moroccans" were those who had grown up in the country, some of whom spoke fluent Arabic, and those who had arrived as a consequence of the Nazi occupation of France. They all mixed well together, but everyone knew who belonged to which group. "That memorable houseboat was the melting pot where lasting friendships were forged, where the finally completed group could successfully face all the obstacles put in its way, by chance or by the concern of the hierarchy over having enlisted women in an armored division," Jacotte wrote in her memoirs.

When the division's toughest infantrymen, the March of Chad Regiment (RMT), arrived at the Temara training camp and heard that there were going to be women in the division, they were appalled. A division colonel, Michel Malagutti, gave the infantrymen a stern lecture: "Here are these women, these young girls, who were in complete security in the United States, living a comfortable life, who chose to leave it all behind to participate in their country's war effort, and who accept in advance the hard life of a combatant. . . . We must adopt them, and help them to succeed."[6]

The colonel, commander of one of the division's three tactical groups, invited a few of the Rochambeau Group at a time to lunch or drinks with his officers, and insisted that they become familiar with the tank structure so that they could more easily evacuate a wounded soldier from within. "He was really nice with us," Jacotte said. "He gave us a lot of moral support." Their instructor took the lesson a step further, and taught Jacotte to drive a tank.

The women's training with the Medical Battalion in Morocco included timed evacuations of "wounded" soldiers, the heavier the better, to test their physical strength. They also underwent simulated air attacks on a convoy to practice getting the ambulances off the road and scattering into the underbrush. And they had division-wide exercises that lasted two to three days. One day it poured rain and the ground turned to mud, trapping all manner of vehicles in the muck. Jacotte said it was like driving in a river of chocolate. Edith wrote in her memoirs that she came back with mud encrusted up to her eyeballs from trying to dig out her ambulance. Never had the houseboat's sole, pressure-less shower felt so good. They also had demining practice, in which one person buried a mine in the sand, and another had to uncover it, following precise instructions. Edith was pleased at the time that they were using dummy mines. She would find out about the real thing soon enough.

General Leclerc came to dinner on the houseboat once, bringing U.S. General Allen Kingman, commander of the U.S. Army's Second Armored Division. Kingman led a group of American military officials to inspect the French Second Armored Division, and Leclerc thought Kingman should meet his women's ambulance corps. Toto exercised her renowned wit and charm for the brass, while Jacotte was simply awed at getting to serve Leclerc at table. The visit and inspection were successful, because the French Second Armored Division was then officially incorporated into the U.S. Army. The Americans requested, however, that the division's black African troops be left behind. The French army was not racially segregated, and its colonial Senegalese troops had been heroes in 1870, in the First World War, in the 1940 invasion, and across North Africa, but the American army was segregated, and the French commanders were asked to "whiten" their ranks. The valued Senegalese soldiers were transferred to the French First Army, which was not under U.S. command. The American command apparently chose to overlook the fact that women were part of the Second Division, since women were not allowed in combat units in the U.S. Army.

The American and French officers mixed fairly well together, despite many cultural divergences. Jacotte and Edith often were asked to accompany Conrad and Toto to American receptions because they spoke English well, and Edith remarked how different in tone the American parties were from the French ones. The American officers were much more casual and rowdy than the French officers, she noted. "Those evenings were always very lively, dotted with stories about their lifestyles, quite different from ours. But, from what I heard on more current subjects, I realized the measure of the phenomenal war effort, in materiel deployed, but also physically and morally, by that vast nation that had come to save us, and had done so with good humor and unlimited kindness," she wrote.[7]

One day Edith slipped in the shower and her foot went through a hole in the half-rotten floor, leaving a grapefruit-sized bruise. She limped around for three days, trying to hide the injury, but her leg turned blue and swollen. Toto noticed and sent her to a doctor, who ordered three weeks of immobility. And then, with Edith flat on her back, the division's imminent departure from Morocco was announced.

The Rochambeau Group was given the task of rounding up all the convalescents staying with families, and told to do so in twenty-four hours. At 6 A.M. the next day, twelve ambulances took off to get the recovering soldiers and deliver them to their regiments. The division had 140 names on its list, and the Rochambeau Group had the locations of only 100, but the word spread, and the soldiers all managed to get back to the training camp before departure. Some of the ambulances had to be driven to Casablanca for shipping to Algeria, and Jacotte was assigned to one, driving in a convoy of tanks. She returned to the houseboat at 8 P.M. from Casablanca, and then turned around at 4 A.M. and left in another ambulance for same city. The back-and-forth driving was good training for her life about to come.

On April 11, 1944, the Rochambeau Group left the houseboat behind, driving in convoy with the rest of the division to their destination, an army camp in Algeria. Edith rode on a stretcher in the back of an ambulance driven by Raymonde. Jacotte drove with Lucie. They were the last in the line, and the accordion rhythm of the convoy's twenty-five kilometer-an-hour pace kept the driving from becoming monotonous. They also had the mission of picking up anything that fell out of vehicles in front of them. Every now and then they'd stop for a bucket, or a tool, and once, Lucie swept up a brilliant green lizard as well. It took them several days to get to their destination, a windswept hilltop called Assi Ben Okba. The women quickly nicknamed it "Bald Mountain." It had no endearing qualities, no tents for the women, and worst of all, no plumbing.

The women didn't mind sleeping on stretchers in the back of their ambulances. But one night Conrad heard a soldier prowling around, an American, and came tearing out of her ambulance shouting at him: "You want my girls?" The soldier, facing a tall, angry white woman, said, "No, I want your wine." Conrad went to the command staff and got tents for the women. Their tents, six women in each, looked no different from those of the other soldiers, except for the ever-present lines of lingerie drying, and the hair styling going on from time to time. On the edge of the camp, there were holes in the ground for latrines, and their helmets served as sinks for splashing up.

The American troops had a circular tent with shower heads installed, and offered to lend it to the women. They used it only once or twice, but the last time, the women lined up to go in to the shower tent, and then had to wait outside as a unit of American soldiers was showering. When it was the women's turn, they undressed as a group and lathered up. The wind blew sand onto their wet skin, but it felt so good to be clean that they didn't care. Then one of the women screamed: Someone was peeping through a hole in the side of the tent. And another! Hysteria spread quickly. Toto ordered them to dress and line up, right away. They marched out in formation, surprising some lingering soldiers. No one wanted to go to the American showers after that. Instead, they got permission to go swimming at nearby Crystal Beach, and that helped keep their spirits up, even though the Mediterranean was cold in April.

Assi Ben Okba, near Oran, Algeria, was the temporary home of thousands of soldiers, French, British, and American, all waiting to invade the European continent. The Rochambeau Group was not the only female unit there: groups of American WACs and army nurses also came and went. The French officers, however, were giving the Rochambeau Group no breaks. Every morning, the women rose to complete their physical training: a jog around the camp perimeter, to the jeers and jibes of division spectators. They spent an hour drilling and marching, and then two hours peeling the medical battalion's daily vegetables. After lunch, they had drill practice again, then vehicle maintenance, then peeling duty again, until 5 P.M. There was one hour allotted per day for "visiting," but the women were restricted to their area of the camp, and no man, whether officer or soldier, was allowed to speak to them without special permission. A command staff adjutant hovered over them, adding new restrictions on a daily basis. At first, the rule was no sitting in the ambulances with a visitor, and later the rule forbade visitors within twenty meters of the vehicles. The hostile atmosphere led to an absolute minimum of casual contact.

The women were, however, permitted to accept invitations to dinner with division officers, and occasionally the American officers asked them to a dinner-dance. They particularly enjoyed the food on those outings, as their daily rations were neither good nor plentiful. At one American dance, a young officer brought Christiane Petit a plate of sandwiches, and then watched in amazement as she ate them all. The American officers who had befriended Madeleine Collomb's family at Safi also were in the area, and took her and Rosette to dinner one evening at an elegant mansion in the nearby port of Mers El Kebir.

At night in the camp, they usually went to bed after dinner. Rosette remarked that if the women had to cross the camp at night, they were greeted with catcalls and insults, the men pretending they were prostitutes from the nearby bordello. "They treated us like whores," she said. "It didn't bother me, I was so innocent." She didn't understand their implications, and when the rude remarks came in Arabic, she didn't understand anything at all. But Madeleine understood Arabic, and the insults were coming through loud and clear. She said she cried over it, and swore she was going to quit the army. "We heard the soldiers saying things like, 'at least we'll get some girls . . .' They made a lot of remarks at the beginning; they didn't know what to think about women in the Army. But we were thinking, 'We signed up to be treated like this?'"

Toto ordered the women to ignore the taunts and insults from the enlisted men, and maintain a respectful attitude toward officers. She wanted at all costs to avoid a charge of insubordination, and possible dismissal from the division that could be the result. They were still on probation with Leclerc; they still had to prove that they could make it in the military. She organized the women into a choral group, with the division's Catholic chaplain, Father Jean-Baptiste Houchet, directing, and scheduled rehearsals during kitchen duty. Before long, the kitchen tent had standing-room-only crowds listening in.

Drilling exercises also drew an audience of spectators. One day when the Rochambeau squad was marching past the colonel on their right, a cheeky officer called "Heads, left!" and they turned the wrong way on the colonel. Another time another officer reversed the left-right call until the women were completely out of step. "It didn't take much to make us laugh," Jacotte recalled.

Edith, still recovering from her accident, observed the drilling practices, and noted that the marching and stiffness of parading was the polar opposite of the way the women moved naturally, which was with suppleness and grace. The lessons they were learning had little to do with anything they had known in their civilian lives, not even the way they moved.

Some evenings at Assi Ben Okba, Toto and Rosette and some of the others played bridge in the back of an ambulance, with the dummy hand responsible for keeping the truck's battery charged so they had a little light. Captain Jacques de Witasse, who would command a tank company in the war, was a regular player. He wrote in his memoirs that the division's men didn't really know what to make of the women at first. "We learned to appreciated those remarkable women who were our ambulance drivers during the campaign. For the moment, we just considered them as kind of fancy comrades, whose presence created the kind of charming ambiance we had forgotten," Witasse wrote.[8]

One evening, after dinner and a session of bawdy songs with the officers of the Second Battalion of RMT, Toto found a new bridge partner in Commandant Jacques Massu. He was a tough young officer from the center of France who had been with Leclerc through his Africa campaign. He was a far remove from the witty Parisian intellectuals Toto was accustomed to, but somehow, Massu put a gleam in her eye. They began an affair that shocked some of the younger women in the group, particularly those in their early twenties who were not yet married and had never had a sexual relationship. Toto was completely unconcerned.

Christiane Petit was among the young and innocent. She accompanied Toto one evening to a dinner with division officers and met a fellow there who seemed interested in her. He even wrote her a letter after the dinner. But when Toto asked her to join the group for dinner another time, Christiane refused. She did not want to get involved with the young officer. Toto was annoyed, but Christiane dug in her heels. "I was a very serious girl. I was not a flirt, fluttering here and there," she said. The young man ended up being killed in the war, but Christiane didn't remember where.

The men's hostility began to fade in the face of the women's relentless good humor and determination to succeed. When a unit of American WACs came through Assi Ben Okba with scintillating military discipline, the French soldiers began to refer to the Rochambeau Group as "our girls." It was a short step from there to the nickname that has stuck with the women for sixty years: the Rochambelles. In choral sessions, they invented a song that began "When I was a Rochambelle" and made up new verses as they went along.

By early May, Conrad believed that they would be leaving North Africa soon, and so invited the women to the town of Oran to visit the hair-

dresser's and then have lunch at the American Red Cross club. The hairdresser was wonderful—it felt great to have clean, styled hair for the first
time in months—but lunch at the club turned out to be peanut-butter sandwiches, which went down less well with the French. On the way back to
Assi Ben Okba, a sandstorm swept in and ruined all the hairdresser's efforts—so much for their ladies' day out. But they had passed Leclerc's test
of training, and while he remained skeptical of their performance in the face
of combat, he agreed to take them on until Paris, where he said he could
find male replacements.

Departure from North Africa was set for May 20, 1944, from Mers El
Kebir. The night before they left, a German submarine was captured off the
coast, waiting to torpedo northbound troop shipments. The news fueled
the tension in the air and underscored the knowledge that the convoy
would be in grave danger of attack by German submarines patrolling the
Atlantic. Then, as the Second Division prepared to board the U.S. Army
transport ships, the American officers in charge tried block the Rochambelles from boarding, citing regulations against women on military transport. Leclerc intervened personally to get them on. "He said, 'They're not
women, they're ambulance drivers!'" and the Rochambelles were allowed to
board, according to Anne Hastings.

Army transport consisted of two former Cunard luxury liners, the
Capetown Castle and the *Franconia*. The Rochambelles were on the *Capetown
Castle*, along with nearly 5,000 men of the division. They slipped anxiously
through the Strait of Gibralter and out into the Atlantic Ocean, joining a
convoy of seventeen Allied ships, including two aircraft carriers, on their
way to England. Jacotte climbed up in the webbing to watch the fleet for
hours on end. As on the previous Atlantic crossing, there was little to do.
Rosette was pleased to get a bath every day, even if it was in salt water. They
had two meals a day, at 9 A.M. and 5 P.M., and Jacotte remembered being
hungry all the time in the fresh salt air. It was, nonetheless, a nice change
from the desert.

The ship also provided empty hours for socializing between division
men and the Rochambelles, now that the adjutant was no longer hovering.
Jacques Branet, a dashing captain from the Third Company, noted their
presence in his journal with a sort of happy wonder that women were there
at all. One of the Rochambelles, Anne-Marie Davion, particularly caught
Branet's eye. "I am seeing the gayest and prettiest (in my opinion) of all

these 'Rochambelles,'" he wrote.[9] Branet's luck was holding, because Anne-Marie seemed to find him attractive as well.

Shipboard orders were to wear life jackets and uniforms, including boots, at all times. That included bedtime. All the women except Christiane and Jacotte disregarded the order and slipped into the crepe de chine pajamas they had picked up at Saks. Toto did a midnight bed check and handed out detentions to the women wearing pajamas. Thus was born the response to all discipline inquiries in the Rochambeau Group: "If you weren't prepared to accept army discipline, you should have joined the Russian ballet!" In other words, no prima donnas allowed. It also led to Toto's Rule No. 5: *Never forget that you are not on a cruise and that you are not part of the Russian Ballet.* Toto's Rules of Rochambelle Order (see appendix) gathered the lessons and experiences of their time at war into a wry and amusing commentary on "What one must do, not do, and had better know about."

The fleet sailed the north Atlantic without incident, and the *Capetown Castle* docked at Liverpool on May 30, greeted by an English brass band. They were transported from Liverpool to Hull, where they saw bombing damage caused by the Luftwaffe, the first they'd seen since the 1940 surrender in France. It was a sobering reminder that their mission would be grim. The women were assigned to a small mansion called Tudor House, in the village of Cottingham, five kilometers from Hull. England seemed so green, so damp after the sepia tones of Morocco and Algeria. The chestnut trees were blooming, and it rained nearly every day. The Rochambeau Group had not been paid in two months, and found the exchange rate of one British pound to 200 French francs was not going to get them far when they did have money. They spent mornings working on the ambulances in the garage, and afternoons in first-aid courses with the battalion doctors.

There was also time to play, and the English were quick to organize dances and dinners for the French troops and drivers. The village mayor and staff were all women, as were most of the workers they met, and were delighted to hold dances for the handsome young doctors of the medical battalion. One evening a French officer was overheard responding to a telephone inquiry about a scheduled dance that "There will be the Rochambelles as well as real women."

"The French are receiving a really terrific welcome from the English," Rosette wrote her mother. "They say there is one man for every seven women, and you can imagine the kind of sentiment they easily inspire."

The Rochambelles were a pretty solid group by this point, but class divisions among them still chafed. Most of them came from the upper classes or the bourgeosie and had similar definitions of politesse. Others did not. In her memoir, Marguerite Marchandeau, whose father was a factory worker, said she always felt like an outsider. As a "simple daughter of the people . . . the social differences that separated me from the majority of the girls did not motivate me to form friendships with one or another," she wrote.[10] Zizon Sicco recounted that Conrad asked her to take one of the women in hand and teach her some proper manners. Zizon protested, "Why me? You know I let slip a curse more often than I should." Conrad replied, "Exactly, my dear Zizon, it is absolutely necessary that she learn to say '*merde*' like a woman of the world."[11] Conrad's motive was that the woman could end up marrying an officer after the war and would need to do him credit. The woman, whom Zizon did not name, did not marry an officer after the war and Zizon thought her "lessons" had been largely ineffective. But swearing correctly seemed to be on Conrad's list of things proper young women should know how to do.

Conrad was also concerned about the women's nutrition. She raided the British and American post exchanges for vitamin supplements and vegetables, scarce on the public markets. The women were introduced to K-rations, wax-covered cardboard boxes containing tinned ham, crackers, some chunks of chocolate, and portions of toilet paper. If they were impressed by the efficiency of K-rations, they soon tired of its contents, and took to calling all army-issued food "beans." They also took advantage of good English tailoring to have the rest of their army-issue fatigues and uniforms cut to fit them. And they practiced parading.

On the morning of June 6, 1944, an English neighbor arrived at their door with a map in hand and a radio. "It's your country . . ." she said. The women were touched, and they all sat down to listen and cry over the D-Day invasion. Tears for not being there, tears for those who were there, tears for those who lost their lives there. It was the beginning of the war to take back the continent from Hitler and his henchmen, and suddenly, France seemed within reach. There were few dry eyes in the Second Division that day.

Leclerc was headquartered at Dalton Hall, a fifteenth-century country estate in Yorkshire. At the end of June, General George S. Patton Jr. came to visit and inspect the troops. Colonel Paul de Langlade described his

The Rochambelles on parade review with the division at Dalton Hall, England.

larger-than-life appearance: Patton wore his habitual jodhpurs and riding boots, equipped with Mexican-style rowel spurs, but the cowboy camouflage was not that of a fool. De Langlade noted that Patton's "gaze was direct and more piercing than the blade of a sword . . ."[12]

The French, with their admiration for panache, adored Patton. He went down the ranks, asking soldiers which individual weapon they preferred. After several had answered this gun or that carbine, he stopped and declared that these were not the responses he expected of Frenchmen. His favorite arm was the bayonet, he said, lunging in demonstration, because when you had finished using it, your target *boche* was right in front of you, dead. And he laughed, and they laughed together. Patton, a devoted swordsman, had attended the elite French Cavalry School at Saumur. He spoke French, and he understood the culture. "The French officers whom circumstances constrained to wearing a foreign uniform under foreign command, remember with emotion that great figure of a soldier and remain honored to have served under his orders," de Langlade wrote.[13]

In early July the entire division was called to Dalton Hall, and each member received the division insignia pin, the gold Lorraine cross on a blue field. They held a formal parade and review of troops, and the Rochambelles looked smart in their dress uniform, a dark skirt and jacket, white blouse, tie, gloves and hat. But while waiting for the ceremony to begin, Rosette and Arlette began idly tossing a "balloon" back and forth. The army did not offer balloons in its K-rations, but it did sometimes include condoms. Toto noticed it at the same time as several of the tank regiment officers. Captain de Witasse described the incident wryly in his memoir: "Toto burst into fury and popped the offending body, which, in turn, caused everyone there to burst into laughter, just at the moment when the Authorities arrived. That gave birth, one imagines, to a thousand jokes of more or less doubtful taste."[14]

While they were stationed in England, Rosette was assigned temporarily to the 501st tank regiment for transport of soldiers to the American hospital nearby. When she reported to the regiment commander, she found that he had not been told she was coming. "For five whole minutes he thought it was a joke," she wrote home. Persuaded that it was serious, the commander set about figuring out where to house her, the only woman in the regiment. He finally put her tent between that of the priest and the doctor. When she went into the mess tent for dinner, all the officers stood up, and she said she quickly took her place at the commander's table, her cheeks bright red with embarrassment. In the mornings, Rosette was assigned to help the doctor, but he had two male nurses and she felt in the way.

"I think my presence is more or less bothersome, since the majority of the patients are there for venereal disease, so I stay in my tent," she wrote.

Three women joined the Rochambelles in England. Polly Wordsmith was a freckled, strawberry-blonde American, now safely out of the reach of State Department dictates; Ghislaine Bechmann had escaped France via Spain, and ended up in London; and Micheline Grimprel was a former Resistant who was spirited out of France after the Gestapo arrested members of her network. They were sent from the Free French organization based at Covent Garden, and while they did not have the advantage the other Rochambelles had in the North Africa training, the three were welcomed into the ranks.

Toward the end of July, in a predeparture move, the division was sent to camp in the mud of a secret bivouac camouflaged in a forest. The battalion doctors' tent was next to Rosette's, so close that she could hear the men snoring in the night. The Americans organized entertainment for the troops, a Western film in English. Rosette, bored, left at the intermission. But they were on their way to France, and they knew it. No amount of English rain or dull films could dampen their spirits.

The Second Division was mobilized for crossing the English Channel on July 30th. It would have been even later, but Patton ordered the division to join his Third Army in Normandy immediately. One of the Rochambelles' favorite officers would not make the trip, however. Colonel Malagutti, who had taken the time to teach the women about tanks, was relieved of his command by Leclerc days before the Channel crossing; they had had ongoing disputes since North Africa and Leclerc dismissed him summarily from the division.

The 15,000-person Second Division left many Englishwomen, all "fiancées" of division soldiers, waving handkerchiefs goodbye. Zizon, who was fluent in French, English, and Arabic, had to translate the last-minute promises between couples who had shared perhaps a great deal, but not a language. Zizon was afraid of being seasick and deeply frightened of heights. But as her ambulance was last to be loaded on the ship, she was posted, to her great relief, on the bridge.

There is a photograph of the Rochambelles on the liberty ship (so-called because it and others like it were delivering freedom to the continent) *Philip Thomas*, crossing the channel, in which Toto is filing her nails, a cigarette dangling from the corner of her mouth. They all smoked then, everyone but Christiane and Conrad. The women's faces were lit with anticipation, with a certain bright, attentive expression of leaning forward into the future.

Toto's bridge partners must have been on a different Liberty Ship, because she played poker instead, and lost her monthly salary of 3,000 francs (about $300 at the time) to a lieutenant-dentist from the medical battalion. She started the war with no money, but her nails were perfect.

On the quay at Southampton: The Rochambelles ready to cross to France. Front of the line to back: Florence Conrad, Suzanne "Toto" Torrès, Biquette Ragache, Raymonde Brindjonc, Anne-Marie Davion, Jacotte Fournier.

On board the Liberty ship Philip Thomas, *crossing to France. Seated, r-l: Edith Schaller, unidentified officer, Anne Hastings, unidentified officer, Suzanne "Toto" Torrès, Colonel Warabiot, Anne-Marie Davion, Dr. Alexandre Krementchousky (with beret and pipe), Jacqueline Lambert de Guise (standing).*

Toto getting ready for action.

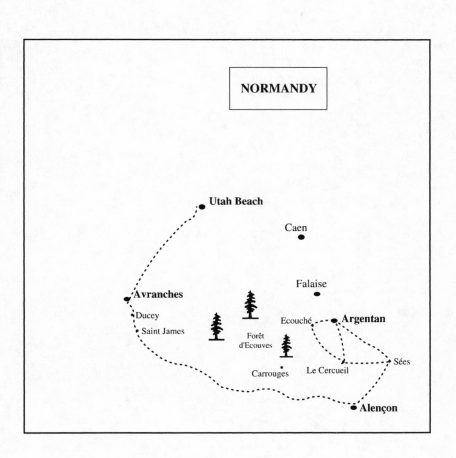

CHAPTER THREE

Fear and the Back Roads of the Bocage

The sky and the sea were crowded and jostling off the Normandy coast on August 1, 1944. Balloons were tethered to ships to interfere with potential air attacks, and ships were anchored in the English Channel against the force of the ripping tides. It was nearly the end of Operation Overlord, when 2 million troops and 330,000 vehicles landed on the Normandy beaches in the sixty days following D-Day. The shifting, tension, and energy offshore were matched on the bridge of the liberty ship, where the Second Division waited to disembark. The Rochambelles had sat on the deck of the ship for three days while the ship inched across the channel, three endless days of heads turning south, searching the horizon for a glimpse of coastline. Finally they were anchored off Utah Beach, but it was 2 A.M., and France remained an elusive shadow in the night.

First they had to get off the ship, and that was not as simple as it might sound. The women and men on the bridge had to climb down the side of the ship on a rope ladder, twisting and swaying in the rolling surf, and jump onto a transport barge that was banging sideways into the ship. Rosette counted that descent as her most anxious moment of the entire war. If her timing was off, she would slip into the sea and then be smashed by the barge as it swung back into the ship. "Fortunately there were huge American Negros to catch us on the way and set us, gasping and relieved, on the bridge," Rosette wrote her mother. Zizon Sicco managed to be the last one in line. With her paralyzing vertigo, she didn't know how she'd make it down. A captain helped at the top, and then at the bottom one of the Americans grabbed her by the waist and swung her onto the deck. It was over before she knew it.

The division's vehicles, including the Rochambelles' nineteen ambulances, had been driven onto the barge from below deck. One of the American soldiers told Edith Schaller to keep the ambulance in first gear through the shallow water and onto the beach, and aim for a narrow path, barely the width of her truck, that climbed up the hillside. She felt a tugboat push the barge close to shore, and at the signal, drove into the breakers.

Toto drove with Crapette Demay and an American officer, moving very fast once they hit land, speeding through darkness on tiny winding roads, noting the "Danger: Mines" signs posted occasionally. American soldiers in the landing area shouted at each newly arrived ambulance to go faster, faster! Rosette barely had time to realize she was back home. Jacotte, her five-year exile at an end, seized the moment. She drove her ambulance onto the beach and stopped dead. "I was almost in an altered state, under the force of emotion. At the foot of the first dunes, I stopped, opened the door, and on my knees, my hands in the sand, I touched my forehead to the ground of my homeland," she wrote.[1]

Then they were off into the night. When they stopped at their encampment, a division officer drove by and tossed a few Camembert cheeses and baguettes to Toto. It was a perfect homecoming gift for the expatriates. One of the division soldiers, Sylvain, played guitar and the women sang old familiar songs. It was good to be home again, worth every difficult moment and every daunting obstacle to be there, bivouacked in an apple orchard in Normandy on a warm summer night. At dawn, Edith climbed onto the roof of her ambulance for a better view and saw the sea drenched in a magnificent scarlet glow of sunrise. "The sun was completely red, and so was the sea and all those ships and contraptions," she said. "It was fabulous."

It was fabulous, and it was frightening. They were diving into the raging middle of the Battle of Normandy, begun with the D-Day invasion two months before. Since then, the Allies had established an eighty-kilometer-wide beachhead on the coast, liberated the Cotentin Peninsula, and begun pushing towards the south and east. The fighting was heavy and intense. The women weren't the only ones in the Second Division with no combat experience, and they wouldn't be alone in finding the meaning of fear.

Leclerc and his command staff had driven straight to Patton's camp from the coast. Generals Leclerc and Patton had a solid working relationship and a similar military style, and Leclerc told his aide-de-camp Christian Girard that he appreciated Patton and the other American generals there. "They're a little bit nuts and that's what it takes to be a good soldier," he said.[2] Over dinner, the French and American commanders conferred on plans for taking back Normandy from the Germans. By early August, U.S.

troops had gotten about 100 kilometers south of the coast and taken the town of Avranches.

Leclerc was already in Avranches when the Rochambelles arrived on August 6, camping in an apple orchard between the outlying villages of Ducey and Saint James with the Third Company tanks of the 501st Regiment. The men were in the orchard on the left side of the road, the women on the right. The ambulances were lined up under camouflage netting. A small German plane had circled over them repeatedly during the day, and some of the other units moved. Toto asked the medical battalion commanders whether they should decamp, too, but orders came down the line to stay put, and to sleep beside their ambulances in full dress. Toto issued the order to remain where they were, but said that the women could sleep in their ambulances if they chose.

Zizon and her partner, Denise Colin, were hot and uncomfortable in their fatigues, and then the mosquitoes starting droning in. They decided to move into their ambulance, and Polly Wordsmith, who had joined the group in England, moved her stretcher over to have a little more room. Zizon took off her heavy fatigues and put on the top of her army-issue pajamas. They had just settled in to rest when hell, in the form of antipersonnel cluster bombs, fell from the sky and exploded in the heart of their camp.

Denise pulled a stunned, deafened Zizon out of her sleeping bag. The ambulance was blazing. Shrapnel had sparked the extra gas can. Zizon ran to get a fire extinguisher. Coming back with it she ran into a captain who shouted at her to take off that light-colored top right away. She tried to argue that she was even paler underneath, "but he had his idea, and I really didn't have the time to insist, so I obeyed and exposed my half-nakedness to the attention of the German pilots."[3]

A soldier handed her the heavy part of his helmet when he saw her bare head, and she ran in her underwear and bra, barefoot with the fire extinguisher and a helmet four sizes too big, to put out the fire. She cut the cords of her hanging sack of clothes and threw it out of reach of the flaming ambulance. When the fire was finally out, she realized how ridiculous she looked and had a fit of hilarity, prompting another driver to run to Toto and report that Zizon had lost her mind. She hadn't. She got dressed and started picking up the wounded. It was the Rochambelles' baptism by fire, and one of the first problems they faced was that tires had been blown out by shrapnel. The ambulances were of no use if they couldn't roll. Raymonde Brindjonc found two of her tires shredded by shrapnel; Christiane Petit's ambulance had lost three. Another woman had parked in a ditch and couldn't get the ambulance out.

They pulled together what was working, got the injured loaded into ambulances, and started moving toward the nearest treatment center. Most of the injured had been on the men's side of the orchard, but the women counted one badly wounded among their team as well. Polly Wordsmith's legs were shattered in the bombing, and she remained crippled for the rest of her life. At first, she refused to be transported until the soldiers all were taken care of, but when Toto saw her condition, she packed her into an ambulance right away. Zizon measured her luck in centimeters. A small banner with the Lorraine Cross, the division symbol, that she had embroidered and hung on the end of her stretcher, was destroyed. "For the first time I was thankful for my small size. If I was just a few centimeters taller, which I often had wished, my feet would have been in the same shape as that flag."[4]

Jacotte loaded her ambulance with five bleeding and burned soldiers and got directions to the nearest treatment center. The directions were wrong, and she drove around in the dark, searching. She saw a group of army tents and headed for them, but the American guard, gun in hand, shouted at her, "Password!" She tried to explain in her gentle, British-accented English that she was looking for the hospital. He kept shouting "Password!" at her and getting angrier, so she left and drove on. She flagged down a passing Jeep and got new directions. She found the hospital entrance, but there the guard said the hospital was full and refused to let her in. She parked and went around to a side entrance, found the head nurse and explained that she had wounded soldiers in the ambulance. If she had to go further on, where could she go? The nurse told her to bring the patients in, that she would take them. Jacotte stayed for a while and translated for the soldiers, then returned to the medical unit's bivouac. It was deserted, dark and empty in the night. A straggler gave her directions and she eventually found the rest of the unit.

It was an ominous start to Jacotte's career as an ambulance driver, but it drew for her a clear and unmitigated picture of the kind of quick thinking and personal initiative she was going to need. The burden of responsibility for the wounded soldiers was going to fall on the individual drivers, on whether they could get through the obstacles, both physical and bureaucratic, that would be thrown in their paths. And fear, if it got in the way, could become yet another obstacle. She understood that she would have to push past it and keep going.

Jacotte wasn't the only one who had a difficult first night. Florence Conrad had gotten lost as well and had driven sixty kilometers out of the way trying to find the field hospital. Crapette Demay, returning to the orchard in the dark, had run over four Moroccan stretcher-bearers who were sleeping on the ground. Fortunately, none was seriously injured.

When Zizon returned to the campsite at dawn, she found her ambulance a smoldering wreck and her clothes and possessions strewn around the muddy ground. Her suede boots had been run over by a tank. Shrapnel had ripped up the interior of the ambulance and sliced through their fatigues. Christiane's ambulance also had taken a beating, and shrapnel had cut through her sack of clothing as well. She unfolded her army pajamas and found a hole run through them from top to bottom, like a paper cutout. She sewed them up and wore them for years after. It was a costly lesson for the group, but one they applied to future operations. They never parked their ambulances in one place again. "It was a mistake to have put all the ambulances in line," Arlette said in an interview. "It was a target."

That night near Ducey, Conrad handed over command to Toto. Conrad was tired, her usual energy flagging. She retreated to serving as liaison with the military bureaucracy and let Toto run the show, which was easier for everyone. The women all had enormous respect for Conrad, but most of them felt she was out of touch, still living in the era of the First World War and insisting on an anachronistic formality of manner. Toto had been running interference between Conrad's old-fashioned ideas and the day-to-day possibilities for several months. Taking charge officially would be simpler for her as well.

"You" Courou-Mangin Guerin also left the Rochambeau Group in Normandy. She was pregnant again, and didn't want to lose the baby. She most likely joined the Army's social services programs being set up to help civilians behind the lines. She was disappointed to leave the ambulance corps, but pleased to be expecting a baby, according to her team partner, Rosette.

The division moved out the next day. The Rochambelles were assigned to the tactical unit commanded by Colonel Louis Warabiot, heading in a southeasterly direction toward Le Mans, with the division's 4,000 vehicles in two columns. The way south wound through fields of dread and horror.

Bodies of dead German soldiers lay rotting in the summer sun, no one willing to bury them for fear of booby-traps. Dead cows and horses, their bodies swollen, their legs stiff in the air, dotted the fields like a harvest of the macabre. The odor of death hung in the air, suspended in dust clouds kicked up by the tank convoys and commingled with the black fumes of their exhaust. Not a single house along the road was left undamaged; families shoveled out the rubble and patched the holes as best they could. Peaceful, verdant Normandy had been shattered in the struggle of the two colossal armies.

Toto and Raymonde were first in a line of ambulances when they came upon a motorcycle soldier who had hit a mine. He had been blown up into a tree, and was hanging there, his legs smashed and bleeding. Raymonde said they put the ambulance under the tree and climbed on top to get him down, but the maneuver blocked the progress of the convoy. Leclerc himself came striding up the line to see what was causing the delay, and poked Toto on the rear with his walking stick. They quickly got the soldier down—he lived, but lost both his legs—and moved the ambulance. "Toto said, well, if he's given me a bruise, I think I'll keep it!" Raymonde recalled. The incident led to Toto's Rule No. 50: *When one sees the General nearby, in operations, do your best to warn the lieutenant, so she can get her ass out of the way of his walking stick!*

Ahead of the French were the Seventy-Ninth U.S. Infantry Division and the Fifth U.S. Armored Division. In a parallel move to the east, the First Canadian Army and the First Polish Armored Division were moving south from Caen, where the long and devastating battle for possession of that city was finally over. The French and Americans were ordered to maneuver in a fishhook, coming up from the south between Alençon and Carrouges, to create a pincer movement and trap the German Army Group B, with its eleven Panzer divisions and forty infantry divisions. It was Patton's plan, and it had the signature of his style, requiring speed, audacity and several good armored divisions. "We are having a hell of a war here." Patton wrote in his diary.[5]

The Second Division targeted a handful of villages on the outskirts of the Ecouves Forest, a 25,000-hectare (10,000-acre) nightmare for the tank regiments. The Ninth Panzer Division had come up from the south of France and hid, camouflaged in the forest, waiting for the 116th Panzer Division to push the French troops into range of its guns. On their western flank, the Second Panzer Division blocked the town of Carrouges. The French edged warily into the woods, with their Second Company tanks leading. Suddenly shells burst straight-on into the first tank in line. Two of its crew were killed and two were badly burned. Company Captain Jacques de Witasse came running, but could not tell who they were, so badly were their faces burned. Jules Boddaert, the gunner, wrote an account of that day. "It was only by saying my name that he recognized me, and his last words were, 'Quickly, old Boddaert, go get yourself fixed up.' I was immediately transported in an ambulance. First aid was given by Madame Torrès, known as 'Toto.' With a great deal of tenderness and gentleness, she reassured me. Afterwards, for me it was a complete blank."[6]

It took seventeen operations in an American military hospital to give Boddaert back a human face. He had third-degree burns over most of his body. Unfortunately, his injuries were not unusual. If a tank was hit, it burned, and the men inside often burned with it. It was perhaps a miracle that any of them survived. The Rochambelles were working night and day to give them that possibility. And not all the injured were French.

Arlette, carrying the torch of her father's hatred for the Germans, found herself taking care of a wounded German soldier through the warm night of August 12. He was the first patient she didn't simply transport, but sat up with and got to know. He showed her photographs of his family, and she had studied enough German in high school to understand what he was saying. "I took care of him. He talked to me all night about his wife, and his little children, and at dawn he died. It broke my heart, and all the hatred, that was gone," she said. "Hate cannot stand in the face of suffering."

The Rochambelles understood early on that suffering was not confined to the Allied forces, and that many of the German soldiers were conscripts forced to fight for the Nazis. Nonetheless, they were the enemy, struggling desperately against the tightening Allied vise, in a terrain that favored defense. Where it wasn't forest, it was cleared fields, but the fields were divided by thick, raised hedges, a Norman system called "*bocage*" in French. The tank divisions kept getting stuck in the fields and attacked by squads of bazooka-armed Germans.

The ambulance drivers weren't having a much easier time of it. On the back roads of the *bocage*, it was vital that the drivers find their way without getting lost, and it was nearly impossible to do so. They had to find where the triage-treatment centers had been set up, while driving in the dark, on

Jacotte Fournier in her ambulance.

unmarked country roads, along invisible borders of German or liberated territory. Directions often conflicted or led straight into enemy lines. Signposts had been removed or reversed: confusion to the enemy resulted in chaos for the Allies as well. Jacotte and Crapette, now ambulance partners, took turns driving, but Jacotte's night vision was better, and she usually took the wheel after dark. They had to remember the way there, and then the way back, and an error in either direction could spell the end not only for them, but also for the wounded soldiers they carried. Jacotte said she searched constantly for landmarks to remember(a white rock by the roadside, an unusual bush, a tree. It was tense and tiring driving.

Sometimes Crapette would sleep on a stretcher in the back while Jacotte drove. Crapette could fall asleep anywhere, and did. Even back at their bivouac, Jacotte would lie awake, listening to not-so-distant artillery. Sleep was in short supply. Either they were in service, or airplanes were buzzing or artillery falling or later in the war, it was just too cold. "That was the worst," Jacotte said. "I was always anxious." But she pushed past it, and kept going.

From August 12 to 15, the Second Division concentrated on pushing the Nazi forces out of the Argentan area toward the north, into the trap being laid by the Allied forces. The German commanders pleaded with Hitler to allow them to slip out of the noose, but he refused, and ordered them to fight on.[7] For a thirty-kilometer radius south of Argentan, the towns were a patchwork of occupation forces. Whose army held which village was life or death information for the ambulance drivers.

One night Edith, now partnered with Micheline Grimprel, who had joined the group in England, were taking a wounded soldier to Carrouges, and were held up by a long column of American tanks. Edith waited to cross, and at one point thought a tank driver had slowed and signaled them to go. She inched out and then heard a loud crunch, and the ambulance was shoved back off the road. The tank didn't stop or give any sign of having noticed the encounter. The ambulance's front right bumper was twisted and the wheel bent. After the tanks passed, an army Jeep stopped and the driver agreed to take Micheline back to their unit while Edith tried to get the soldier to the hospital. Micheline stood and waved goodbye as they sped off. Edith limped into Carrouges, turned the soldier over to the hospital, and went looking for a garage.[8] She found one with a promise of an overnight repair, and checked into a small hotel (a bed!) and had a big omelette for dinner (no rations!). Edith's love of comfort and good food would lead her into trouble time and again during the war, and she didn't regret a moment of it.

The next morning, the ambulance repaired, she stopped at the hospital to pick up bottles of rubbing alcohol, ether, and other medications. Then she set off to find Micheline and their reconnaissance unit, called "the Spahis" from their formation in North Africa. A motorcycle soldier had a map and tried to help, but wasn't up to date on the latest troop movements. She continued on, feeling the emptiness of the streets like a shiver down her spine, but an occasional pedestrian assured her that Allied troops had been through that way. Then, at the entrance of a village, she felt a deafening blast. She floored it to get into the village and stopped at the first house, where an old man sat on a stoop, and asked if the French soldiers were around. He turned and went into the house without answering. She continued into the village square, and German soldiers poured out of a building, guns drawn and pointed in her direction. She ducked her head out of instinct and a shot rang off her helmet. She jumped out of the car.

"Ach, es ist eine Frau." The lieutenant who had just shot at her became positively polite and agreed to take her to the commandant when she unleashed a torrent of German at him. Raised in Alsace, Edith was fluent in French and German as well as English. The three would serve her well in the war. She argued to the German officers that she belonged to the International Red Cross, was not a belligerent party, and should be released immediately. After a short discussion, they agreed to let her go, escorted by two soldiers who would take her beyond the German lines, if she promised not to reveal that they were there. "I promised. A German promise is not a French promise," she wrote. Edith and the officers returned to the ambulance, which had been stripped of its equipment and the bottle of ether smashed, an event they could smell from several meters away.[9]

The lieutenant asked for two soldiers to accompany Edith, and an older one stepped forward right away, followed after hesitation by a younger one. Ten kilometers down a tiny, winding road, the older German leaned over and pointed out three American soldiers on the edge of a wood. They were part of the Fifth U.S. Armored Division. Edith got out, arms held high, and ran to them, shouting her unit identification as she approached. They told her the French troops were on the other side of the forest. They all turned as the two Germans came running toward them, arms in the air, to surrender. The Americans didn't want them, they were going on an attack. They suggested that the Germans run back to their lines, and said they wouldn't shoot until after twenty paces. Edith, translating from English to German and back again between the men, stopped, horrified. She said she could take them to the rear lines of the American troops and turn them over as prisoners there, and they all agreed to that. The younger one scowled a bit and got an elbow in his ribs from the older one. It seemed to Edith that being taken prisoner was the older German's hope and desire all along. She dropped them off in a prairie full of Americans and wished them luck, then slipped back into the French troop convoy just as a whistle sounded the departure. With barely a moment to let out her breath, boom! Her windshield went flying, shattered from inside out. She was hit by a bit of shrapnel behind her right ear, and the back of the ambulance was shot to pieces. The soldier in the vehicle behind her had accidentally stepped on the firing pedal of his 37mm mortar launcher when he jumped in to go.[10]

Edith sat on the edge of the road for a few minutes, waiting for the ringing in her ears and the shaking in her hands to stop. She had been shot twice that day, and had had the amazing luck to have no injury more serious than a piece of shrapnel lodged behind her ear. She also had been taken prisoner by the enemy, talked her way free, and turned over two German prisoners, leading to Toto's Rule No. 34: *Know how to spend a few hours with the Germans without deserving to have your head shaved.* It had been enough to unsettle any soldier, but Edith did not scare easily. And at the moment, her main concern was finding Micheline.

Born Marie-Louise Charbonnel, nicknamed Maryse, using the nom de guerre of Micheline, she was twenty-six years old and strikingly beautiful. The daughter of a career army officer, she had driven an ambulance on the eastern front in 1940 and then worked for the Resistance during the occupation under the code name of Scarabee. She married another Resistant, Jean-Marie Grimprel, and became Maryse Grimprel. She was the only Rochambelle to take a nom de guerre, a tactic sometimes used as a measure of protection against reprisals on families. It is quite a stretch to imagine that the Nazis would identify the medical battalion's ambulance drivers and then seek to punish their families. But the clandestine and the imaginary had been the tools of Micheline's previous career, and perhaps she did not notice that the terrain had changed.

While a Resistant, Micheline's network had been broken up by the Gestapo and she was forced to flee to avoid arrest. She was airlifted from Angers, France, to London in March 1944, along with an injured British pilot and a French Resistant carrying the seventeen-meter-long map of the Normandy coast and Nazi gun emplacements that became a key to D-Day planning. In London, she argued heatedly with the Resistance group leader Marie-Madeleine Fourcade that she should be sent back into France, and Fourcade refused.[11] Micheline quit the Resistance in a pique, worked in the Free French offices in Covent Garden for several months, and then joined the Rochambelles in England in July 1944, just before they crossed over.

Now Micheline was missing, and Edith was getting very worried. With her ambulance out of action, she got a ride with an army Jeep into Ecouché and found three ambulances parked outside the hospital. She ran over to ask a couple of stretcher-bearers if they had seen Micheline Grimprel. They hadn't, but before the conversation could continue, a blast of mortars slammed down around them. Edith dove under an ambulance and waited for it to end. She slid out and found the two stretcher-bearers she had spoken to moments before dead on the ground. Later she learned that the bombardment was from the Americans, shooting over the heads of her Spahi unit to dislodge the Germans still occupying Ecouché. She had driven too far into town.

She eventually found her unit, but no Micheline. She worried through the night. Micheline should have been back, should have hooked up with the unit, or at the least, been seen by someone by now. At dawn, Edith set out on foot, tracing the route Micheline might have followed. Argentan was four kilometers away. Finally, off the side of the road, she saw a dark shape with a red cross visible on the side. It was an ambulance, destroyed, the hood smashed, the interior partly burned. A dead man was on a stretcher in the back. No sign of Micheline. She walked into Argentan and knocked on the doors of empty houses. A group of old men hiding in a cellar told her all the women and children had left town, and that in the night they had heard tanks. The village priest said the Germans had pulled out in the night, but that he had not seen any uniformed women. She walked back to the Spahi bivouac in yet another apple orchard, and sat down in a corner to cry. She was starting to fear the worst.

Florence Conrad went out and interrogated every villager she could find, and ended up with two possible versions of what happened to Micheline: The first story was that an armored car attacked the ambulance, she got out, hands in the air, and was taken away by the Germans. The second story was that she was taken dead from the ambulance and buried on the spot, but no one knew where. The second story made no sense, as the Germans were not taking the time to bury anyone.

Micheline had told Edith that she was carrying papers for the Resistance, and Edith suggested that that was unwise. Edith thought Micheline was impulsive and rash. "She didn't think, she just acted." During the attack on the orchard near Ducey, Edith and Micheline were a couple of fields over, and Micheline tried to run right into the bombing. Edith told her to wait until the attack was over to go help. Edith said she felt older, wiser, more experienced than Micheline, and she regrets not having insisted that Micheline get rid of those papers. But were the papers her downfall? At that point in Normandy, Resistants were joining the Second Division and action was overt rather than covert. Edith also felt a little guilty that they had separated, against the rules. Micheline might not have run into trouble had she stayed with Edith.

Micheline may have gotten wrong directions on where to take her patient, or may have gotten lost and wandered into enemy territory. The distinction between German and Allied turf was changing all the time. On the afternoon she disappeared, August 13, a squad of Spahis sneaked into Argentan and hung the French flag at the town hall, but then had to pull a quick retreat, outnumbered and outgunned by the Germans. Did Micheline drive into the retaken town unknowingly? Two days later, U.S. troops took the town. "It all went so quickly," Edith said. "One didn't know where the Germans were." The fluidity of possession created great peril.

There was some indication that Micheline joined the 10,000 French women held as political prisoners at the Ravensbruck concentration camp north of Berlin, but none of her names was recorded there on the Germans' meticulous lists. She supposedly then was taken to the Soviet Union by the Russian troops who liberated the camp. More than 50,000 French men from Alsace and Lorraine who were conscripted into the German army also were missing at the end of the war, fate unknown. Many thousands were believed to be held in prison camps in the Soviet Union, but the Stalin regime left little room for discussion of the issue. Raymond Dronne, a division veteran and assembly member after the war, brought up the possibility of Micheline Grimprel being in Russia to Soviet leader Nikita Khrushchev

Zizon Sicco (l), Denise Colin

during a 1950s visit to France, but Khrushchev denied the existence of prison camps. Reports of a French nurse meeting Micheline's description in Soviet camps surfaced in the 1950s, and a note in her handwriting slipped under her mother's door in Paris in 1961 fueled the belief that she was still alive, but she never was found.

Micheline's disappearance and Polly's terrible injuries put a somber and frightening frame around the ambulance drivers' activity from the start of the war. Some of them had thought long and hard before joining the group about whether they would be able to face the fear; others found out about it when fear was sitting on their shoulder, making their hands shake and their imaginations run wild. It was at that moment that all of them found the essence of courage.

"When I was ignorant of the real dangers of the war and when I willfully abstained from thinking about it and focusing on it, I imagined that fear had no place in an honest character. I would willingly class warriors into two categories: the 'good guys' who were never afraid, and the others, the cowards, worthy of all scorn," Zizon wrote. "Now I know that fear is not incompatible with the greatness of a soul, and that heroism and the composure of the brave often mask some hard-repressed trembling."[12]

Zizon discovered the insidious onset of fear and panic, alone one night in an apple orchard. "At night there were so many real and imagined dangers. At night you dreaded everything, even on a night as lovely as when we arrived at Ecouché." It was a beautiful, clear evening: Denise was sound asleep in the ambulance, and Zizon was trying to fall asleep outside. Then she saw four men in the field next to theirs, creeping strangely toward the company's camp. Why were they acting so oddly? If they were French, they had nothing to hide. And if they were not French, they must be German! She must alert the doctors. But the men would see her if she moved. She was slipping into a state of panic, heavy breathing, heart pounding, reason fleeing. The light was fading; she couldn't see them anymore. Where had they gone? She slid off the stretcher onto her stomach and began crawling toward the doctors' tents. A rocket burst in the sky and she took advantage of the brief glow to try to spot the men. They had not moved from their initial position. They had not moved because they were not four German soldiers trying to sneak an attack on the medical company. They had not moved because they were apple trees, cut to strange shapes by the bombing and silhouetted in the darkening sky. She crawled back to her stretcher, mortified, glad she had not arrived at the doctors' tents, grateful for the rocket burst, and hoping she would not hallucinate like that again.[13] Fear, she realized, was just another state of mind.

Summer days were long, with daylight fading between 9:00 and 10:00 P.M., but once it was gone, there was no illumination at all. They had to drive without lights at night to avoid drawing enemy fire, and a twelve-kilometer corridor between Sées and Le Cercueil (French for "the coffin," and for many, it boded ill) was particularly hazardous. The carcasses of burned-out tanks, half-tracks and Jeeps littered the shoulders and sometimes the middle of the road, and driving through it in the pitch night was a blind man's bluff. Zizon and Raymonde were each driving with stretcher bearers one night as Toto and Denise had set up a medical station to treat the many wounded from intense fighting there. Raymonde said she was driving slowly in the dark, with an ambulance full of burn victims, when suddenly Zizon came barreling down the middle of the road and ran smack into her. Zizon was a little near-sighted. "She only saw me at the last moment," Raymonde said. The collision jammed Raymonde's gears, and she couldn't get the truck moving again. "The wounded soldiers started complaining like crazy." Finally she got it going in third gear and roared off down the road.

But Zizon's ambulance was immobile. She and the stretcher-bearer, Henri, would have to wait for help to come. She was getting jumpy sitting like a target on that road. Crack, crack—what was that? Only Henri chewing gum. He told her not to worry, and pulled out a revolver. It only has two bullets, he said, so if the Germans approach, I'll shoot you first and then myself. She explained the Geneva conventions on medical personnel being unarmed, that they could be shot just for having that gun.

She became more worried that Henri would panic and shoot her than she was over the possibility of Germans in the area. Finally Raymonde returned to pick them up, and Zizon took the wheel, as Raymonde was exhausted. Before they could move, something smashed hard into the ambulance and Zizon heard Denise's voice: "It's her, captain!" Denise had persuaded Captain Ceccaldi to come looking for Zizon and they had crashed into her in the dark. Denise was bruised in the wreck, Ceccaldi uninjured. His Jeep had lost a wheel and ended up in a ditch. The ambulance's radiator was smashed and pouring water, and gas was leaking as well. They sent Henri and his revolver to walk the eight kilometers back to camp and bring help, while they sat and stared morosely at the three new wrecks on the corridor. Division mechanics, working at the speed of light, had them up and running the following day.[14]

At that point, Zizon wondered if she would have signed on as an ambulance driver if she'd known how gory it was going to get. "All the blood, the wounds, the dead, could I really stand it? Had I ever imagined that I would be picking up men blown to pieces, be spattered with their blood, and then have it dried on my hands for hours afterward? Had I ever realized what war wounds were like, the burns that transform a man into a swollen monster, and all this repairing of flesh and bone that is the surgery of war?"[15]

The next day, Zizon and Denise were ordered to join a tactical unit nearby, but there was a mix-up in instructions, and they started in the direction of Argentan. A motorcycle soldier stopped them just before the village and turned them around. It was still in German hands. They went back the way they came and tried another direction, toward a village called Fleuré. Another motorcycle soldier cut them off and asked if they'd lost their minds, Fleuré was still in German hands. They went back whence they came and on the way saw a tent in a field, the advance general headquarters. A captain suggested they get out of there before Leclerc found them parading up and down the front line looking for their unit. They returned to Ecouché and found everyone there except Toto and her team.

Toto and Raymonde had been working thirty-six hours with no rest. On August 14, they led a convoy of a half-dozen ambulances from Sées, where the bombing was intense, to Ecouché, where the tactical unit was camped. They were driving a market truck, converted into an ambulance by the Germans and confiscated by the Spahis, marked with a big red cross on the sides, but no national insignia. Night fell before they could reach Ecouché, and Christiane Petit insisted that they stop rather than blunder about in the darkness. Toto called a halt in the woods by Saint Christophe-le-Jajolet. Raymonde was so exhausted she was shaking, and she was afraid if Toto saw her trembling, she would cut her from the ranks. Raymonde slumped against the ambulance door and fell into a deep sleep.

Shortly before dawn, she was awakened by Toto, who murmured that the Germans were there, and not to get out of the ambulance. Raymonde looked out the windshield to see the hulking dark outline of an enormous Panzer, just in front of them. A Jewish Austrian doctor on their team, who took the nom de guerre of Valéry when he fled the Nazis, slipped silently from the back of their ambulance into the forest. Toto got out to talk to the

German commander. Raymonde got out as well, and a German soldier approached her.

"He said to me, 'You know, mademoiselle, war is a sad thing,'" Raymonde recalled. The Panzer was in a convoy of tanks and vehicles covered with soldiers, hanging on every which way they could. The German soldiers began checking the ambulances, and Raymonde knew there was a half-track of men doctors and stretcher-bearers at the back of their convoy. Toto stepped in front of the soldiers forcefully, insisting that there were only women ambulance drivers, no need to bother inspecting.

Those who knew Toto would have no trouble believing that she could single-handedly stop a Panzer division. She had a razor-sharp tongue backed up by steel-plated courage. "She nailed everybody, men, women," said Rosette. "She was very intimidating." She also was Jewish. And she stood on the edge of the forest in the misty dawn and faced down the Nazi commander, denying him inspection of her ambulances and demanding right of passage.

The German commander wanted to take the women prisoner, but there was literally no room in his six Panzers and twelve armored vehicles— the remains of the 116th Panzer Division. Toto held her ground, insisting that they were neutral noncombatants with the Red Cross. Raymonde said the problem both groups faced was that there was no room for either to turn around. The German commander finally agreed to leave them, if they would promise not to move for two hours. The sun was starting to come up as the German column pulled out past them. Toto and Raymonde climbed onto the roof of their truck and saw that the convoy was heading in the direction the Spahi unit had taken the evening before. Christiane remembered that Colonel de Langlade's tactical group was camped nearby, at Montmerrei, and climbed onto the hood of the half-track to lead the convoy of ambulances to safety. It was August 15, the Catholic celebration of the Assumption, and Christiane had begun praying to the Virgin Mary the minute she saw that Panzer. Some of the other drivers thought Toto ought to keep her promise to the Germans and stay put for two hours. She shrugged off their reproaches.

When they reached the tactical unit encampment, Colonel de Langlade, an officer of the old school whose manners were already smooth as silk in that early morning, told Toto in a patronizing way to calm down.

"He didn't believe her at all," Raymonde said. "He told Toto, 'You've had a fright, dear lady, but that certainly wasn't the Germans.'"

Commandant Massu, Toto's bridge-playing boyfriend, knew better. Coffee cup in hand, he interrupted before Toto could lose her famous temper in the direction of a superior officer. "If Madame Torrès says she saw the Germans, it was the Germans," Massu said. A reconnaissance plane was called to go up and check it out, and the German tanks were found trying to hide in a nearby farm courtyard. Toto and Raymonde and the rest of their group continued on to Ecouché.

The division fought around Ecouché for another week, pushing the Germans into what was becoming known as the "Falaise Pocket," as its center was the town of Falaise. The pincer movement was turning into a sack, and the Allies were slowly closing the neck of the sack. The remains of German Army Group B were being squeezed inside, but the pincer movement suddenly was halted for several days by the U.S. command staff, and in the delay, some of the German troops slipped out. When the Allies finally closed it, they took 50,000 Germans prisoner. Leclerc wrote a letter to General de Gaulle, who had just arrived in France for the first time since 1940, updating the Second Division's situation. He reported that in the Falaise battles of the previous week, the division had seen 60 of its soldiers killed and 550 wounded.

During the Falaise battle, the Rochambelles worked around the clock, evacuating wounded soldiers through the hazards of shelling and bombardment. Rosette got a letter from her mother while they were there, admonishing her for having gone rowing on a lake in England with some young officers. It was far too dangerous to the social reputation of a proper young lady, her mother said. Rosette, her helmet on against incoming artillery, had a good laugh. The contrast between past and present dangers was ironic, and Rosette felt the gap widen between her previous life as a civilian and her current station as a soldier. At any rate, neither handsome young officers in rowboats nor lethal artillery barrages would give Rosette pause. She said she was simply too busy to stop and be afraid.

She also had an eye for amusing moments in the war, and her letters to her mother reflected that (and purposefully did not mention times of danger or despair). Driving the ambulance full of wounded soldiers near Ecouché, Rosette ran into the engineering truck in front of her when it turned suddenly off the road. She slammed on the brakes, but the impact still was brutal. "I was full of remorse for the wounded, who added to my despair by insulting me thoroughly: 'You should be ashamed to be an ambulance driver when you don't know how to drive!' I would be, they told me, responsible for their deaths," she wrote. She and Arlette got the soldiers to the hospital nonetheless, and the doctor said their days were not numbered. "Arlette and I let loose a sigh of relief. We would have to try to be a little less sensitive."

One day near Ecouché, they had to bury several division soldiers and the chaplain was not there, so Toto asked Christiane to preside. She grabbed her prayer book and went to work. "I said the prayers that came to me. It wasn't a real mass. But the soldiers were very touched that there were at least some prayers," she said. If it wasn't a "real" mass, then it was all right for a woman to say it, following the same pattern of logic that held that the Rochambelles were not "real" women, they were ambulance drivers.

During that intense fortnight, two of Edith's ambulances were destroyed, and Toto and Raymonde had taken the Spahi-confiscated market truck to help fill the gap in vehicles. What the Spahis didn't find was the cache of Calvados under the stretchers. The women were pleased: a shot of Calvados—brandy made from apples—would be just what the doctor ordered for the lightly injured. They also were handing out eye drops to relieve the grittiness. It was dry that summer, and the troop movements and heavy vehicles seemed to grind a constant dust into the air.

One morning, in yet another apple orchard, Anne-Marie Davion asked Jacotte and Crapette if they would like some coffee. They were about to have some, to share a pleasantly ordinary moment in the midst of tension and chaos, when the shrieking whistle of an incoming mortar sent them facedown flat on the ground, eating dirt, praying this one wasn't for them. It wasn't. But the camp next to theirs had one dead, eleven wounded. "It was in moments like that when you had to gather all your force and know how to dominate your emotions, in order to act in the most efficient way possible," Jacotte wrote. "Our 'profession' included knowing how to cover up your sadness and be brave, but we often had very heavy hearts." [16]

Jacotte and Crapette got lost one night around the same area and decided to await the dawn at an abandoned farm rather than wander in the dark. But shots rang out nearby, and shadows seemed to lengthen and twitch. On that night, fear became a motivating factor: they decided they would rather take their chances on the dark road back to the medical company's tent. The doctor on duty was surprised to see them at that hour, but with one look at their red eyes and tight lips he led them wordlessly back to a couple of empty stretchers. They managed to get a couple of hours' sleep before the captain charged in at 5:00 A.M. and shouted at them to jump up and follow him.

The lack of sleep was the most difficult thing to overcome for Jacotte. She didn't mind the hunger and the dirt, or not being able to bathe, but having no sleep for days on end was stretching her nerves. She and Crapette chewed GI-issue gum, smoked cigarettes and drank instant Nescafé to stay awake.

The division relied on fresh food from the local farmers to round out their rations, but the Rochambelles found little cooperation from the Norman peasants. One farmer sent his eight-year-old daughter to sell eggs, milk, and chickens to the army, and one day Zizon asked her if she was pleased that the French soldiers had replaced the Germans. The girl replied "Oh, yes! The Germans were bad to us. They didn't pay like you do."[17]

The First Company counted itself lucky in its cook, an Italian who had had a restaurant in Rabat before the war. Zizon described his method of persuading the Normans to come up with supplies: He went along to farms on their route and announced that he needed food for the troops. The farmers would respond that they had nothing to give him. "That's no doubt because you sold too much to the *boches!*" he would reply. "Fine, look, I need five kilos of butter, twenty dozen eggs and twelve chickens. The price is such and such, and I'll pay you that. Think about it. I'll be back in a half-hour. If you still have nothing, I'll demand the double and it'll be free." He carried a rifle with him and toyed with it in a convincing way while speaking. When he returned, the supplies were always ready.[18]

The war also brought cultural differences across the regions to light. "In Normandy the peasants certainly weren't pleased with us," Anne Hastings said. "What they did say is first there were Germans, then you. They obviously thought we were disturbing them. They never offered us anything, you had to pay for every egg."

The Canadians defeated the last German Tiger brigade on August 16 and liberated the town of Falaise. The neck of the Allies' sack closed on the Germans on August 20, and with it, the Battle of Normandy was over.

Losses on both sides were high. Some 200,000 Germans were killed and another 200,000 taken prisoner.[19]

On the Allied side, an estimated 36,000 soldiers died (20,000 of them Americans) and 140,000 were injured in Normandy. A quarter of the deaths occurred on D-Day alone. For the Leclerc division, its first two weeks of war saw 141 dead, 78 missing and 618 injured.[20] One of the missing and one of the wounded were Rochambelles.

The Second Division's experience in Normandy had manifold effects, both consolidating the tactical groups as effective fighting units and the overall division as part of the U.S. Third Army. Another result was an end to the contempt and hostility in which some of the division men had held the women ambulance drivers. Their performance under combat in Normandy erased the most entrenched doubts. "We admired the Rochambelles for their courage and their devotion," Dr. Guy Chauliac said. "They made a place for themselves even though we didn't want them. The Rochambelles were excellent, remarkable."

Among those who changed his mind in Normandy was Leclerc. "He held them in great esteem," Chauliac said. (François Jacob, the other division doctor from Rabat, was severely injured in the bombing near Ducey, evacuated by ambulance drivers from another unit, and spent a year in hospitals, recovering. He went on to win the Nobel Prize for his research discovering the role of DNA.)

Toto recounted in her memoir that one day a tank regiment officer who had tried his best to block the women from joining the division approached her. "You know what I thought of this female section and the pessimism of my predictions for its behavior under combat? Well, this is what I think now." He stood at attention, removed his beret and made a deep bow, "à la D'Artagnan." Toto was touched. He became a good friend, and a few months later, she picked him up wounded off the field and got him to a hospital.[21]

Colonel Pierre Billotte, who led the tactical unit from August until mid-September, noted in his memoirs that the Rochambelles "rivaled the men in audacity" in the Normandy operations. Audacity seemed to be a Second Division trademark. Luckily for the French, it was a quality Patton admired, both in strategy and in people. Before Normandy was even wrapped up, Leclerc was in to see him about the prize: Paris. "Leclerc of the 2d French Armored Division came in, very much excited . . . he said, among other things, that if he were not allowed to advance on Paris, he would resign. I told him in my best French that he was a baby, and I would not have division commanders tell me where they would fight, and that anyway I had left him in the most dangerous place," Patton wrote in his diary on August 14. "We parted friends." [22]

Leclerc's aide, Christian Girard, wrote that in that meeting, Patton promised Leclerc Paris, and that he motioned to his compatriot, Major General John S. Wood, and said, "Look at Wood, he's even more annoying than you are."[23] Patton wrote that he was in charge of 450,000 men in the war. Leclerc had just 15,000 men—and thirty-three women, at that point— but did not hesitate to make demands on Patton.

Leclerc was in a delicate position. He was on his home turf, but could not hope to win the war alone. He owed everything the division had, from Sherman tanks to Thompson machine guns, to soldiers' uniforms, boots, and even their rations, to the Americans. But liberating France was in the French soldiers' hearts as well as heads, and emotion could not be distilled from logic in the heat of the war. Conflicts with the Allied command were inevitable. The question of Paris was one of those points of discord, and by the third week of August, it was on everyone's mind. Parisians felt the pull of home like a powerful magnet, while the politically inclined were calculating the postwar gains of liberating the capital.

The Allied command did not favor an approach to Paris. It was not strategically significant, it was not practical to send an armored division into an urban setting, and worst of all, the army would then be responsible for feeding and supplying the population of Paris once it was in Allied hands. The Allied command wanted to bypass Paris and push on toward the Rhine. Leclerc and de Gaulle, however, were adamant that the Second Division should take Paris, and take it now. The Resistance in Paris had begun an endgame uprising that could turn into a massacre without military backup, and had sent messengers to Normandy to urge the army to move immediately on the capital. Leclerc ordered a small reconnaissance unit to check out the situation, and then went to see U.S. Army General Omar Bradley. He came back on August 22 with a smile on his face, and, barely out of his Jeep, gave the order: immediate departure for Paris.

When most women go to Paris, they think about what they're going to wear. The Rochambelles were no exception. Zizon was in a particular fix because her dress uniform had been shot up and burned at Ducey. All she had were fatigues. Toto said she could take advantage of a lull in the action to run to a PX the following day and get a new uniform. She would have to leave at 5:00 A.M. and get back early. "I went to sleep with the comforting perspective of being able to contribute to edifying the Parisians on the well-known elegance of the Rochambelles," she wrote.[24]

But she was awakened at 3:00 A.M. They were moving out for Paris, and the army did not care how Zizon would look when she got there.

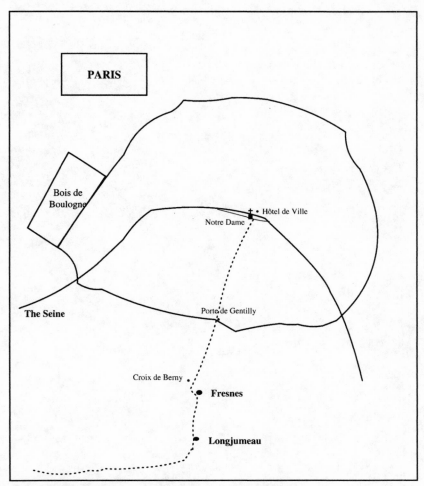

The Rochambelles' route to Paris, August 24-25, 1944

CHAPTER FOUR

City of Light Rekindled

Paris was home for many of the Rochambelles and the Second Division soldiers and officers, and absence had sharpened their affection for the city to hugely sentimental proportions. For others, it was the first time they had set foot in the city of legend, city of light. Paris, repository of France's soul, treasury of its historical jewels, and wellspring of its vainglory, lay at its liberators' feet on the morning of August 25. But the insouciant Paris they had left behind had changed, four years of occupation having stripped bare the shelves, emptied the store windows, and strangled the flow in the streets. Ordinary bustle and hum had been muted by the staccato of jackboots on the paving stones.

During the occupation, Parisians had become accustomed to not seeing the Germans in the capital, to looking right past them as though they did not exist. But in the first ten days of August 1944, as the Allies pushed southward from the Normandy coast, Parisians watched closely as the Germans began burning papers, removing archives and evacuating German civilians. The capital sensed a breeze of liberation blowing its way and edged into a state of nervous anxiety, excited at the prospect of freedom, worried about possible destruction, concerned about the political aftermath.

By August 15, the moribund economic life of the capital had ground to a standstill. No subway trains were running, electric power was cut to ninety minutes a day, little to no cooking gas was available. German soldiers at street barriers began confiscating every bicycle they saw. The railway train engineers had gone out on strike on August 10, but no passenger trains had been running for weeks at any rate. Then the city police went on strike, and that had a strong psychological effect on Parisians. By August 18, mail service disappeared and Resistance posters began appearing on walls.[1] The only thing running in the streets was rumor, spinning around the date the Allies would reach the capital.

The changes in the capital were not only physical. Four years of occupation also had distilled political differences into sharply divergent camps, and nowhere was that more evident than in the ranks of the Resistance. If the occupation was a long dark night, the dawn of liberation was being viewed in very different colors. Historian Adrien Dansette defined three goals of the Resistance: a unanimous goal of national insurrection against the occupier, a less-unanimous goal of political revolution to oust the Vichy regime, and a highly contested goal of social revolution to redraw the economic map of France.[2] In broad strokes, the far right hoped to reinstate the order of pre-war institutions and the far left hoped to install a worker's republic along Soviet lines. The center, a precariously thin turf, was rapidly being occupied by de Gaulle.

De Gaulle had managed to pull all the major Resistance factions under an umbrella eventually called the French Forces of the Interior (FFI) in 1943, and put the legendary Jean Moulin, a prefect turned Resistant, in charge of them. It was a fragile coalition, in which individual political interests were barely outweighed by the national interest of liberation. By the summer of 1944, the Resistance had prepared the terrain for victory, and the Paris regional commander, Henri Rol-Tanguy, a communist union leader, was maneuvering sharply to put the left in power. De Gaulle was conscious of the delicate political balance at hand; Leclerc and his soldiers instead were focused on the military task of cleaning out the Germans.

This was the Paris the Rochambelles were on their way to discover. First they had to get there, and German defenses in the suburbs around the capital were strong. The U.S. Fourth Infantry Division swung around to the eastern side of the city, charged with taking control of the bridges across the Seine. Leclerc sent his tactical groups on different routes through the southwest and southern suburbs, and urged them to swiftness. German resistance stopped the division on August 24 just south of the capital.

The Second Company was caught by a German antitank battery outside the town of Antony, about ten kilometers south of Paris, where a tank had its cannon muzzle shot off by an 88mm shell. A civilian resident showed the Second Company soldiers how to get behind the guns, and they filed through the back streets to within 100 meters of the enemy. Just then, the Germans noticed they were there, and started turning their big gun around to shoot. It swung slowly, but the French tank gunner was quick, and one well-aimed shell took out the German battery. The intersection at Croix de Berny would soon be theirs.

At Longjumeau, Toto and Denise set up a temporary treatment center for the influx of wounded soldiers, while Raymonde and Zizon drove their ambulances alone, one stretcher-bearer between them and a local member of the Resistance to help them get around. On the night of August 24, they were exhausted by the time some American soldiers stopped them outside Dourdan, about forty-five kilometers southwest of Paris. German troops were still in the area, it would be dangerous to continue through the night. Zizon and Raymonde slept in one ambulance, the men in the other. They were awakened before dawn by flashlights shining on their faces and commotion outside the ambulance. Some black American soldiers were looking at them, laughing loudly. Zizon tried to find her sense of humor but failed, and explained that they really needed to sleep. The soldiers left. At daybreak they discovered the source of their hilarity. She and Raymonde had slept with the windshield open, and the exhaust from passing tanks had left their faces encrusted with a fine black powder. They were unknowingly in blackface.

Jacotte and Crapette had driven through a raging thunderstorm the night of the 23rd, and normally Jacotte was afraid of lightning, but that night she was hoping for more so she could see the road ahead. Jacotte asked Crapette about her nickname once, and got a terse reply: Crapette was her name and that was that. She didn't ask again. It also was the name of a popular card game at the time, but Crapette played a lot more music than cards. At any rate, Jacotte and Crapette were becoming fast friends, and would remain partners throughout the war. "She was an exceptional young woman," Jacotte said. "She left a memory for everyone who ever knew her." They drove across the town of Chartres at 2:00 A.M. in a streaming rain, and yet the streets were lined with people who had turned out to cheer them on.

On August 24, they worked around the fighting at Croix de Berny, which, aside from the Second Company's tank battle, was well defended by Germans behind the high walls of the Fresnes prison. Finally that night they were sent to get some rest, and told to park the ambulance in a nearby field for safety. They were just tucking into their stretchers when a mortar hit nearby and peppered the ambulance with shrapnel and mud. Several soldiers were hit; one of them died in Jacotte's arms. She and Crapette took

the injured men to the Longjumeau treatment center in lights-out conditions, avoiding the gaping holes punched in the road, as well as the wires
hanging down from trees, set to trigger hidden mines. It was a very tense
ride, and they stayed the night at the hospital rather than return to Fresnes.

Rosette and Arlette, meanwhile, had another little accident, this time
driving off the road in the dark into a cannon. It caused no damage, and
they recovered the road fairly easily, but the bump apparently knocked a
duffel bag off its hook on the outside of the ambulance. In that duffel bag
were the baby clothes, diapers, and supplies Arlette had carefully selected in
England to prepare for her impending marriage to Georges Ratard. They
had arranged their personal belongings outside and on top of the ambulance in order to leave more room for injured soldiers inside. They discovered the loss the next morning, as they were working with the wounded in
the suburbs. Arlette was inconsolable, going on and on about the baby
clothes to Rosette. The next day, Georges Ratard found the bag and
brought it to them. "Whew! The future little Ratard will have a wardrobe
and we can go liberate Paris with a light heart," Rosette wrote with a touch
of sarcasm.

The Americans had told Leclerc that he couldn't move an armored division more than twenty-five kilometers a day. To get to Paris, he pushed
them nearly 200 kilometers in a little over two days, and they had fought
hard through the day of the 24th. They needed to rest and regroup. Leclerc
saw that he would have to wait for morning to approach the city, and he
couldn't stand it. He was afraid the U.S. Fourth Division would get in first,
if its eastern approach were less well defended, and then the Americans
would go down in history as the liberators of Paris. Leclerc pointed at the
first captain he saw and ordered him to get a company inside the capital that
night. It was Raymond Dronne's Ninth Infantry Company. Three Second
Company tanks were told to accompany them, and the soldiers left behind
in the suburbs listened to sketchy reports over the radio along the way.

Gaston Eve, a twenty-four-year-old Anglo-Frenchman, was driving the
tank *Montmirail*. A Resistant rode with them to guide them through the
suburbs. As they progressed closer to the city, windows in buildings lining
the route began to open at the sound of the tanks and vehicles passing by.
"Windows were opening, and hundreds of people started coming out,
thinking we were the Americans. No one wanted to believe we were a
French division. An amazed old man kept repeating, 'Impossible, impossi-

ble . . . ' The people gave us bottles [of wine] and asked where we were from in America," he wrote.[3]

Daylight faded as they reached the Seine, and turned left along the quay to the Place de l'Hôtel de Ville, where Paris city hall stands. On the island in the river, the cathedral of Notre Dame began ringing its bells, and nearby churches joined in. A tank radio operator signaled to the division behind in the suburbs, told them to listen to the music, and held his microphone up outside the tank. The church bells of Paris were ringing, chiming out the news that liberation had, at long last, arrived. Paris was on her way back to independence.

A French radio journalist reached Dronne that night and interviewed him on the scene, emphasizing to his audience that it was French troops liberating the city, and then turned to Dronne's adjutant and said, "Let's see where this French soldier is from, where were you born, young man?" And the soldier replied, "Constantinople."[4] Simple formulas never applied to the Second Division. In the morning, a Paris newspaper had a photograph of the three tanks outside city hall, and the tank crews saw it and laughed aloud with pleasure. It had to be true, they were really there: it was in the newspaper.

At first light on the following day, August 25, the rest of the division rolled toward the capital. Paris was in view and they were all in a state of high anticipation. They did not know how defended the city would be, or what it would cost to retake the capital, but they were on their way.

Toto and Raymonde entered the city through the Porte de Gentilly in the stillness of early morning, and as word spread, people came pouring into the streets. Women in hairnets and nightgowns, unshaven men, barefoot children, everyone throwing themselves onto the French troops. Some sniper fire from rooftops scattered the crowds briefly but did not stop the great embrace. Tank driver Gaston Eve remarked later that he had never been kissed so much in his life, before or after, as on the day of liberation.

Jacotte called the crowds "a human tide." The Parisians threw themselves at the soldiers, and at the ambulance, and then backing off in surprise when they saw that the drivers were women. "As soon as they approached us, people were visibly surprised to see a woman at the wheel," she wrote. She couldn't believe it had been five years since she had been home. She pulled the ambulance up in front of Notre Dame behind the rest of the column, and joined many of the soldiers in a silent, heartfelt prayer of thanks. "If everything had ended right then, life would have been worth living."[5]

A tank battalion was sent down to Place Saint Michel, and discovered a nest of enemy artillery around the Senate building and the Ecole des Mines at the Luxembourg Gardens. Some 600 German troops were holed up and shooting, and a Panzer defended the entrance. A group of French militiamen, Nazi supporters, fired on the French soldiers from the Lycée Saint-Louis on the Boulevard Saint-Michel. A tank maneuvered into position behind the Panzer and shot, ripping off its rear tread. The crew abandoned the vehicle and disappeared into the city. The battalion commander, Colonel Joseph Putz, brought in a German prisoner, a colonel, to order remaining troops to surrender.

"What I find really strange about this war is that everywhere there's a mix of civilians and military," Rosette wrote her mother. "As soon as the shooting stops, you see the kids come out of the hedges, the guys start weeding their cabbages. We feel like we're the band of crazies who despite their insanity cannot prevent normal life from continuing on its parallel course. The tanks gathered at the Boulevard St.-Michel, ready at that moment to charge on the Luxembourg, were covered with children as though they were going on parade."

Further north, at the Place de la Concorde, a pitched tank battle went on for over an hour until the German tanks in the Tuileries gardens surrendered. One division commandant, Jean Fanneau de La Horie, joked afterward that at one point, only he and the obelisk were still standing, that everyone else in the plaza had hit the ground when the firing began.

Aiming at the Hotel Meurice, where the German high command was headquartered on the Rue de Rivoli, Captain Jacques Branet's Third Company was moving carefully up the street, infantrymen hugging the sides of the buildings, dashing across the exposed arches. Grenades tossed from upper windows landed inside several tanks in the street. One crew threw a grenade back out before it exploded; another wasn't so lucky. As Branet and his men advanced, a grenade suddenly burst in front of them, showering them with shrapnel and deafening them with the blast. Branet's ear was bleeding and he had bits of metal sprayed into his body. He was taken to a Red Cross infirmary at the Comédie Française, where he stayed for about an hour, when he decided that he was fine and got up to return to the fight-

Anne-Marie Davion with German officer's hat on radiator grill, in Paris

ing. Branet had promised Anne-Marie a captured German helmet for a
hood ornament after she had complained to him about the Germans using
French *kepis* as vehicle trophies. When Branet was wounded, he ordered his
driver to follow through on the mission.

The German commander of Paris, Dietrich von Choltitz, was taken at
his headquarters in the Hotel Meurice and agreed to call a cease-fire at 3:30
P.M. He surrendered officially to Leclerc. Anne-Marie got her helmet, the
highest-ranking hat Branet's driver could find. She stuck it on the radiator
grill of her ambulance. Jacques and Anne-Marie didn't try to keep their romance a secret, but nor did they flaunt it in front of the others. Jacques
would lean back, smoking his pipe, while Anne-Marie chattered vivaciously
around him. He was quiet, solitary by instinct and structured by preference,
while she was sociable, creative, and joyful. It was an attraction of opposites,
but the attraction ran deep.

With von Choltitz's surrender, Paris was back in French hands, and the
city erupted in joy and celebration. The liberation of Paris had not been
without cost, however: the division counted 71 dead and 225 wounded in
the fighting. Among the wounded was Marianne Glaser, a Rochambelle
who, with her fluent French, English, and German, had been requisitioned
as a translator by the Americans since Utah Beach. She was shot in the arm
while walking in the city. It was not a serious injury, but it sidelined her
from continuing with the army. On the German side, the division reported
3,200 dead and 12,500 prisoners. The American infantry brought in another 5,000 German prisoners.[6]

Underneath the surface exhilaration, postliberation political wrangling
had already begun. At the Montparnasse train station where Leclerc and de
Gaulle had established headquarters, the two men found themselves pulled
in many directions at once. U.S. Army General Leonard Gerow ordered
Leclerc to take the Second Division out of the city and start cleaning out
the northern suburbs. At the same time, FFI leader Rol-Tanguy stuck his
name on subsequent copies of the official surrender document, next to
Leclerc's, as though von Choltitz had surrendered to him. The FFI, with its
large communist base, was claiming the liberation for itself—with no mention of the Second Division—in posters and broadsheets. The FFI certainly
had been instrumental in the city's liberation, and had seen about a thousand members killed in the process, but they were not alone. De Gaulle decided to stake out his own territory by holding a parade of the Second

Division down the Champs-Elysées the following day. When Gerow forbade participation by Leclerc and his troops, Leclerc sent him to de Gaulle, who asked to "borrow" Leclerc back from the Americans for a day. Gerow was furious.

The sniper fire that interrupted, but did not halt, the August 26 parade was a metaphor for the political scene at hand. The Gaullists were trying to recover and claim France's national glory, and there were many, of different political stripes, who did not want them to have it. And there were others whose first thoughts focused on revenge, on punishing those who had not suffered during the occupation, on eliminating those who had actively supported the Nazis. Now that Paris was liberated, long-harbored resentments burst to the surface.

The most visible targets were women who had consorted with the enemy. They were stripped naked and had their heads shaved, then were daubed with tar and marched through the streets. The national humiliation thus could be personified, fault could be laid at a feminine door, and the rest of the country could proceed with a clear conscience. For the male collaborators, humiliation was not part of the punishment formula. Many of them, men in powerful positions who had used the occupation to profit financially or socially, were simply shot dead. The FFI acted with impunity against its targets. Not all of the victims were in fact collaborators, and there were errors of identity as well as personal vendettas carried out under political cover. There was also an element of class warfare in some of the attacks: chateaux pillaged in the countryside, luxury apartments looted in the city under pretext of "collaboration." Historian Robert Aron estimated that between 30,000 and 40,000 French were killed in acts of vengeance after liberation.[7]

That was the backbite, the chilling hangover that followed the liberation. Joy was the order of the day itself. On August 25, people in the streets jumped on every vehicle they saw. When Zizon and Denise's ambulance broke down in the middle of a crowd, they thought they would never get out of there. The ambulance had not been running smoothly, and when it quit altogether, it was immediately swallowed up by the masses, while Zizon tried to explain that they were broken down and that they needed to hurry to keep up with their convoy. A young man finally understood and got the crowd to move, opened the hood, and pulled out the carburetor, jammed full of mud. They cleaned it, the ambulance started up, and off they went.

At every stop men were jumping on the running boards. It was early morning, no one had shaved, and all the whiskery kisses they were getting were raking their skin raw. Both Zizon and Denise had one red cheek, on the window side.

The chaos in the streets had not yet begun when Marie-Thérèse Pezet, a dark-haired, thirty-one-year-old law student, was walking to mass at Notre Dame on the morning of August 25. The streets were empty and quiet. When she reached rue Saint Jacques, she looked in amazement at a vehicle rolling slowly up the street. "What kind of toad is that?" she wondered. It was the first Jeep she had seen. A column of tanks and vehicles continued up the street behind it, and Marie-Thérèse stood transfixed. People started pouring into the street, shouting that Leclerc had arrived! Leclerc had arrived! The column stopped for a few minutes, and soldiers were shouting out family telephone numbers to the crowd, could they call and let them know that Jean, Pierre, Georges, was in Paris. Just in front of Marie-Thérèse, an ambulance came to a halt, the driver's window rolled up despite the heat. She walked up to the truck and tapped on the window, asking if there was someone she could call for them. The window opened slowly, and Marie-Thérèse was astounded. The driver and her partner were women! It was Jacotte and Crapette. Jacotte declined, politely, and closed the window. But that was it for Marie-Thérèse. If women could be in Leclerc's division, she was doing nothing else until she joined.

Most of the Rochambelles gathered at the Place de l'Hôtel de Ville. Rosette and Arlette went over to the Préfecture and saw von Choltitz escorted in. Walking along the quay, they were stopped by a car full of Resistance members, who said they wanted to kiss an American. "I told them I was French. They left, saying, 'Merde! Just our luck!'" Rosette recounted. Rosette later went on a tour of the city with one of the division doctors in a Jeep, "with Paris barely liberated, where there was still shooting going on, where we passed German tanks burning. The boulevards were practically deserted. FFI cars were tearing around at insane speeds. In the Tuileries a bunch of cars had been abandoned. Anyone could take them, and soldiers, Resistants and civilians were helping themselves," she wrote. A young woman wearing a Red Cross uniform approached Rosette with a single question: How could she join? She was Tony Binoche Rostand, married to

Rosette Trinquet (l) and Arlette Hautefeille, in Paris

the grandson of the writer Edmond Rostand. When she joined the group, the women called her Cyrano's granddaughter.

Arlette, meanwhile, had been hanging around Notre Dame when a striking young woman approached and asked if she could do something for her. "I'd really like to take a shower," Arlette told her. She didn't recognize the woman, but she was Elina Labourdette, a glamourous young film star at the time. She took Arlette to her parents' apartment on the Ile de la Cité to get cleaned up. The elegant apartment had a rooftop terrace overlooking the Seine and the Cathedral of Notre Dame. "I'd never seen anything so beautiful," Arlette said. She chattered happily to Elina, explaining that she and her fiancé wanted to get married but didn't have a clue how to get it done in the middle of a war. Elina volunteered to help.

Florence Conrad took charge of the legal details, and Elina and her parents arranged to hold the reception at their apartment. Conrad took Arlette to see General Koenig, who gave his permission, then to the archbishop of Paris, who refused to marry them at Notre Dame, saying it was reserved for royalty. Conrad offered to lend Arlette her daughter's wedding gown, and took her to an apartment she had kept in Paris to try it on. The building's concierge hemmed the dress, Elina Labourdette's mother loaned Arlette a veil, and the outfit was complete. Georges found a white shirt to wear with his dress uniform, and Arlette went with a police officer to open a jewelry store so that they could buy rings. The tank brigade's command staff organized the music, the church, and the priest. "I didn't do a thing," Arlette recalled. "I was on a little cloud."

The night before the wedding, on August 27, Rosette, Arlette, Georges, and a few other division officers were invited to the Labourdettes' for dinner. Rosette and Arlette arrived in their fatigues, just slightly blood-stained, and found themselves seated with Jean Cocteau and Robert Bresson, the celebrated directors of French cinema, as well as the actor Jean Marais and the painter Christian Bérard. Cocteau stood, lifted his champagne glass, and proposed a toast to the division soldiers, comparing them to archangels at the barricades, untouchable by bullets, heroic in history. Cocteau later referred to the division as "that team which sees with but one eye and beats with but one heart."[8] Bresson promised to make a star of Rosette in a film after the war, but it wasn't her ambition. She assured him that she could not act. Georges Ratard talked Marais into sign-

Arlette Hautefeuille in her wedding dress, on the Labourdette's rooftop terrace. Photo courtesy of Madame Arlette Hautefeuille Ratard.

ing up with the division, and he drove an army tanker truck for the rest of the war.

When Arlette and Georges arrived at the mayor's office of the 4th arrondissement on August 28, they found American flags decorating the hall. Because the officials had dealt with Conrad, and the accompanying officers wore American uniforms, they had assumed it was an American wedding. The FFI sent an enormous bouquet of red-white-and-blue flowers. The mayor had been appointed to his post the evening before by the Resistance, and had never performed a wedding. He interrupted the ceremony repeatedly to ask the assistant mayor how to proceed. They went to Notre Dame des Victoires church for the religious part of the ceremony (in France, couples must be married first by the state, then may be married by the church as well), and then to the Labourdettes' for a reception, a feast with food not seen in Paris in years. For their honeymoon, the Labourdettes loaned the couple a studio apartment they had on the Quai des Orfèvres. Arlette had a week's leave from the Rochambeau Group, and Georges took a day or two. Arlette remembers the sheets were crepe de chine and so slippery that the pillows kept falling on the floor.

There is a black-and-white photograph of Arlette in her wedding dress, standing on the Labourdettes' rooftop terrace. A breeze has just lifted a corner of the veil, Paris stretches out in the background, and Arlette's face is radiant. It was a miracle of a wedding, set in a celestial moment in history, pulled together by the goodwill and energy of friends and strangers, all in a mood for celebration. Arlette would later say that theirs was the first wedding in free Paris.

Zizon had dreamed of the glory of liberating Paris, but now that they were there she just felt exhausted. Also she was still in her dirty fatigues. Then Toto loaned her an extra dress uniform, and Captain Ceccaldi offered to take her and Denise to Montmartre to dinner in his Jeep. "Paris is somber. Paris is calm. Paris is sinister, but, at last, it's Paris!" she wrote.[9]

By this time, the other women were snickering and calling Zizon "la Pompadour," because Ceccaldi had developed a crush on her (the Marquise de Pompadour was the powerful mistress of Louis XV). Ceccaldi tried at one point to have her transferred to a less dangerous duty, but incurred such wrath on her part that he gave up.

Dinner with Ceccaldi didn't turn out so well either. His Corsican driver knew a restaurant of "compatriots" that he swore would be stocked with black-market bounty, a tempting thought after nearly a month of K-rations. They arrived, knocked on a locked door and heard a rude and violent response. The driver shouted his name and banged on the door, which then opened to "an army of cousins" full of tears and embraces. They promised a delicious dinner of cabbage and chicken stew. A pastis cocktail was served. But first, the cousins needed to go settle a score with a neighbor. The Corsicans slid on their FFI armbands and departed. Shots were fired, shouts were heard, and the group returned, pleased, to ask what Ceccaldi thought of that? The captain said he didn't think before eating. Sure, they said, but first there's another little score to settle, this one requiring the Jeep and driver. Off they went before Ceccaldi could stop them. They promised to be quick. They returned at 4:00 A.M., surrendered the Jeep and driver, and the very hungry Ceccaldi, Zizon and Denise went back to the encampment to hunt up some rations.[10]

When they first arrived in Paris, the Rochambelles were bivouacked at the Jardin des Plantes, where the Paris zoo was then located. On the second night, the Germans flew over and bombed the quays of the Seine, presumably aiming for the bridges, but instead hit the Halle aux Vins (wine market) next door to the Jardin des Plantes, which sent up a great flambée of alcohol. "Our greatest fear was that the lions would escape," Rosette said. Bombs they were getting used to. Hungry lions were another matter. The next day the group moved to the Jardin de Bagatelle, in the Bois de Boulogne, on the western edge of Paris.

Edith and Lucie were not pleased with the new location, so far from the action of the city. After enjoying a swim in the lake, washing out some clothes, and scrubbing down their ambulances, they felt they'd done their bit. But a heavy iron gate locked them in at night, ostensibly for their own security. They had parked their ambulance against the back wall, and climbing up to have a look, found a tree branch hanging close enough to shinny down the other side. They took the first ambulance in line on the street and they were off, around the Arc de Triomphe, down the Champs-Elysées, drinking in the vision of Paris waking from its nightmare of occupation. The men wore bits and pieces of uniforms; the women seemed to have found only tulle and voile, and to have concocted floaty, fluffy little

Rochambelles bivouacked at the Bagatelle Gardens, August 1944. First row, standing, l-r: Lucie Deplancke, Arlette Hautefeuille, Toto. Seated, back row, l-r: Michette de Steinheil, Edith Schaller, Antoinette Berger, Marie-Thérèse Pezet, Christiane Petit, Nicole Mangini.

dresses out of them. Lucie, born and raised in Paris, and equipped with the street smarts and cheek that made her the "*titi Parisienne*" of the group, knew exactly where to go. Edith had lived in the capital only briefly, once in boarding school and then later in nursing school. Down to the Concorde, the Tuileries, around Place de la Madeleine, up the boulevard des Italiens, everywhere the shop windows were decorated with little *bleu-blanc-rouge* flags. Around Palais-Royal and over the Pont Neuf, they pulled up in front of Notre Dame and jumped out of the car to marvel at its majesty.[11]

Lucie dropped Edith at her cousin's apartment and arranged to return at 5:00 A.M. to pick her up. Edith and her cousin visited through the night, caught a couple of hours' sleep, and then Lucie was back. They sneaked back into Bagatelle through a small door in the gate, already opened at dawn, and slept until someone came to see if they were ill. They pretended to participate in the day's exercises, dreaming of the night. They did it over and over again, partying with Lucie's friends at the Paris Opera, visiting old acquaintances, and enjoying the release from both military discipline and enemy occupation. Edith doesn't remember how many times they sneaked out at night and caught up their sleep with naps during the day, until one day Toto called them out: they had been caught. They were dressed down verbally and put on telephone duty. The telephone was in a restaurant at the entrance of the Bois de Boulogne, and the restaurant was perfectly empty and dreary. Lucie picked up the telephone and called her friends, and Edith called her cousins, and they invited them all to bring lunch to the Bagatelle. The friends and cousins arrived with arms full of roast chickens, ham, cakes, and wine and everyone sat down at a terrace table to feast. Midway through a joyous meal, Edith looked up and froze: Toto was standing there, glaring with disapproval, and the table fell silent. Someone invited her to join them, she hesitated briefly, and then turned and left without a word.[12] The party picked up again gradually. Paris was free and life was so sweet after the occupation that it seemed pointless to be glum. Edith and Lucie made an effort to be very, very good for the next few days, and Toto didn't say anything to them. Orders were loosened up to allow the Rochambelles leave in Paris when they weren't on ambulance duty.

Rosette went shopping. Prices were high for food and drink, but other luxuries were no more expensive than in Morocco or England. On the Rue du Rivoli, she spent several months' pay on some handkerchiefs, stationery, a scarf and an enamel insignia pin. Paris was starting to feel crowded. "The Americans have arrived now and people keep confusing us with them, which is annoying the first time it happens and exasperating on the tenth 'Bravo little Americans,'" she wrote.

Jacotte and Crapette, meanwhile, had been selected by the First Medical Company Doctor Alexandre Krementchousky to work for him directly. He moved them from the Bagatelle campground and put them in a house with a piano, which Crapette used to entertain them splendidly. Krementchousky and Crapette had known each other before the war, as both were from Russian Orthodox families from Limoges. Jacotte developed a tremendous respect for Krem, as they called him. He spent most of his time in the front lines, so as to give medical aid more quickly. He had been with Leclerc since the battle of El Alamein in 1942. "He had a complete disregard for danger and a natural serenity that gave courage to everyone," Jacotte said. "He was an extraordinary man."

A distant cousin spotted Jacotte at the wheel coming into Paris and asked if her family knew she was there. The cousin undertook spreading the news, calling her father, who called Jacotte's younger sister, Suzanne. Suzanne went out and ran across another Rochambelle, Rosette, and gave her her address to give to Jacotte, which Rosette did. Then Toto got permission from Captain Ceccaldi for the Parisians of the group to go see their families, and took Jacotte to Suzanne's address, on Rue Royale. Suzanne was there, along with a number of other people who had taken refuge in the building. Suzanne told her that their parents and other sister Yvonne were in the countryside at Herblay. Suzanne insisted on riding her bicycle to their family apartment on the Avenue Wagram to get the bottle of champagne they had put away years before in anticipation of an eventual reunion. It was a long and dangerous ride, and she nearly was shot by a machine gunner at Saint Augustin.

To be back in Paris, reunited with her sister, after five years away, was an overwhelming moment of happiness. "It was indescribable," Jacotte said. "So much emotion! It was more emotion than joy." She and Suzanne embraced warmly, but they were with a group of people, and couldn't really express their feelings. Later, after the others left, and Suzanne was making up a bed for Jacotte, they started to try to cover the distance. "We didn't know where to start or where to finish, after five years," Jacotte said. Suzanne had gotten very thin. Her family had no garden or connections to send them fresh food, and rations were down to almost nothing. Herblay was still under German occupation, and then the U.S. Army took over the Fournier estate. It wasn't until September 7 that an officer offered to give Jacotte's mother and father and Yvonne a ride to Paris. They were flabbergasted to find Jacotte there, and more amazed to learn she was in the army. "They were astounded," she said. "Even more astounded because I was someone who could not look at a scratch or cut, I had to turn my head. They thought I was in New York, they believed I was safe in the United States."

She hadn't sent word ahead because she didn't want them to worry. The family had one night together, and then the division left Paris. Jacotte wrote them from the eastern campaign, reassuring notes that included little of what she was actually doing. "We would be coming out of hell, but I didn't talk about hell."

One of the highlights of the Rochambelles' Paris stay was Leclerc's visit to their Bagatelle camp. The women stood at attention, and Leclerc inspected their ranks and reminded them that he had agreed to take them on as part of the division up to Paris. The women held their collective breath. "But . . . I'll keep you," Leclerc said, remarking on their efficiency, competence, and value to the division. Toto hissed "Attention!" at the women, afraid they were going to be extremely unmilitary and jump for joy. She thanked Leclerc, he left, and then they all whooped and jumped for joy. "When he turned his back, there was a great 'Hurrah!'" Jacotte recalled.

Leclerc especially thanked Florence Conrad, calling her "the Providence of our wounded."[13] When the division moved on, Conrad stayed in Paris to help with division patients at Val de Grace hospital. Even from the rear she got out front, obtaining penicillin from the Americans for her patients before the rest of France had even heard of it. Conrad's favoritism of Second Division soldiers caused some resentment among other wounded in the hospital, and some of the nurses distributed Conrad's largesse beyond the division to smooth things out.

Janine Bocquentin was one of those nurses. She applied to join the Rochambelles and was told there was no room for the moment. She was a registered nurse, and was asked to work at Val de Grace until a place opened up among the ambulance drivers. Janine enjoyed her work at the hospital, much of which was providing moral support to men who were far from home. "Our role was to replace the family. All those people from North Africa had no family nearby," she said. "We were like their sisters."

Leonora Lindsley rejoined the Rochambelles there as well, and was sent to Val de Grace. She had been working with the American Red Cross since being eliminated from the Rochambeau Group in New York, arriving in France in July 1944. Once the city was liberated, Leonora moved to an apartment her mother had kept there since before the war, and lived there while working at the hospital. She had been there for a month, and she and Janine Bocquentin became friends. They were sympathetic young women caught in a complex moment of judgment and reprisal.

One day at the hospital, an officer from the Second Division who had lost both his legs asked for their help. Another soldier had passed by his open door and recognized him from early in the war, when he had been a pro-Nazi militiaman and had arrested the soldier's father. He begged them to get him out of there before the soldier took revenge. They borrowed the hospital guard's civilian jacket and took him to Leonora's apartment, but they had no way of providing the constant care he needed. "It was crazy, what we did," Janine recalled. At that very heated moment, accusations were flying, people were being shot on the street. "It was terrible, all those arrests. Leonora wanted to save him," Janine said. At the liberation, she had seen an older German soldier hiding in doorways, trying to escape, and the FFI tracking him down. "They trapped him like a rat, and they killed him. It was horrible." The ex-militiaman eventually turned himself in to the authorities and was tried and acquitted, largely because Leclerc testified on his behalf. Janine said he told her later that the officials interrogated him by dropping him repeatedly on the stumps of his legs. Leonora Lindsley's mother got in touch with him after the war and bought him a wheelchair.

The division's presence in Paris attracted fresh recruits, bringing its total up to 16,000, including a handful of new ambulance drivers. Leclerc formed four new companies and two squadrons from the ranks of Resistants and others, and a new tactical group was organized to encompass them. Another 100,000 former FFI nationwide had joined the First French Army, under the command of General Jean-Marie de Lattre de

Tassigny. The French have a saying that describes those late summer days of 1944: *Voler au secours de la victoire:* that is, Fly to the aid of victory. There were perhaps 20,000 FFI members in the Paris area in August 1944, but more than 123,000 Parisians applied for official recognition of their resistance work once the war was over.[14] The myth making had begun: every French man and woman was a Resistant, few if any had collaborated, and the nationalist beat went on. De Gaulle encouraged the attitude in the interest of social cohesion. "Il faut savoir oublier," he said. One must know how to forget.

When attractive, intellectual Marie-Thérèse Pezet went for her interview with Suzanne Torrès, Toto looked at her name and asked if she knew Ernest Pezet. Of course, Marie-Thérèse replied, he's my father. Toto was delighted; Ernest Pezet, a longtime deputy, lawyer, center-right party founder, and foreign affairs specialist, was a friend of her husband's. Toto asked if she didn't have any good friends who wanted to join the Rochambelles. She nodded toward a group of women in the waiting room. "Have you seen these marvels who want to sign up? I am not going to accept just anybody."

Marie-Thérèse, politically astute from the cradle, understood. "She was afraid of taking on women who had slept with Germans and wanted to launder their reputations a little. Also she had to beware of women who wanted something else. She needed young women or girls with a good education, but not too good, if you know what I mean. You had to be friendly with the boys, be a little bit of a social worker."

Marie-Thérèse called her childhood friend Marie-Anne Duvernet, a registered nurse, and asked if she would like to join Leclerc's division. Marie-Anne shouted with joy. They became partners in the ambulance group, and made a good team. Marie-Anne had been living in an attic room to avoid her sister and brother-in-law, who had cozied up to the Nazi command and had been entertaining German officers regularly in the Duvernet parents' spacious apartment. Marie-Anne couldn't stand it, and joining the army was a perfect riposte to their misplaced loyalty.

First, Marie-Thérèse had to tell her father she was leaving. Ernest Pezet was a larger-than-life personality who dominated his family as well as his political party. A member of the Lille Group of the Resistance, which had gathered many intellectuals and political elites, he and Marie-Thérèse had skirted danger more than once during the occupation. But she felt she lived in her father's shadow, and the Rochambelles offered a way for her to strike out on her own. She packed her bag and left it with the concièrge, and then told her parents she was joining the Second Division. Her father remarked only that she wasn't such a pillar in the face of blood. She said it didn't matter. "That's how I got out from under his paternal authority. My personality was thus detached from him." He wouldn't say it, but he was enormously proud of her, and sent dispatches of her ambulance career to the local Brittany newspaper whose district he represented in the National Assembly.

A spunky, freckle-faced redhead from Caen, in Normandy, also joined the group. Danièle Heintz was a twenty-two-year-old nursing student when Allied bombs began crashing down on Caen at 1:30 P.M. on D-Day. She and her brother, André, went straight to Bon Sauveur Hospital, helping to carry wounded and assist the surgeons. With each enormous blast of a bomb, the meter-thick walls of the hospital tilted, shuddered, and then righted themselves. Danièle met a nun who had been buried in rubble by one explosion, and disinterred by the next. They urgently needed a signal to the bombers that the building they kept trying to destroy was a hospital. André suggested putting a big red cross out on the hospital grounds, but where would they find red cloth? Danièle took some white sheets down to the operating room and drenched them on the bloody floor. They were quickly red. They made a cross of them in the garden, and as they finished, an Allied Piper Cub flew overhead, circled, and tilted its wings in recognition. The hospital was not bombed again.

Caen, however, endured daily Allied bombing from June 6 through July 9, destroying 80 percent of the town and killing an estimated 10,000 persons. All through Normandy, American and British bombers had pounded the German installations, but in the process also destroyed many ancient towns, St. Lô, Le Havre, and Valognes among them. An estimated 50,000 civilians were killed in the bombing throughout Normandy.[15] Historian John Keegan quoted a British soldier who walked into Caen after the battle and found "just a waste of brick and stone, like a field of corn that has been plowed. The people gazed at us without emotion of any kind; one could hardly look them in the face, knowing who had done this."[16]

Some French remain resentful of what they believe was overkill on the part of the Allies. Danièle was philosophical about the destruction.

"At that point, the method was to crush. So they crushed. At the time, that was the tactic," she said. German resistance remained strong in and around Caen, and so the bombs fell, and the town residents fled, took to their cellars, or died.

Danièle got a taste of ambulance driving while still in Caen. One day a haggard man walked into the hospital and begged the staff to send aid to a group hiding in the Carpiquet quarry on the outskirts of town. They had been bombed and strafed by an airplane several days before. Danièle helped load medicine and bandages into two Red Cross ambulances, both driven by women. A doctor and nurse joined them, and they set out with Red Cross flags flying. They would have to cross the front between the Germans and the Allies to get there, and they had gone only a few kilometers before a mortar came smashing down next to the ambulance. They jumped into the roadside ditch, counting two flat tires on each of the ambulances. The firing stopped, and they started off again, driving slowly on the ruined tires. Once at the quarry, they spent two hours treating injuries and infection, and made the difficult choice of eight patients they could transport back to the hospital. But they made it back, and Danièle was hooked.

"That mission probably decided my engagement beyond Normandy," she wrote in an unpublished memoir. "I had gotten through the Battle of Caen, luckily for me, without being a victim. I had endured, for better or for worse, the 'baptism of fire.' Confronted with all the violence and suffering, I had done my best. Fear certainly had not spared me, but the thought of dying didn't scare me either. I must, it seemed to me, continue to help others."

Danièle and her brother spent a month after the Battle of Caen helping to uncover, identify and rebury bodies, and then they read that the Second Division was moving toward Paris. Danièle hitchhiked to Rambouillet and ran into a neighbor and director of the Caen Red Cross. He sent her to Florence Conrad, who asked if she could drive. She lied and said of course. Her first time behind the wheel was driving a 1.5-ton Dodge ambulance from Rambouillet to Paris. She did all right. "I had watched my father drive," she said.

While the war was not won in Paris, its liberation had turned the political tide within France in favor of the Allies. On the ground, German troops were still entrenched in eastern France. The division lined up in convoy once again on September 8, eastward bound. Leclerc had sworn on March

2, 1941 in Koufra, Libya, during the fighting for North Africa, that he would not lay down arms "until the day when our colors, our beautiful colors, fly above the Cathedral at Strasbourg." Strasbourg, the easternmost city in France, was the capital of the Alsace region, which had been annexed by the Germans. Leclerc's goal became known as the Oath of Koufra, and the division members considered it their mission and duty to carry it out.

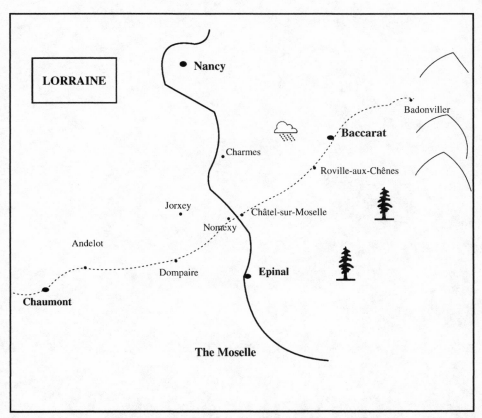

The Rochambelles' route through Lorraine, September 9-November 17, 1944

CHAPTER FIVE

Romance, the River, and a Few Close Calls

The war picked up again outside Paris with a battle at Andelot, a town northeast of Chaumont in the Champagne-Ardennes region, just east of the Marne River. Commandant Jean Fanneau de La Horie's tank regiment took the town and some 800 prisoners, who were seated in rows, elbow to elbow, in a meadow when Toto and Raymonde arrived. It was too much for one regiment officer, a Jew whose family had been deported to concentration camps. He ran toward the German prisoners and began slapping and kicking them individually, going down the line. His friends brought him gently away, and he collapsed in tears.

Between Chaumont and Andelot, Edith and Lucie were driving down a narrow road, closely watching the forest for a sign of the enemy. They came out of the woods into a clearing, a muddy field where a tank regiment was beginning an attack on a German-held village. A couple of division soldiers waved them over to tell them there were some injured soldiers down a dirt road a few hundred meters back. They needed to turn around, and Edith got out of the ambulance to guide Lucie. The shoulders of the road might be mined, and so they had to be careful not to go off the paved surface. Soldiers in a vehicle in front of them shouted encouragement, and Lucie executed the narrow turns with precision. Edith suddenly felt her eardrums blow and saw a fountain of flames shooting up under the ambulance, which flew up into the air and landed on its nose. Lucie, ashen, was gripping the steering wheel. Edith ran over and jerked open the door and slid her out of the driver's seat. The blast had come from an anti-tank mine designed to blow up a couple of tons of armored steel. It was in the middle of the road, where twenty or so military vehicles had already passed safely until Lucie triggered it in turning. The ambulance was shredded with shrapnel, as were both of their sacks of clothing, jammed under the front seats. The duffel bags had blocked the direct spray, saving Lucie from serious injury. She was deafened, shaken, and in shock, and soldiers in a nearby Jeep offered to take

her to the field hospital straight away. Edith stared at the ambulance in dis-
belief, and then looked around and saw two bodies on the ground, spread-
eagled. It was the young men who had waved them over. She had been
standing practically next to them, and she was uninjured. She realized that
the front wheel had blocked the exploding shrapnel from hitting her, but
the young men had been struck straight on.[1] Lucie spent a week resting in a
hospital, and Edith was assigned her third ambulance of the war.

Driving across the same field, Raymonde and Toto's ambulance got
stuck in the mud. They carried metal sheets hung on the inside walls of
the ambulance for that eventuality, and put them under the wheels to get
it out.

Danièle and her partner Hélène Langé, known as "La Grande Hélène"
to distinguish her from Hélène Fabre, were in a convoy not far behind
Edith and Lucie, and they too had been warned about mined shoulders.
Her tactical group had identified a circular route to use if the ambulance
needed to take someone back to a treatment center. Danièle drove carefully,
the convoy inching along the narrow road, both sides bordered with tall
hedges, until it suddenly opened onto a wide field. On the other side of the
field stood the village, where the church spire was now in flames. As they
reached the field, the twenty or so tanks in front of them spread from a
single line into a fan formation, heading for the village in a ballet of armored steel. It was Danièle's introduction to combat, and she found the
beauty in it somehow disconcerting. She was still a novice when she and
Hélène were sent to pick up some wounded soldiers at a nearby intersection. When they arrived, no one was there. Artillery fire rained down
nearby, so they clung to the sides of the ambulance "like complete idiots,"
Danièle said. A Jeep pulled up and an officer with a walking stick shouted at
them: "Put your helmets on! What are you doing here! Your role is not to
hang around, get the hell out of here right now!" And he sped away. A soldier approached and asked if they knew who that was, and they said they
didn't. That was General Leclerc, he said. Before they had time to be impressed, shrapnel from a nearby explosion struck the soldier down. Danièle
and Hélène had found their victim at their feet. They picked him up and
took him to the treatment center. "It was a great lesson in movement, in
usefulness, in not standing still. Leclerc gave us that lesson at the start,"
Danièle said in an interview. "Action was the secret. You had to move. You
couldn't stand there wallowing in fear."

Marie-Thérèse and her partner, Marie-Anne, also were brand-new on the job.

Marie-Thérèse recalled her first evacuation, picking up two wounded soldiers and then putting a third soldier, who was dead, in the ambulance as well. She gripped the steering wheel and cried for the dead soldier the whole way back to the infirmary. "I cried for that young man, for that young life cut so short," she said. "It was a moral shock, I think." When Marie-Thérèse and Marie-Anne arrived at the infirmary, set up in a school on the village square, medical battalion staff yelled at them for having transported a dead person. It was against the rules. Another division unit was in charge of picking up bodies, confirming identification and notifying families. One of the doctors said to her afterwards, "Marie-Thérèse, you're brave but an idiot. You should have told them he died in transit."

Marie-Thérèse wrote her family that she had simply wanted the soldier to have a decent burial. And he did. When the village priest buried the soldier later that day, all the village inhabitants turned out to honor him, though he was a complete stranger to them.

The division continued in an eastward direction, liberating Vittel, the prewar spa town. Its previously chic hotels had been turned into barbed-wire prison camps for thousands of British and American women civilians caught in France when their nations joined the war. Leclerc greeted them with warmth. "In 1940, we were admirably received by the English. The Americans have given us arms. We are particularly happy that it has fallen to us to deliver you," he said.[2]

Across the plains of Lorraine from Vittel, the Germans began consolidating troops from the south and west, keeping the Vosges Mountains at their backs. It may have felt like the war was over in Paris, but since time immemorial, eastern France has made the call. Patton knew it, and marched eastward with his Third Army. He was repelled at Pont à Mousson with a loss of nearly 300 men. The French Second Division advanced in a parallel south of the Americans, and met the Germans at Dompaire on September 12.

Madeleine Collomb and her partner were sent to a U.S. heavy artillery unit that was helping the French at Dompaire, as the Americans had no ambulances there and had requested backup. When they reported for duty, the American commander said, "I didn't ask for a nurse, I asked for an ambulance driver." Madeleine persuaded him that they were in fact ambulance drivers, but the American doctor couldn't get used to working with women. "The doctor was so afraid for us, being women, that he went with us on each evacuation," Madeleine recalled. "After two days, he said, look, I don't want the death of women on my conscience. Go back to the French."

The night before the attack at Dompaire, Danièle was talking to Lieutenant Louis Gendron, a tank commander, about life, religion, philosophy. Danièle had been a prize-winning philosophy student in high school, and she was an ardent Catholic as well. Gendron shrugged at her ideas. "He said, 'At any rate, I'll be dead tomorrow. I'll be wounded, and I'll die.'" Danièle was shocked at his certainty. She argued against his fatalism, she argued for the existence of God, she fought his conviction with weapons of eloquence and reason, but she could not shake it. The following day, the battle erupted around Dompaire. The Germans had been swinging up from a base at Epinal, attempting to attack the American troops from behind. Instead, they met Jacques Massu and Pierre Minjonnet's tank regiments and were torn apart. Some sixty German tanks were left on the field, burnt shells.

After the fight, Danièle asked after Lieutenant Gendron. He had indeed been killed. "I felt ill," she said. "I wasn't able to do anything, either to help him die, or to help him believe [in God]." She doesn't believe Gendron was suicidal. Morale in the division was sky-high at that point. "I believe his death was not voluntary, but was somehow destined," she said. "I think it's extraordinary to be able to have a premonition of that sort."

Patton was so pleased with the Second Division's performance at Dompaire that he invited Leclerc to lunch with General Wade Haislip in a muddy field nearby, and popped a bottle of champagne. His men had captured a stock of 50,000 bottles, and Patton wrote in his diary that he had distributed it to the troops. Haislip, as commander of the U.S. Army's Fifteenth Corps, had been Leclerc's boss since Normandy, and they had become good friends. After lunch, Patton strode over to his Jeep, laid his cigar carefully on the hood, dug into a bag, and pulled out two medals. He called Leclerc over and pinned them on, and gave him a pack of five Silver Stars and twenty-five Bronze Stars to distribute to his men for the Dompaire operation. Leclerc, who loathed fuss and praise, seemed bothered, and Haislip grinned at him. "But you have done great things for the honor of the American Army," he said.[3] Leclerc returned the favor before the end of the war, pinning the French Croix de la Legion d'Honneur on Haislip. The March of Chad Regiment also made Haislip an honorary corporal, backhanded praise from the regiment's rugged infantrymen.

In front of the division lay the Moselle River, a 500-kilometer-long, meandering waterway that had served through history as the gateway to the resource-rich plains of Lorraine and Alsace. Patton had been there in another wet September, twenty-six years before, and knew that getting across the river was critical, difficult and dangerous. Now he wanted the U.S. Seventy-ninth Infantry to cross at Charmes, and the Second Division to traverse further south, at Châtel-sur-Moselle, a bombed-out village of some 1,400 inhabitants.

On September 15, Captains Jacques Branet and Raymond Dronne led their tank and infantry companies across the river, wading through water up to their thighs. The bridge had been blown by the Germans when they pulled back to the east. Jacotte stopped her ambulance on the western bank of the Moselle to remove the engine's fan belt before crossing the river, as she had been taught in the mechanics course in New York. Crapette and Dr. Alexandre Krementchousky and Raymond Worms, a nurse, were with her as they drove up the river bank into Châtel and stopped beside an old hospice built atop the buried ruins of a medieval fortress. It would do for an infirmary for the medical company.

The village mayor, Pierre Sayer, greeted the French troops with enthusiasm. He was thirty-seven years old, the town doctor, and head of the local Resistance group. Châtel's residents had heard about the liberation of Paris three weeks before, and of the Allies' victorious sweep toward eastern France, and hoped it was their turn. Dronne sent out some men from his Ninth Company to check who was in the area, and the mayor called out the village men to rebuild the bridge. Soldiers strung a footbridge across the river in the meantime, and marked the ford crossing for vehicles with two stakes and a white cord tied across the river. The patrols brought back a few German prisoners and reports of a splintered enemy presence to the east, but nothing more than rain looked imminently menacing.

The next day, U.S. intelligence reported that 142 Panzers were massing at Rambervillers, twenty-five kilometers due east of Châtel. It was thought that their direction would be north to the city of Nancy, where the Seventy-ninth U.S. Infantry Division would be going once it crossed the Moselle. But to the south, a German Panzer company still held the town of Epinal, seventeen kilometers away and on the western bank of the river.

The Second Division companies were in a precarious position, with only a few hundred men and a dozen tanks, but they decided to stay put.

Rain was still falling the following day. At the time of day the French call between dog and wolf, that elusive moment of transition from day to evening, a woman called the mayor's home: Panzers were pouring into her farmyard! Branet radioed his tank company, and they blasted away, destroying the German tanks as well as the woman's farm. The Germans had gotten to within a kilometer of the Second Division's perimeter, and from there, they launched a barrage of mortars, aiming for the half-finished bridge.

Jacotte and Crapette sheltered behind the hospice's thick wall, pinned down by the mortars on one side and a German machine gunner shooting from the other side, covering the approach to the footbridge. Wounded soldiers started streaming in, some on foot, some carried by the medical company's stretcher bearers, until there were too many to fit in the hospice. They had to put several soldiers on the ground outside, just as the rain started up again. They covered up the men as best they could. They had the only ambulance east of the Moselle, but there was nowhere they could go until the shelling and shooting let up.

Branet's tanks began pushing the Panzers back into the woods. The two companies opened up with all the artillery they had. Mortars echoed with deafening percussion, machine guns spat and sputtered, tracer bullets cut fiery arcs across the darkening sky. The Germans had fifteen to twenty Panzers and their heavier version, the Tiger. One of Branet's Shermans lost its tread; another was mired in the deep forest mud, but suddenly the Germans stopped firing and seemed to pull back. Branet was pleased.

Jacotte and Crapette loaded the ambulance and drove it down to the footbridge across the river. It was quiet. If the machine-gunner was still there, he gave no sign. They handed the injured soldiers over to stretcher-bearers, who carried them across the bridge to ambulances waiting on the other side. Other Rochambelle teams would drive the soldiers to the nearest field hospital. Jacotte and Crapette made a dozen trips back and forth. At midnight, the medical company cook came and found them. He had made a rabbit stew, it had been sitting since the beginning of the attack, and they had better come eat it right now! There were a couple of cardinal rules to army life, and one of them was: Don't upset the cook. They followed him.

But Branet got a call from regiment commander de La Horie, who was on the western side of the river. Orders were to evacuate Châtel immediately. "I thought I'd misunderstood!" Branet wrote later.[4] But another Panzer brigade and two German infantry battalions were on their way to Châtel. Branet and Dronne would be encircled if they stayed on the eastern bank. Orders were clear: pull back, now.

Jacotte and Crapette had just sat down to eat by the light of a single candle, numb with fatigue. Before they could take a bite, Krementchousky threw open the door and yelled, "Drop everything, we're pulling out!" Jacotte and Crapette piled in the ambulance. Sayer's wife, Marie-Thérèse, and their six-year-old son, Bernard, were put in the back. Branet urged Sayer to come with them as well, but he refused to leave: he felt it was his duty as mayor to stay. A half-track—a sturdy armored vehicle that was half-Jeep, half-tank—hooked up to tow the ambulance through the river. With the rain, the river had risen too high to drive across. Branet's tank company was behind the ambulance, and everyone moved in the dark, as silently as possible, trying not to give the enemy a fresh target.

At the western bank of the river, the half-track slipped in the mud and, unable to back up with the ambulance in tow, maneuvered around in a circle to re-approach the bank where the ground was more solid. Jacotte kept the line taut between them; that was all she could do to help get them to ground. She also kept glancing behind her. The grinding column of tanks had entered the river and was coming up fast. Could the drivers see her in the dark? Unlikely. She thought, this is the end of the ride. After all the bombings, the attacks and the bullets, I'm going to be crushed by our own tanks. The first tank in line bumped her fender and then slowed, just in time. The half-track clambered up the bank and pulled Jacotte's ambulance with it. They had made it, by a split second.

After the war, the village of Châtel put up a granite monument to the men who didn't make it that night. The monument names thirty-five soldiers from the Second Division, and Pierre Sayer. On Monday morning after the retreat, Sayer was carried off by a group of French militiamen, as the Nazi collaborators called themselves, and was turned over to the Gestapo. He was shot the following day, along with four other Resistance members, their bodies left in a nearby forest.[5] Fifty-five years later, his son Bernard Pierre Sayer read an account of the struggle for Châtel at the Leclerc Memorial in Paris, and called to thank the ambulance driver who took him across the river that night. It was Jacotte.

Danièle and Hélène were having a difficult time with the river as well. They were asked to pick up some wounded soldiers on the eastern side of the river between Charmes and Châtel. They were to cross the river at the old Roman ford, a wide and shallow crossing that was marked in Roman times by a sculpture of a man on a horse, both riding on the back of a man-serpent. The statue, removed to a museum, had been replaced for the moment by an army sentinel. Danièle started across the ford into water about a meter deep, and Hélène, a more experienced driver, said "Slow down!" Danièle's immediate and mistaken reaction was to brake. The ambulance stalled out and would not restart. A Jeep passed them going in a westward direction and a soldier shouted at them to move: the tank company was retreating with German Tigers in pursuit. Danièle and Hélène would very much have liked to move, but the ambulance resisted all effort. A half-track driver spied them sitting there and came to their rescue. As they were towed up the riverbank, the water spilled out of the exhaust and they were able to restart the engine. They picked up the wounded soldiers and followed the dozen tanks back westward across the river. That night, they slept in a school in Nomexy, on tables that were even less comfortable then their stretchers.

"It was the first time we had retreated," Danièle said later. "It seemed strange to us. We had always gone forward before."

Rosette and Arlette had arrived at Nomexy to find the town draped in Lorraine crosses and French flags. Arlette was not feeling well, and was getting very jumpy under fire. They were called to an evacuation at the village of Iqney, and followed a doctor's Jeep through a hail of 88mm mortars, feeling like a painted target on the empty road. They found the house they were looking for, and a young boy, injured by the bombing, lay in bed bleeding. His parents stood on either side, watching him bleed to death. The doctor asked angrily why they could not at least have put on a tourniquet and saved his life. The parents were ignorant peasant farmers, Rosette said, and had no idea of what to do. She felt sorry for the boy, who died.

After another run to the treatment center with some wounded soldiers, they returned to Nomexy and found all the flags and crosses had disappeared. The division had retreated from Châtel, and the residents of Nomexy had quickly chosen discretion. "I was astounded to see the streets empty and the houses undressed in so little time," Rosette wrote.

With the retreat, Jacotte and Crapette and the rest of the medical company pulled back to Jorxey, a village about ten kilometers west of the

Moselle. Since their assignment to the medical company, which had its own Jeep, stretcher bearers, and cook, Jacotte and Crapette had only to drive the ambulance. The other Rochambelles were scattered among various tactical units and often had to do their own support work. The medical company, moving with the fighting front, generally took over village cafés to set up an infirmary. The cafés tended to be located on a square, where there was room to park the ambulances in front; they had a large room where stretchers could be laid out, and they had water. Such was the situation at Jorxey. Jacotte and Crapette had fallen into an exhausted sleep in the back of their ambulance when Krementchousky came banging on the door and said they had to get up, it was an order! They did, groaning, and found the emergency was that a local farmer's wife had cooked up a big meal for them, with cabbage and potatoes and a mirabelle tart (it was plum season), their first proper meal in days. They ate with relish, and then slept for the rest of the afternoon, to return for more of the same fare that evening. The woman who served them was called "Tante" or Aunt, by her niece, and Jacotte and Crapette began referring to her as "Tante Mirabelle." Two mirabelle tarts later, they baptized the ambulance *Tante Mirabelle*, and the good farmer's wife assisted in the ceremony. (The name of their ambulance was later to prompt many an Alsatian to give them a bottle of mirabelle brandy, a homemade potion of some renown.) They pulled out at 5:00 A.M. the next day to retake Châtel, crossing the river via a temporary pontoon bridge the engineers had managed to put up. This time, the Germans began launching mortars at their very approach, and it was hard fighting to retake the town.

Edith and Lucie, newly released from the hospital, caught up with their Spahi unit at Nomexy. They parked their ambulance behind the house closest to the river, and ran, heads down, with their stretchers to pick up the wounded soldiers on and around the footbridge. The infirmary behind them was in a school, and it was rapidly filling up with the injured. Then the hail of mortars started marching right across the river toward their ambulance. Lucie ran for shelter and Edith got the ambulance out of there fast, just as a shell destroyed the house they had been using for cover. She drove toward some garages they had seen, thinking they might provide a good place to park, and found Lucie talking to a young soldier in the doorway of one of the garages. As she approached, the soldier lit a cigarette and Lucie leaned over to light hers off the flame. At that very moment, a jet of

Jacotte Fournier (l) and Crapette Demay in front of a stack of fertilizer in Lorraine.

blood spurted from his neck and he collapsed, dead. A fragment from an exploding mortar had sliced his jugular. Lucie covered her eyes with her hands and went rigid with shock. Edith pulled her down into a homemade bunker where some local residents were hiding, and stayed there with her, talking her back to a state of calm.[6] Lucie was having a few too many close calls.

And she wasn't the only one. A couple of American officers, driving up in a Jeep while Nomexy was under attack, were hit by a mortar. One of the men had his leg blown off. Raymonde Brindjonc took his necktie for a tourniquet to stop the bleeding ("I always used their ties as garottes," she said). The man was conscious, but heavy, and as Raymonde tried to pull him over to the ambulance, they fell into a ditch. As they rolled down, a mortar slammed into the place they'd been standing a moment before. Both of them would have been killed if they had not fallen. Years later, the American officer told a division veteran that he had never forgotten the big blue eyes of the woman who saved him that night.

At Epinal, the U.S. Fifteenth Corps attacked the remaining Panzer divisions and sent the survivors flying for the shelter of the Vosges Mountains. The division pushed the Germans out of Châtel as well, and the columns of tanks moved out in an eastwardly direction.

Tank company commander Captain Jacques de Witasse, meanwhile, had broken a couple of ribs and separated his collarbone in a Jeep accident, and like many before and after him, plotted his escape from the hospital when it was time to be transferred to the rear. He was transported in an American ambulance, supposedly driving from Vittel westward, but he directed the American driver eastward instead until they arrived at his company's camp near Charmes. "The American ambulance driver quickly understood that he had been had, and furious, started letting loose imprecations in the best Texas style," Witasse wrote. "To calm him down, the *Austerlitz* [tank] crew gave him a marvelous reception in which the Lorraine mirabelle had a leading role. The American left several hours later, completely happy, and alone in his ambulance, which seemed to have a tendency to weave a bit as it headed in the approximate direction of Vittel."[7]

After Châtel, Georges Ratard took Arlette to see a division doctor, who confirmed what she already knew: she was pregnant. Georges wanted her to quit, and she was ready. She said she didn't mind leaving the Rochambelles in the middle of the war. "I was happy," she said. "I didn't regret leaving, because I was expecting a son." She was convinced from the start that the baby was a boy, and that was important to her. Arlette was Rosette's second partner, after "You" Guerin, to leave the Rochambelles because of pregnancy.

Toto's only comment was that if Arlette had come to her sooner, she would have helped her avoid a pregnancy just then. Arlette later said she was utterly naïve at the time, that she didn't have a clue how to avoid getting pregnant, and wouldn't have tried anyway. Rosette, however, said that on the day of her wedding, Arlette asked several Rochambelles how to prevent pregnancy, and no one knew. They told her to ask Toto, and apparently she never did. Innocence bordering on ignorance was close to the rule among the women. Rosette recounted that one afternoon in a soldiers' cantine, a fellow stuck his head in the door and said, "Quick, they're distributing the *capotes anglaises!*" (Literally, this would be an English bonnet, but was also slang for condom.) One of the Rochambelles stood up and said "Great! I don't have anything to wear!"

The army wasn't much more sophisticated than the ambulance drivers. When Arlette returned to Paris for demobilization, the army had no procedure for discharging a soldier because of pregnancy. "They didn't know what to do," she said. They took her military clothing, so she didn't even have a coat. Elina Labourdette loaned her a fur-lined coat for the winter, and Arlette moved in temporarily with a cousin in the city. Rosette was assigned a new partner, Nicole Mangini-Guidon, an elegant blonde who had joined the group in Paris. Rosette was pleased to have Nicole as a partner, even though Nicole did not know how to drive. She had a wonderful manner of dealing with the injured soldiers. "I have the impression that her young and fresh beauty, and her compassion, comforts them," she wrote. Rosette took over all driving duty, and the soldiers never knew their other "driver" wasn't quite up to her job.

From Châtel, Anne-Marie and her partner Michette de Steinheil were sent to Zincourt, a few kilometers east, to pick up some wounded soldiers. On the way, they ran across Leclerc, who asked where they were going. They said Zincourt, and he said, go on then, giving them his habitual little push behind with his walking stick. Branet's company was behind them, and Branet quipped over the radio: "Don't worry, the Rochambelles are out front." Anne-Marie and Michette found the streets of Zincourt empty, not a soul around; the village had just been deserted by the Germans. Then residents started coming out from behind their doors and greeted Anne-Marie and Michette as conquering heroes. Branet and his tanks arrived to "take" the village and found the women having lunch in the center square. Michette said they only had to transport one man, a civilian, from that town. They weren't supposed to take care of civilians, but if there were no wounded soldiers, it was hard to refuse.

Anne-Marie and Jacques Branet were an established couple at that point, and their affair was an open secret in the division, even if they were careful not to let it show around others. "They were very, very discreet," Michette said in an interview. "They didn't flirt openly." Anne-Marie was married at the time; her husband had been active in the Resistance and then joined the First Army. But her heart was no longer in the marriage, she confided to a friend. And then she met the classically handsome Branet, who, in Leclerc's description, was adored by his men and esteemed by his bosses. Anne-Marie did not fail to enjoy his company, and, having been married, she was not in the same state of lamentable ignorance as the others.

The war, with its inherent elements of camaraderie, courage and sacrifice, was inevitably a crucible for romance, but the women insisted that any liaisons be carried out with great discretion. The stakes were too high for both the women and the men to play around carelessly: social reputations carried consequences, venereal disease was common and pregnancy outside of marriage could spell ruin. At the same time, an undercurrent of affection between some Rochambelles and division officers was often in the air. "Of course there were people losing their hearts to each other all the time," Anne Hastings remarked.

Other women developed deep friendships with their fellow soldiers, relationships they would not have dreamt of wrecking on the shoals of sexual attraction. For Jacotte and Crapette, their buddies became the tank crew that always seemed to be right in front of them in convoy. *Malmaison*'s crew was led by Lieutenant Eric Foster, who was half English and half French, and included Drouillas, a Chilean; Chevalier, a Swiss, and Jacques Salvetat, from the south of France. One afternoon, the *Malmaison* crew invited the two women to "tea." They all pretended to be in an extremely elegant environment, instead of sitting on a board in a muddy field. Salvetat peeled an apple for each of them and the women offered them cigarettes, which everyone was running low on at that point. "What a privilege it was to get to know them," Jacotte said. "They were boys of great character."

And even if one of them was sweet on Crapette, and everyone knew it, nothing was ever said or done. "We never had the slightest flirtation with the boys. There was no misunderstanding," she said. "We were friends, that's all. There was never any hand-holding or smiles. It simplified things that way. They considered us as untouchable."

Had they been further back in the line, possibly there would have been time and inclination for flirting and seduction. But they were on the front. "We couldn't have done what we did if we had had other ideas in our heads," Jacotte insisted. Jacotte's viewpoint was that of the majority of the women. Toto and Anne-Marie, both separated in distance and affection from their husbands, were exceptions.

Danièle, for example, had never been permitted to wear her hair down. When she joined the division, she wore her waist-length braids wrapped around her head, in the Alsatian style. The mores of the time dictated that she could go to war, but she could not wear her hair loose. It would have been considered an indicator of her moral condition. "We were very naïve in that era," she said. "On one hand we were raised with sort of Scout ideals, that counted a little, as did the religious education of the time. The attitude of the girls was very important. Madame Conrad did not accept just anybody. All the girls were very well-mannered. We always said, 'We are not A.F.A.T. [the auxiliaries]! We are Rochambelles.'"

Danièle noted that the women and men *vous-voyéed* each other, a linguistic device the French use to create distance and demonstrate formality, rather than the casual and informal "tu" form of you. "We were with 20,000 men and not one of them would have touched us," she said. Janine Bocquentin seconded Danièle's assessment. "We were friends and comrades," she said. "I never heard of girls who slept with the boys. We weren't there for that. We were there to experience an extraordinary moment, in my case at any rate. It was a great adventure."

Friendship amongst the women also was cemented by this time. They had stood the test of combat, and the knowledge that they could trust one another with their lives forged links that never would be broken. Rosette wrote her mother from Lorraine, where the farmers maintained pungent stacks of fertilizer, that she was deeply satisfied. "This morning, walking in the stinking streets, I suddenly realized how happy I am with the life I'm leading, how warm it is in friendship, how rich it is in surprises. What a fine job it is to help men who are suffering. It is easy to overcome fear when you have a precise task to accomplish and you try to do it to your best ability."

Rosette didn't hesitate to dive right into action if she was needed. Captain de Witasse recalled a day of fierce fighting near the village of Anglemont, when one of his tanks was hit and called for an ambulance. Nearby, de Witasse could see Rosette, whom he described as "young and ravishing," but he was reluctant to send her into the middle of the firefight. He didn't need to. "Rosette heard the call for help on the radio. She headed down the road, crossing the barrage of German artillery encircling Anglemont (that day the artillerymen were firing with heartfelt enthusiasm on both sides), and returned a little while later, under the same conditions, with an ambulance full of wounded."[8]

Not everyone in the medical battalion was so stoic. Rosette recalled one doctor whose talent for disappearing at the first sight of danger was well known. He tried to reprimand her for a cracked windshield on the ambulance, which had in fact occurred because of a small accident. Rosette didn't feel like owning up to yet another accident, so she said a machine gun had done it. The doctor called her on it, saying the crack was nothing like the damage automatic weapons fire makes. "How would you know?" she snapped. The doctor turned pale and left.

The Rochambelles' tactical group changed commander for the fourth time after Châtel, when Colonel de Billotte was sent to Paris to organize and train a new battalion of Resistants. The new commander, Colonel Jacques de Guillebon, a graduate of the elite Polytechnique School, was quickly characterized by his haughtiness. "Our Rochambelles, in whom the sense of observation was tightly allied to that of humor, awarded him the nickname 'Bec d'Ombrile (Umbrella Nose),' which has stuck ever since among us," Witasse wrote.[9] Rosette explained that Guillebon had a habit of standing stiffly, with his nose in the air, and communicated with the lower ranks as little as possible. The nickname was his reward.

Patton and Leclerc were ready to drive straight to the Rhine, continuing the fast-moving momentum that had spelled their success up to now. But the food, munitions, and gasoline supply line had not kept up the pace. They were short on all counts. Patton estimated that his army was lacking 140,000 gallons of gasoline, and he was told that 3,000 tons of supplies were being diverted to Paris on a daily basis to support the civilian population.[10] Patton raged and fumed at the Allied command's inability to furnish his troops with what they needed, but nothing he did had any effect. For most of the month of October, the Allied forces sat in the mud and rain of Lorraine, giving the Germans time to regroup, resupply, and reinforce their defenses. Leclerc was as frustrated as Patton.

"Leclerc spent a month being unbearable," Danièle recalled. "He was dreadful, all the time at his maps. He strained like a dog on a leash."

On top of the downtime, Leclerc was ordered to detach from Patton's Third Army and put his division under the orders of U.S. Major General Alexander Patch's Seventh Army. Leclerc didn't know Patch, but was reassured by the fact that General Haislip also was transferred to the Seventh Army.

For the long wait, a half-dozen Rochambelles were assigned to stay at a deserted village called Roville-aux-Chênes, but upon arrival they found the tank crews had already occupied all the comfortable housing. Toto requisitioned the combined village hall-school building for sleeping quarters for the women. Some Second Company soldiers, feeling a bit guilty, helped them sweep and clean out the room, and the women worked hard getting it in shape. As they were finishing, a couple of soldiers from the *Austerlitz* tank crew, having found uniforms in the hall attic, disguised themselves as firemen, put on false mustaches and masks, and knocked on the door. "Putting on a 'gendarme' accent, they demanded to speak to 'Madame la Commandante,'" Witasse wrote. "Toto arrived and they explained that the village hall could not, under any circumstances, become a house of 'working women.' Therefore they had to leave the premises, right away. Out! Toto exploded with a fury that was in no way pretended. Her girls, upset, formed a circle around the two rogues, and, equipped with brooms, became absolutely threatening. The two fellows pretended to try to escape, and then pulled off their mustaches. It ended in a gigantic burst of laughter."[11]

Toto and the women spent several days resting and trying to find food in neighboring villages, and eventually invited some officers and tank crews to dinner. They realized, to their dismay, that the men's meals were far better than the women's: the tank regiments had support personnel assigned to forage duty. The foragers hit a wide-ranging territory, buying or stealing—whichever was necessary—chickens, ducks, whatever produce the local farms still had available. The ambulance drivers had no experience in this, and mostly confined themselves to being creative with K-rations. Witasse wrote that the combined lunches and dinners nonetheless inspired the men to clean up a little. "Our ambulance drivers were often invited by the tank crews, who, on those occasions, made a great effort to receive them in a dignified manner. A kind of competition developed, which brought about the happy effect of obliging the personnel to put on clean clothes, and allowed us to establish the bonds of friendship, so precious in combat."

At Roville, the women also had frequent musical evenings of singing popular songs and duets. Marie-Thérèse remembered Lucie, Michette, and Raymonde as having particularly good voices. Some of the division officers also would join in.

One October day Florence Conrad arrived to summon Toto back to Paris. The army was trying to organize its women's corps and had decided to cut Conrad's four stripes of a major to the two stripes of a lieutenant, and take Toto from two stripes down to one. Conrad had assigned herself and Toto their ranks at the beginning of the Rochambeau project, and they had sewn their own stripes on. Neither of them were about to take any off. Toto went to Krementchousky, who sent her to Leclerc. Leclerc sent a blistering letter to Paris confirming their ranks in the division. Florence and Toto went to the A.F.A.T. headquarters and were sent from office to office until they finally ended up in front of the commandant, Hélène Terré, who had received Leclerc's opinion. Their stripes were reluctantly confirmed, and Toto returned to the front.

When she got back, she found Edith asking for a change of partner. Edith later said she had finally figured out what the rest of the Rochambelles already knew: Lucie was a lesbian. "It took me a long time to understand. I just didn't get it," Edith said later. Lucie did not try to hide her sexual orientation, and the other Rochambelles said it had never caused any conflict in the group. Lucie had been married and had left her husband after an affair with another woman. When she wasn't having near misses with death or being reprimanded by her commanding officers, she was a lot of fun, and Edith missed her afterward. "She was terrifically cultivated. I missed her because she was so funny," she said.

Lucie also was fast, and the faster you got the soldiers onto the stretcher and out of combat, the safer you were. Edith found she was pretty quick, too. "I had discovered that I was quick, that I wasn't afraid, and that I managed to do my work well."

At Roville, the Rochambelles were assigned a new driver who had tried to join the war as a regular soldier. Michelle "Plumeau" Mirande had worked with the Resistance during the occupation, and when her group joined the division, so did she. One day, she was on guard duty when Leclerc happened to walk by and ask her a question. She responded, and he jumped and said that that was a woman's voice. "But I am a woman, General!" she replied. She was sent directly to the Rochambelles, furious to be sidelined as a driver. Plumeau, so nicknamed because of her feathery hair, didn't want to join a women's unit. "But when she understood our work, she accepted it," Raymonde said.

With little to do to fill the days, Rosette went shopping. In Nancy, the nearest big city, she bought some fur-lined gloves, socks, and insoles for her army boots, which were too large for her feet. She and everyone else in the division complained that the GI-issue boots absorbed water like a sponge. She also got a plaid scarf, but Toto didn't like it and Rosette wasn't allowed to wear it when Toto was around. Toto could be overbearing about the women's personal appearance: she told Janine Bocquentin that she wasn't feminine enough, and to make more of an effort. Janine shrugged her off.

In a village near Roville, they found a public shower, and Rosette was in line behind a soldier whose boots and socks gave her pause. "I confess I was a little afraid when I saw the state of his feet. He hadn't taken off his socks since Paris!" But for a shower, that rarest of comforts, she braced herself and went ahead. While at Roville, Rosette and Nicole named their ambulance *Bessif* (The Force) to stay in keeping with the other "Moroccans," whose ambulances bore Arab names such as *Baraka* (Blessing) and *Mektoub* (It is Written). Rosette said she never followed through with painting the name on the ambulance. She felt part of the "Moroccans" because she had joined from there, but she was not an Arab speaker and had only lived in Morocco for three years before the war.

The rain did not stop falling, the ever-present stacks of fertilizer left a permanent odor in the air, and everything, everywhere, was muddy. Jacotte said that one night her boots were so caked with mud she couldn't get them off, so she hung her feet off the edge of a bed and slept on her stomach. They began putting snow chains on the ambulances to get them out of the muck. Marie-Thérèse remembered gathering branches and small logs to build a wooden platform behind the ambulances so that they could arrange their blankets on the stretchers to sleep at night. Without the platform, the stretchers sank into the mud. Once wrapped, with one blanket on the bot-

Anne Hastings (standing) and Anne-Marie Davion checking the oil in their ambulance.

tom for insulation and two blankets on top for warmth, they slipped the stretchers back in the ambulance and climbed inside to sleep.

"It is so wet that we have to winch the tanks up hill," Patton wrote. He was bivouacked to the north of the Second Division, waiting for the rain to clear so that the bombers could flatten the fortress at Metz. "Metz, the strongest fortress in the world, is sticky but we will get it as soon as we can get the air."[12]

Finally, at the end of October, Leclerc got the green light from Haislip for an attack on Baccarat, home of the crystal factory and core of a German command center that defended Alsace to the east. Leclerc decided to attack through the Mondon Forest, north of the town, and his unexpected approach coupled with extra heavy artillery crushed the Germans there. Marcelle Cuny, a young woman Maqui fighter, rode in the commander's Jeep to lead the tactical group into Baccarat by the back roads, mortars falling all around them.

Edith was now partnered with Anne Hastings, the French Harvard student who was married to an American. One day they were driving on a narrow track in the Mondon forest toward Brouville, expecting an ambush at any moment, wondering where the Germans had gone. A couple of tank soldiers on a rise at the edge of the forest signaled to them, and they tried to drive over, but the grass was too wet and the tires slid. They got out and climbed up on foot. The soldiers were part of a tank unit, and their lieutenant had taken a direct hit by a shell. His torso was hanging out the top of the tank and his legs were in the bottom. They helped get him out and laid him on the ground, which ran red with blood. Edith and Anne wiped their hands on the wet grass, shaken and upset, and returned to their ambulance. There were men still living who would need them, and all their concentration had to be funneled in that direction.[13] They found the fighting centered on Brouville, where the German and French troops dug in to pound each other with shells through the rain and mud. For several days, the ambulance drivers slipped up and down the dark forest roads, carrying the wounded to treatment centers, and the mortars fell in the incessant rhythm of the rain.

Christiane Petit and her partner Ghislaine Bechmann, who had joined the group in England, were attached to the Spahi reconnaissance unit along with Dr. Benjamin Moscovici, a Romanian, who referred to his female ambulance drivers as "*drôles de cocos*," or funny kind of guys. Because they did reconnaissance, the Spahis were far in front of the rest of the division, and after one mission at Nonhigny, the ambulance drivers had to take wounded soldiers through a no-man's-land to an American field hospital. An undefined space between the lines was the worst place to be. They could as easily be shot by their own troops as by the enemy. In the darkest parts, Ghislaine walked in front of the ambulance with her fingers muting the glow of a flashlight to give minimal guidance. Christiane was relieved when they reached the hospital, where they surprised the U.S. Army staff. "The American who met us, I can still see his face," Christiane said in an interview. "Two girls, twenty-five years old, who arrive out of the middle of the battle with all our wounded. He said, 'We don't have any girls here.' There weren't any anywhere."

After their work there, the commander of the Spahis' regiment gave Christiane and Ghislaine the honor of permission to wear the Spahi's red cap, citing "courage admired by everyone." They also received citations for their evacuations "under particularly violent fire" at Nonhigny. Christiane enjoyed wearing the cap a little more than Toto thought she should, and this led to Toto's Rule No. 41: *When sent temporarily to another unit, do not insist on wearing that regiment's headgear when the lieutenant is patrolling nearby.*

Another day, Christiane and Ghislaine were called to take Raymond Fischer, a division soldier, to the hospital. He was suffering from hepatitis and was badly dehydrated. Fischer, who had signed up with the division in Paris at the age of eighteen, became obsessed with getting some tea. He wrote in his memoirs that Christiane and Ghislaine tucked him into a stretcher between their two twin beds for the night before leaving for the hospital, and brought him some tea. "Divine nectar, sublime brew, served by the Graces, and though it did not render me immortal, as the Greeks would have wished, it revived my will to live. And in that feminine barracks, I was filled with bliss."[14]

Fischer, a native of Alsace who had hidden in Normandy to escape conscription into German ranks, drove one of the medical battalion's armored halftracks, which picked up wounded soldiers in conditions under which the Rochambelles' nonarmored ambulances should not go. He said in an interview that he heard about the Rochambelles before he met any of them, as they had a tall reputation in the division. "Their name ended in 'belles' and they often were. The officers liked them a lot, and the Rochambelles had a slight favoritism toward the officers," Fischer noted with the wry resentment of an enlisted man. Having women in the division was "marvelous," he said. "If anything happened to us, we knew we had devoted women by our sides."

The attack on Baccarat signaled a return to the roar of pounding artillery, shells smashing down for hours on end, bullets zinging past any rounded corner. But the division was delighted to get moving again, and so were the ambulance drivers. One day Toto and Raymonde picked up a wounded soldier from a field and then saw that the German gunners who had hit them also were dead, except one, who was injured. They put the wounded German in the ambulance with the wounded Frenchman, who immediately started protesting that he wasn't going to share his ambulance with the enemy. Toto gave him a generous shot of morphine and he passed out.

The Rochambeau Group often took German wounded to hospitals. "The poor kids, fifteen, sixteen years old, shot full of holes . . ." Jacotte remembered. However, some were not poor kids at all, but dedicated Nazis, as Jacotte discovered. One day she was asked to transport a dozen German prisoners in her ambulance to the rear of the American lines. She didn't like the look of one of them, and though the prisoners had been searched by the French soldiers, she checked his pockets again, and found a grenade. "Then, we had the feeling they were the enemy. Then, they could go jump on a mine and I wouldn't care," she said.

Marie-Thérèse picked up some German teenagers, sixteen and seventeen years old, outside Badonviller. "They were blond, they were young, you would have called them children. And they cried, calling 'Mother, Mother . . .'"

And sometimes, in the back of an ambulance, the French soldiers were able to overlook their differences with the Germans. Anne Hastings recalled having several wounded French and one injured German with her one day. She asked if they were hungry, and the French men said they were, so she gave them food. And the French soldiers said, "What about the *Fritz?*" "*Fritz*" was a slightly less rude way of referring to the Germans than "*boche.*" "I gave them cigarettes—as though that were good for their health!—and again they said, 'What about the *Fritz?*' And I thought that was quite nice. It made things less nasty," she said.

Baccarat was at last liberated on October 30, and Leclerc was pleased with both the speed of the campaign and low number of casualties the division had suffered. With the town in friendly hands, Edith and Anne went to visit its renowned crystal factory, tramping in with their muddy boots and bloodstained uniforms, and felt the intensity and fragility of beauty in a way they never had experienced before. Edith recounted the piercing contrast between the filthy horror of the war and the brilliant fineness of the vases and goblets around her. "Here, all was light, beauty, creativity, while outside, all was ugliness, ruin and suffering," she wrote.[15] Marie-Thérèse bought her family a seventy-six-piece service of Baccarat glassware at the factory and had it shipped to Paris.

Even when the battle was over, explosives buried in the mud remained treacherous. A soldier stepped on such a mine, and Marie-Thérèse and Marie-Anne were called to take care of him. The American field hospital was set up in a high school at Lunéville, northwest of Baccarat, but the Rochambelles were not supposed to go there. They were required to take the injured to the treatment center closer to their lines. Marie-Thérèse decided to ignore that rule and take the soldier straight to the hospital at Lunéville. He was badly wounded in both arms and legs, and the women had could not stop the hemorrhaging. At the hospital, the American nurses—all men—carried him directly in to surgery, but the doctor was not optimistic about his chances for survival. The women left and had no news of the soldier afterward. They believed he had probably died, but that they had done their best for him.

The war also had its lighter side, and for Marie-Thérèse and Marie-Anne, it was a moment of warmth and respite in an old farmhouse outside Baccarat. It had an old-fashioned fireplace in the middle of the large common room, and the inevitable stack of fertilizer in the courtyard. The Lorraine farmers measured their wealth in the size of their stack, and this one was stinking large. The farmhouse owners apparently had fled the Nazis, and had tried to hide their stores before leaving. Some division soldiers did not take long, however, to find the entrance to the cellar hidden under the stack of fertilizer. Along with some fine bottles of wine, they found urns full of butter and goose lard and sacks of potatoes. They caught a dozen or so chickens, wrung their necks, plucked their feathers and put them on a roasting spit over a big fire. They fried the potatoes in a big washtub full of fat, a treat the French hadn't had in the lean years of occupation. It was a veritable feast, and Marie-Thérèse and Marie-Anne were the only Rochambelles around to enjoy it.

At the end of the meal, the men brought out some mirabelle brandy they had found, and poured shots for everyone. Just then, a couple of soldiers burst in the room: a patrol had been hit, and there were wounded to evacuate. One of the men at the table said that since women don't down their brandy in one shot, they could pass theirs over to him. Naturally, Marie-Thérèse and Marie-Anne stood up and shot the potent brandy. Then there was work to be done, and Marie-Thérèse, who was utterly unaccustomed to heavy drinking, insisted on carrying out her duty.

"Marie-Anne," she pronounced carefully, "open the barn door." She drove the ambulance out of the barn and picked up a doctor to accompany her, as Marie-Anne sensibly bowed out of the mission. The doctor shouted as Marie-Thérèse drove over an anti-tank ditch and straight on without blinking. They got the soldiers, who were not too seriously wounded, and drove them to the treatment center. The doctor hopped out of the ambulance at the center and requisitioned some strong coffee for Marie-Thérèse. He wasn't risking the ride back on the fumes of mirabelle brandy.

Toto had a bad cold and a worse case of the blues one afternoon in mid-November, stuck in a convoy held up between Baccarat and Badonviller, and decided to go sit in a rare patch of sunshine on a village square. She took out her jackknife and sat on the edge of a wall, cleaning her fingernails, when an infantry soldier approached, laughing, with a fashion magazine he had found in the ruins of a house. He opened it and pointed at a photograph: there was Toto, in a long white evening gown and gloves, perfectly coiffed, bejeweled and elegant. "It was very funny to see Toto in such a different life," Raymonde said. They laughed over it, and Toto kept the magazine.

In fighting around Vacqueville, a village northeast of Baccarat, Jacotte and Crapette's ambulance was shot straight through. Crapette caught some fragments, but wasn't seriously injured. They were glad the back of the truck was empty at the time. A few minutes later, the back windows of the ambulance were blown out by the percussion of antitank cannons shooting from their side. The women covered the windows with cardboard. The following day, the *Malmaison* tank crew member Jacques Salvetat came round to the infirmary and squatted quietly in the corner, smoking his pipe, and Crapette said, "So, Salvetat, what can we do for you today?" He replied, "Umm . . . we were worried about you yesterday." He wanted to be reassured that they were fine. Crapette and Jacotte smiled and told him not to worry. They were touched by his concern, but felt they were in no more danger than anyone else in the division. The next evening, they were asked to take a woman about to give birth to the hospital in Baccarat, and upon their return, found the house where they had been staying flattened by a mortar.

As the division liberated villages along their path, village residents returned to their homes. Marie-Thérèse, writing in a November 7 letter home, remarked that she felt tremendous sympathy for them. "I will never forget the scenes we are now seeing, these poor people returning to their villages, pushing their poor little handcarts, and finding nothing, or almost nothing, and yet thinking to hang a flag on what remains of their houses."

Badonviller was one such town, and the fighting there was fierce. Zizon and Denise were near Badonviller one afternoon when a soldier on a motorcycle asked them to evacuate a badly wounded member of General Leclerc's guard unit. The route was still under fire, but they raced behind the motorcycle through the bombing and found the soldier. He had been shot in the heart and both arms, caught by a horizontal spray of machine-gun fire. They got him into the ambulance, and Zizon sat behind the wheel, with him holding desperately onto her hand. She was trying to maneuver the ambulance around craters in the road to avoid aggravating his injuries, and it wasn't easy to do with just one hand, but the soldier would not let go. "Let me hold it, you know very well that I'll never hold a woman's hand again," he said. Eight kilometers down the road, they unloaded him into a treatment center, and the doctor on duty yelled at them for having run the risk of picking him up. "Can't you see that he is going to die?" the doctor said. Denise responded with vehemence that their job was to pick up the wounded wherever they were, not to make life-and-death judgments in advance. The bitter exchange ended cordial relations with that doctor for the rest of the war. The ambulance was so bloody that Zizon and Denise had to wash it down with buckets of water and throw out the stretcher before returning to their post. "On the way back, I cried like an idiot, collapsing under the weight of so many deaths. Denise just said to me calmly, 'How many will you have to see die before you can manage some serenity?'"[16]

Newly promoted to lieutenant colonel, de La Horie led his troops into Badonviller on November 17 in a surprise attack on two German battalions there, killing 200 men and taking 600 as prisoners. The next morning he stopped his Jeep to speak briefly to Marie-Thérèse. They often had conversations on literature or history, the kind of talks that were food for the soul for intellectually starved Marie-Thérèse. De La Horie was "charming, cultivated, and good-looking, and also married and a good husband," she said later. That morning he told her that things were heating up nearby, and that he had to go. Jacques Branet was among the soldiers in a Jeep behind him, and they drove off to the village of Brémentil, three kilometers north. The officers were standing in a house, discussing plans, when a mortar blasted through the window and exploded at their feet. Branet got up, dazed, and found de La Horie unconscious. Krementchousky happened to be there, and he threw de La Horie into his Jeep and raced for the infirmary at Badonviller. On the way he passed Leclerc's car, en route to a meeting with de La Horie. They were all too late. The colonel was dead; a piece of shrapnel had pierced his heart. Leclerc and de La Horie had been classmates at the St. Cyr military academy, and they had made the long march across North Africa together. Leclerc went to say goodbye, kissing his old friend on the forehead before turning heavily back to the war.

The news flew rapidly through the division, and Anne-Marie ran into the infirmary, crying and shouting. "De La Horie is dead, and Jacques is, too! I have to go see Jacques!" A couple of ambulance drivers calmed her down. Branet was not dead; he was fine. It was the only public display Anne-Marie ever made over Branet, whose discretion in her regard was extreme. "He was a little cold, even with her,"said Marie-Thérèse. "I never saw any gesture that could be translated into tenderness or affection. He was a good-looking man, very old France, from the Parisian bourgeoisie, very distinguished."

Anne-Marie and Marie-Thérèse had attended the same Catholic school and had belonged to the same Scout troop when they were teenagers, and now by coincidence were in the Rochambeau Group together. But Anne-Marie never confided anything about Branet to Marie-Thérèse. She did talk to Toto, however, and Toto tried to help her. Anne-Marie wanted very much to marry Branet, but his ultra-Catholic family opposed the match, as she would be a divorcée.

The same morning that de La Horie died, a battle erupted at Petit-mont, the next village up the road from Brémentil. Michel Phillipon, radioman on the *Montereau II* tank, wrote that he was in a convoy of tanks, followed by a couple of ambulances, when they fell under attack. The lead half-track (HT) was hit, with one man dead, three badly wounded, and the vehicle on fire. Then shells hit the tank *Iena*, killing three men and injuring two. The tank also started to burn. "Courageously, the Rochambelles went to get the wounded from the HT. They wrapped them in blankets, and placed them provisionally on the grass, waiting to be able to evacuate them. Then they came to load up Dornois and Dollfus [crewmen from *Iena*]."[17] The remaining tanks opened fire, and by nightfall the village was theirs, and the wounded soldiers were recovering in a field hospital. Fighting in the area cost the division nearly 300 casualties.

The soldiers were young, some of them not even the eighteen years required to join the army, some of them away from home for the first time. Military culture tends not to leave room for emotions of sadness, fear, and loss, while those were often precisely the emotions of a war experience. The young men came to the Rochambelles for moral support, for encouragement, for telling secrets, and for shedding tears. Marie-Thérèse remembered two childhood friends who enlisted in Paris, and who told her the story of their lives: They had loved the same girl, and she had chosen one of them, and instead of the choice destroying the friendship, it had made it stronger. In Lorraine, one of the young men was killed. The surviving friend came to Marie-Thérèse and wept long tears of grief on her shoulder. He was nineteen years old. "He needed a compassionate heart, a friendly ear," she said.

As the division wrapped up the area around Baccarat, winter began to close in. The first snow had fallen and stuck on the ground, and the tank regiment began confiscating white tablecloths and bed linens from villagers to camouflage their vehicles. Patton's troops had finally taken Metz, after a twelve-day assault and 2,000 bombing runs, and were moving into the northeastern corner of France towards Belgium.[18] Another U.S. unit came up from the south to meet the French at Vacqueville, in the foothills of the Vosges Mountains. The infirmary was the only room with a table, and the

American and French command staffs spread their maps out there to consult before going their separate ways. An American officer kept taking a draw from a whiskey flask every time artillery hit nearby, and offered some to Jacotte and Crapette. They refused. It was 7:00 A.M.; they hadn't yet had their coffee. Besides, Jacotte said later, had they needed a drink every time they heard a little artillery, they would have been drunk throughout the war. And they had work to do.

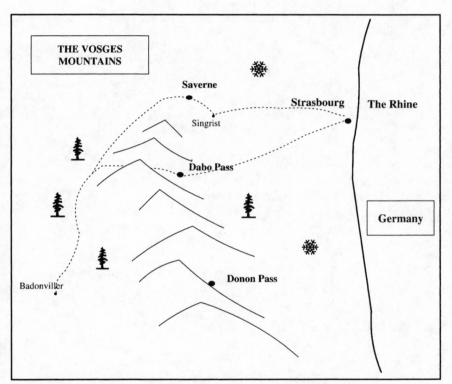

The Rochambelles' route to Alsace, November 20-23, 1944

CHAPTER SIX

A Warm Kitchen and a Cold Cellar

Between the Second Division and Strasbourg stood the blue pines of the Vosges Mountains, where the Germans sat with all possible geographical and tactical advantages. Two infantry divisions of the Seventh U.S. Army's Fifteenth Corps were working hard to break through German defenses around the central Donon pass, so General Leclerc looked to the north. The only place it was known to be impossible to cross in winter, and thus was likely left undefended, was the narrow pass at Dabo, 660 meters high. Leclerc sent Jacques Massu's tactical group to Dabo and, once he got through, two others to the Saverne and Petite Pierre passes, further north. The French were ripping holes in the German line.

Edith knew the Dabo pass road from vacation trips with her parents, and the idea of getting a convoy of heavy tanks and armored vehicles around its hairpin turns on icy roads was nothing less than terrifying. They crawled up the narrow forest track in the dark, one foot on the brake and one on the clutch, trying to keep from sliding into the vehicle in front and behind. At dawn, they reached the pass, and exhaled. The descent, which should have been slightly easier, became a slalom to avoid some dead horses, swollen and rotting in the snow, apparently victims of a mortar. A half-track in front of them had pushed the bulk of the horse carcasses off to the side of the road, but they had to drive over piles of gore. Edith said it turned their tires red.

They were bivouacked that night in a village on the western edge of Alsace, and Edith and Anne ran to the sole, tiny hotel to reserve a room for the night. They dined in the hotel restaurant on soup, omelettes, and sautéed potatoes, nicely complemented by a crisp Alsatian wine. Edith was happy to hear the accents of home, and the hotel owners were delighted to see some French soldiers. They climbed up to their room feeling warm and satisfied, and found their things outside the locked door. Someone else from the division had picked the lock and stolen their sleeping quarters. The hotel owner found them some cots in the attic, where they slept very well, despite their annoyance.

Alsace was home for many division members, and arriving there held a particular poignancy for them. When the Germans invaded France in 1870, they annexed Alsace to Germany and held it until 1919, when the Versailles Treaty ending World War I gave it back to France. With the 1940 invasion, the Germans had again claimed Alsace as theirs. The Alsatians in the division carried a double emotional charge, fighting for their nation but also very much for their region. Roland Hoerdt, a *Romilly* tank crew member, was one of them. Just as he arrived in Alsace, a small injury was becoming very painful. He had cut his finger on a tin can, and it had become infected and swollen, and no matter how silly it seemed in the midst of a war, it was making him miserable. His lieutenant told him to go to the Rochambelles to get it taken care of. "The ambulance came, and I hesitated to get in: I explained, I am Alsatian, I have waited more than four years for the moment to take Strasbourg, this is not the time to leave!" Zizon and Denise said they would get him back quickly. They rushed to the nearest field hospital, marched Hoerdt to the front of a large room full of wounded soldiers, and demanded immediate treatment. Just because Hoerdt was a fearless tank operator who didn't blink in the face of heavy artillery didn't mean that a doctor with a scalpel wouldn't scare him to death. "I was sweating big drops and I confess I was afraid when I saw the surgeon arrive with his lancet, and if my charming ambulance drivers hadn't held me by the arms, I think I would have run."[1] The doctor lanced the infection, wrapped it in a big bandage, and Zizon and Denise got Hoerdt back in time to invade Strasbourg.

The division had gotten across the Vosges Mountains so quickly the Germans didn't even realize they were there yet. Marie-Thérèse and Marie-Anne had come through the Saverne pass, bringing up the rear with Yves Ciampi, a division doctor whose parents were famous classical musicians. Their unit was posted at Singrist, a village outside the town of Saverne, with a mission to block any attempted German attack from the rear. Instead, they found that German cars and trucks kept arriving from the eastern side, the road from Strasbourg. Division soldiers erected a barrier of tree trunks to slow down approaching traffic, and positioned a tank and machine gunner at the end. Any vehicle that tried to run the barrier would end up in their sights. They picked up a few cars like that with no problem, but then a car stopped in the middle of the trap, and a German man in civilian clothes, accompanied by some German officers, jumped out and started firing a machine gun in the direction of the village.

Marie-Thérèse was a little way down the road, behind the ambulance, unloading blankets for the infirmary they were setting up in a farmhouse. She felt the blast before she knew what was happening. "Fortunately I didn't take the burst straight on but in ricochet," she said. "I was thrown into the ditch. It was a very violent shock." She had been hit in the left foot, but at first couldn't feel her leg at all. Division gunners opened up on the German civilian and the officers, killing most and badly wounding the civilian, who died a few hours later in the infirmary. The bullet had not penetrated Marie-Thérèse's leggings, boot, and three pairs of socks, but had bruised her Achilles tendon to such an extent that she was never able to play sports again. Ciampi had a look at it, bandaged it, and put a splint on her ankle for support. Marie-Thérèse couldn't bend her foot, but she could get around.

Soon afterward Ciampi got into some mirabelle brandy, found a trumpet in the farmhouse, and started blasting "Vous N'Aurez Pas L'Alsace et La Lorraine," a World War One song that had been dusted off, along with the artillery, for this second go-round. The refrain:

Vous n'aurez pas l'Alsace et la Lorraine
Et malgré vous nous resterons Français
Vous avez pu germaniser la plaine
Mais notre coeur vous ne l'aurez jamais!

(You won't have Alsace and Lorraine
And despite you, we will stay French
You managed to Germanize the plain
But our hearts you never will have!)

Later that evening, a German fuel truck arrived at the Saverne end of the village, and division soldiers opened fire on it. It burst into flames with an intense explosion and the driver and passenger burned to death inside. "It was a completely crazy night," Marie-Thérèse said. She went and hid in a barn to rest for a couple of hours when the pain in her foot got too bad. "I didn't want them to see me cry."

The next day, they continued eastward. The telephones were working in villages they passed through, and operators told the division that some of the commanding German officers had taken their families to the mountains to get them out of Strasbourg in case of Allied bombing. The Alsatian operators gave as much information as they could about where the Germans were in the city. Captain De Witasse's company put a fluent German speaker on the phone to Nazi Army headquarters in Strasbourg and managed to get some information out of the unsuspecting German on the other end. The Germans no more expected the Allies to get past the Vosges than the French had thought the Germans could cross the Maginot Line four years before.

Leclerc's instructions to the division on the drive to Strasbourg had been simple: get there fast. They raced across the Alsatian plain in two days, with Massu's tactical group out front, and gathered in four separate approaches to the fortified city. Leclerc got back the code of confirmation at 10:10 A.M. on November 23: Colonel Marc Rouvillois's unit was inside the city.

Edith and Anne, attached to the Rouvillois group that day, drove right up under one of the massive seventeenth-century fortresses, waiting for a bombardment. None came, and so they kept going, straight into Strasbourg from a northerly approach. They stopped outside a military barracks, and women came out into the streets to greet them. Edith was starting to feel confident that she would have a hot meal and a bed that night, but a Spahi signaled to her. Four men had been wounded and there was a great deal of resistance up ahead. Anne had been given temporary leave to join her husband, as his American unit was in the area, and Madeleine Collomb joined Edith instead. They picked up the wounded soldiers and headed for the Strasbourg hospital. Edith knew where it was, and they got there quickly.

Trouble was, the hospital was still in enemy hands. Edith hadn't thought about that, but when she drove up to the gate, two German soldiers were posted on guard. Thinking fast, she leaned out the window as she approached and yelled at them in German that she had wounded aboard. They opened the gate and she drove in. A nurse and a nun met them, and Edith switched to Alsatian, not knowing whose side they were on. But the nurses noticed what the guards did not: the ambulance was not German. "You're French," they whispered. Edith nodded. "Praise God!" said the nun, her eyes filling with tears. Madeleine and the nurses unloaded the wounded soldiers and Edith asked the nun to take care of them, not to give them to the Germans. The nun told her not to worry. They returned by ring roads to their Spahi unit, and were told that one soldier was missing. It was dark by then, and Edith couldn't go looking until morning.[2]

Early the next day, Edith started looking for the missing soldier, asking passers-by on the path they had taken the previous day, but learned nothing. She went back to the hospital. This time, two Alsatian civilians were guarding the gate. Inside, the four French patients were recovering, but had no information on their missing comrade. Someone suggested she check the morgue; the hospital's chapel was being used for that purpose as of the previous day. She pushed on the door and found it blocked. The body of a young man, with golden curls and brilliant blue eyes staring into nothingness, lay in front of the door. His shirt was gone, he had no visible wounds. She pushed a little harder to move him from in front of the door, and saw that he had no feet. He had bled to death. She felt sad that no one had been there to tie a tourniquet for him, to perform the simple kindness of saving his life. And she wondered why he had been left there in front of the door. She felt for a light switch, and understood in a jolt. Bodies were piled up all over the room, on top of each other, at all angles, up to the low ceiling in one corner. She tried to look for her missing soldier, walking past the stacks of dead men, but the air in the room was too close, too still. She left, and leaned against the wall outside to try to breathe again.

She remembered the hospital cook she had met the day before, a big, jolly man with a white chef's hat, and thought he would be a good antidote to the nightmare of the chapel. He invited her into his warm kitchen, and she stopped over each pot, breathing in the savory fragrance of simmering stew, sauerkraut, beans with ham, sausages, cabbage. It smelled delicious, but contrary to her nature, she did not feel hungry. Finally he persuaded her to have some soup and omelette, and she felt among the living again. She left, and driving past a building with a makeshift sign that read "*Kranken-haus*," German for "hospital," she thought: what if the missing soldier is there? She bounced in without hesitation and found eighteen German officers standing at attention. They looked at each other, the officers impeccable and correct, Edith in her dirty olive-drab. "I had a full stomach and an empty head," she remarked later. A dozen German nurses in starched whites stood to the side, disapproving. It appeared to be the occupying medical corps. An officer approached, stopped neatly in front of her and said: "We demand to be taken prisoner."[3]

She stood speechless, wondering what to do with them. They wouldn't all fit in her ambulance. She could make them march behind, but all the way to the barracks? The officer suggested he collect their arms to turn over. Edith agreed. A couple of the men went upstairs and came down with arm-loads of sabers, pistols and revolvers. She had been told that medical units had no right to carry weapons. She looked outside to see if any assistance might be in view, and saw a line of American soldiers creeping around the corner, guns at the ready. Worried that they would shoot first and ask questions later, she shouted out the window in English: "Hello boys! Hello boys!" The GIs stood up and recognized that she had the same uniform as they did, if not the same accent. They came into the clinic, and she explained the surrender and that she expected correct behavior from them. They sent for transportation, keeping their eyes glued to the pile of weapons on the table.[4]

Getting into Strasbourg was not easy for the rest of the division. Marie-Thérèse discovered fear on a narrow track leading up to Fort Kléber, on the south side of the city, where fighting continued over two days. She and Marie-Anne were sitting in the ambulance, having a smoke, when suddenly they had tracer bullets coming through the ambulance across their laps. "I had the fright of my life. The officers yelled at everyone to get in the ditches. I can still see myself, nose in the mud, wondering what the hell I was doing there." Then calls for ambulances came and they jumped up and ran to collect the wounded.

Fighting continued, even after they were in the city. Several of the Rochambelles had become close friends since their musical evenings in Roville with Jean "Jaboun" Nohain, who, at forty-five years old, was an honorary big brother as well as their musical adviser. He was a writer, singer and radio star, a celebrity in a pre-television age. Trying to wrench an army barracks away from the Germans in Strasbourg the first day they were there, Jaboun's tank was hit and an artilleryman badly wounded. Jaboun got out of his protected position to help the soldier and was shot. A good part of the left side of his face was gone. Marie-Thérèse and Marie-Anne re-arranged an already full ambulance to fit him in, and Marie-Anne sat in the back holding bandage after blood-soaked bandage to his head, while he screamed in pain and begged them for some morphine. At that moment, they had none. Their instructions were to follow the mud track they had taken into town to find the next treatment center behind lines, as the closest one had been bombed.

"It was a nightmare to drive an ambulance full of wounded who were suffering," Marie-Thérèse said. Jaboun was getting all the other wounded soldiers agitated with his screaming. She decided to take the main road instead, as it would be faster. They came almost immediately upon an American ambulance, broken down behind lines, with one lightly wounded soldier in it. Marie-Anne suggested they get some morphine from him, but the American driver refused to give them morphine unless they took his patient. They put one of their less severely injured soldiers in the front, and Marie-Anne squeezed into the back with the American soldier. She promptly gave Jaboun a shot of morphine. He subsequently went through several operations in the States, and returned to France to became a television star. "Of his wound there was practically no trace," Marie-Thérèse said, but some facial paralysis left a slight speech impediment, enough to become a Nohain signature. Younger comedians later made fun of his way of speaking, and whenever Marie-Thérèse saw them do that, she got furious and had to turn off the television. "If they knew how he got that . . ." she said indignantly.

But the small injustices of life were something Nohain understood. After the war, he wrote a play, *The Fireman's Ball*. He explained that he named it thus in memory of the tank crewman who was killed that day in Strasbourg, Henri Etchegaray. Whenever they had talked about the unfairness of this or that, Etchegaray would always say, with a shrug of his shoulders, "Like at the fireman's ball, it's always the same ones who dance." Nohain danced his way to the age of eighty and then died in January 1981. Marie-Thérèse went to the funeral, and Nohain's son, Dominique, asked her to sit with the family in the front pews of Notre-Dame de Passy. "You're the one who saved him," he told her.

Between the Vosges and the Rhine, Zizon and Denise had to stop for repairs to the ambulance and were left behind by their unit. Attempts to find it led into dangerous territory several times, and finally, as a last resort, they decided to go to headquarters and admit to the brass that they couldn't find their unit. Denise still had her beret, which looked more official, so she went ahead, hoping to discreetly find a lieutenant to direct them. But Captain Christian Girard, Leclerc's ever-present aide-de-camp, ushered her in to Leclerc himself, who was poring over a map of Strasbourg. Massu had just entered the city and Leclerc was too delighted to be cross with an ambulance driver. He showed her the route to take, and off she and Zizon

Marie-Thérèse Pezet and Marie-Anne Duvernet crossing a river in Alsace, November 1944.

went, as fast as they could, weaving around the heavy American vehicles coming up behind.

Outside Strasbourg, Madeleine and Paule were with the Fourth Company of tanks pinned down by heavy fire when the company commander, Captain Jean de Castelnau, was badly wounded. Madeleine and Paule nosed the ambulance next to the crippled tank, climbed up, and got Castelnau into the ambulance with such grace and speed that the infantrymen of the March of Chad Regiment, taking cover in the roadside ditches, burst into applause. Their ambulance windshield then was shot through and both Madeleine and Paule were cut by glass, but it was not enough to stop them. "The other wounded soldiers were yelling, Paule, Madeleine, take us, don't leave us here," Madeleine said in an interview. But they said they had to get the badly injured Castelnau out of there fast. They ran him to the ambulance at the end of the line, and Zizon and Denise took off with him toward the treatment center. Then Madeleine and Paule went back to get the others.

Zizon and Denise, with Castelnau in the back, were crossing a temporary bridge made of two wide planks when they came under fire, their flag shot right off the hood of the ambulance. In front of them, a Jeep stalled, and they were stuck, sitting ducks on the bridge, until it got going again. The American soldiers below were yelling at them to go faster, faster, while Zizon tried to negotiate the planks without shaking up the other wounded soldiers, one of whom was screaming in pain. When they got across, they found that Castelnau had died.

The next day, Captain Charles Ceccaldi called Toto in and said Paule and Madeleine were to be punished, as they were missing a wrench from their mechanics kit. Toto started to protest. "I understood that our Chieftain had heard a little too much praise of them, and that his male pride was hurt, when he responded 'Exactly! They might be heroines, but they sure are damned troublemakers!'"[5]

Jacotte said that she didn't think Ceccaldi was as bad as Toto made him out to be in her memoir, but that he just didn't know how to command women. Neither did the other officers, she noted. "Either they became super-authoritarian or they were clumsy," she said. "He wasn't clumsy."

At Fort Ney, another of the old stone fortresses ringing Strasbourg, the German military governor General Franz Vaterrodt holed up and refused to surrender unless forced to do so. The French had only one squadron, one infantry company and one battery of 105mm artillery, not much against a fort. Then up the road came a U.S. artillery company with some 155mm howitzers. The French asked if they would mind firing a few at the fort. They let loose a barrage of heavy shells, and a half-hour later the German governor surrendered. The combined exercise, though impromptu, had been effective.

German defenses at the Strasbourg airfield held up Rosette and Nicole's unit until division tanks routed hundreds of Germans out of their trenches. They surrendered, offering their watches and pens to their captors. Rosette didn't want to have anything to do with war booty, but other division members were not so principled. She recalled running into one of the Ninth Company soldiers later that evening who said, "My dear, your watch is not very attractive, wouldn't you like another?" And pulled up his sleeve to reveal a dozen different watches on his arm.

Rosette's experience of liberating Strasbourg contrasted sharply with Edith's. She got in the city on November 24 and found that the infirmary had been set up in the former Café de la Wehrmacht. She loaded up wounded soldiers as usual, and at one point had two French and two Germans in the back when she was delayed on a city street. While waiting to move again, she opened the back door to rearrange some supplies and a group of civilians came around. "I had the clear impression that the people showed more compassion for the *boches* than for the French," Rosette wrote. "They talked to them, comforted them, brought them water, apples, schnapps . . . the sight of it put me in a rage, and it was without any niceness at all that I asked the population to get away from my vehicle."

That first evening in Strasbourg, Marie-Thérèse and Marie-Anne were sitting at their tactical group's command post, a house in town with a garden. They were sipping confiscated champagne with some officers in one room, while in the room next door, another officer was interrogating a German civilian prisoner. Suddenly a tank lieutenant burst into the house, shouting, "I want him, leave him to me! " The lieutenant was Alsatian, and had just returned from learning that some of his family had been deported by the Nazis. He grabbed the prisoner and shoved him out into the garden before anyone could react. "We heard two shots," Marie-Thérèse said. The prisoner was dead. "I was so upset and shocked. It was, actually, a murder. Even the enemy deserves an interrogation, a defense. He could have been innocent."

That same evening, Edith found Anne and discovered that they had free time, and should find their own sleeping quarters. Edith considered the possibilities and decided they should start at the top, La Maison Rouge, Strasbourg's finest hotel. The desk informed her that they were hosting only military that night, and Edith and Anne quickly presented their credentials. The room had two beds and a bathroom with a bathtub. Ecstasy! They soaked themselves clean, put on fresh uniforms and went off into the night. The Strasbourgeois were beginning to celebrate their liberation, and French flags were popping up in every window. They went to Edith's favorite restaurant, L'Aubette, and found it full of Spahis. They failed to recognize their Rochambelles at first, clean and dressed up as they were, and they all had a cheerful dinner together. The next day, the division moved out, heading south, Edith driving alone as Anne was sent elsewhere.

She was not alone for long. A replacement partner was sent her way at Neudorf. Suzanne Evrard arrived in spike heels and a chignon, false eyelashes, and serious makeup. Edith started missing Anne immediately. Suzanne took the wheel, but after a while she asked to switch, and got a small suitcase from the back of the ambulance. Edith marveled at the bag full of pots, tubes, brushes, nail polish, and lipstick. Suzanne said she was a beautician, and proceeded to take off her perfect makeup and reapply it in a slightly lighter skin tone, while Edith alternated between keeping up with the convoy in front and watching the transformation in the seat next to her. They ate dried biscuits that night and slept in the ambulance, and in the morning Edith splashed her face dismally with cold water, her helmet as basin, as usual. Suzanne began to meticulously reapply her mask of makeup, and Edith was starting to get depressed, when Anne arrived, her jaw dropping at the sight of Suzanne. They had a good laugh over it afterwards.[6]

Once the center of Strasbourg was liberated, the Spahis of the Bompard platoon cobbled together a *bleu-blanc-rouge* flag to hoist on the spire of the cathedral, fulfilling Leclerc's Koufra oath. They used a butcher shop's blue tablecloth, a captain's white shirt, and a Spahi's red cloth belt to represent Strasbourg rejoining the French nation. The Second Division had taken Paris and Strasbourg, the two largest urban centers of combat, by repeating the same tactic. They showed up inside the cities before the Germans even knew they were on their way. Leclerc was turning *Blitzkrieg* around and throwing it right back at the Germans.

Strasbourg was back in the French fold, but the rest of Alsace was still held by the Germans. The worst fighting of the war, under the most bitter conditions, lay in front of the division. To make matters worse, Leclerc was also fighting off a transfer of the Second Division to de Lattre's First French Army. Jean-Marie de Lattre de Tassigny, whose 150,000 troops had landed in Provence in August, was coming north to Mulhouse, and Leclerc was ordered to detach from the U.S. Army and place his division under French command. He was loath to do so, for many reasons. Girard explained the problem in his memoir:

> De Lattre's quartermasters continue to obstinately apply the same [outdated methods] that have failed a hundred times. They have learned nothing and refuse to evolve. Their stubbornness annoys the Americans, who have their own methods and don't see why they should be the ones to conform to the habits of a small minority. . . . We are, for our part, always very welcome, because the General has decided, by realism and by logic, to adopt American methods. The result is that we obtain what we need without difficulty. It is absurd to try to live in a society of which one has need, in perpetual rebellion against customs that have proved their efficiency.[7]

Hostility between de Lattre and Leclerc was heartfelt. The two men detested each other, and their rare meetings were marked by closed-door arguments. Leclerc went up the American chain of command trying to halt his transfer, even getting Patton and Haislip to appeal for a reprieve from the Allied commander-in-chief, General Dwight D. Eisenhower, but Eisenhower said that the request had come from de Gaulle, and that the Allies were bound to respect it. The more Leclerc struggled to get out of it, the louder de Lattre insisted that he report immediately for his orders. Leclerc and his staff expressed their great regret to their U.S. commanders. "If our relations have been, at moments, a little tense, which is normal during operations, we have in the end gotten along very well with the XVth Corps," Girard wrote.[8]

The Rochambelles, like every other soldier in the division, were only vaguely aware of the changes of command. It was not their problem; their commanders were captains, not generals. "We were at grasshopper level," Jacotte said. Nonetheless, leadership at the top set the tone for morale in the lower ranks, and more important, assigned the division's position in the campaign. Their fate would now be in de Lattre's hands.

As the division moved out of Strasbourg southward into the Alsatian countryside, the weather turned dead cold. It was the end of November; darkness fell early and lifted late. Leaving the comforts of Strasbourg with slight regret, Edith nonetheless was eager to get to her hometown, Colmar, and see her family.

Edith and Anne followed their Spahi reconnaissance unit in a slow crawl to Erstein, twenty kilometers south of Strasbourg, on November 27. It was dark by the time they reached the outskirts. No one was in the streets, no lights were on, and clouds obscured the moon. Edith was tense; it didn't feel right. Where were the Germans? When the convoy halted, the ambulance came to a stop just in front of a cemetery. It didn't add to the mood.

They checked with the artillery soldiers in front of them. No one thought that they would move or attack that night, but just stay in place and wait for daylight. The men were checking out the village to make sure it was clear. Edith and Anne knocked on the door of a little house, whose owner said they could sleep there, and that there was a restaurant just up the road. They thought they would try to get a quick sandwich. Edith pushed the restaurant door open a crack and surveyed the room: no German uniforms. They walked in and felt every eye upon them, as do strangers in a village café even in ordinary times. Edith said in Alsatian that they were ambulance drivers with the Leclerc division, and the place exploded with joy. They were passed from embrace to ample embrace and showered with questions. The Germans were gone, they said, but where were the French? In Alsace, it was always one or the other. Edith and Anne tried to wolf down their sandwiches while answering questions and telling what they knew, and then someone started to sing the Marseillaise, and that was it. Edith felt tears in her eyes. Someone put on an old Alsatian folk song, they grabbed the women in a dance, and sentiment was getting the better of the evening, when suddenly Edith saw a Spahi at the door signaling her to come. "The Germans are back," he whispered.[9]

The moonlight was back as well, and they ran as close as possible to hedges and houses to get back to the ambulance, and as they did, rocket fire opened with full force in their direction. Edith listened for the French response and heard none. Then, finally, the French artillery answered, and she began to breathe again. She and Anne dashed to the house where they had left their toiletry bags, and found the owner on the steps outside, bags in hand. He put his finger to his lips. "Two Germans have taken the room," he said. They slipped silently back to the ambulance and watched the fireworks in the distance. One of the Spahis came to their window to deliver a succinct disciplinary lecture on their absence. Edith listened without resentment; she knew they deserved it. They waited in the night, Edith watching the tombstones in the cemetery and imagining a German behind every one. Anne tried to reassure her that nothing had moved.

Finally the column started to inch forward, and Edith was relieved to get out of there. At an intersection, the Spahis turned north to return toward Strasbourg, but an officer stopped the ambulance. There were wounded soldiers to transport. As they maneuvered the ambulance in the other direction, a mortar slammed into an armored vehicle that had stopped to let them pass. The young men occupying it were splayed across the truck, broken, smashed, bleeding. They loaded the ambulance rapidly and turned toward Strasbourg. Erstein had a fine hospital, but it wasn't in French hands, so they began the long ride north, guided by the light of a flashlight only, with at least one soldier who was bleeding so heavily that they knew he wouldn't survive the trip. A short way along, they saw a guardhouse for a railroad crossing and decided to take a chance that help might be found there. The guard came out and told them to bring the soldier in and put him on the kitchen table. His wife ripped up a bedsheet and they worked quickly, got the bleeding under control and a dose of morphine in the soldier, and returned to the ambulance. The guard warned them to be careful: they had a choice of crossing a bridge or going through a forest. The bridge had been badly damaged by mortar fire, and the forest was surely full of Germans.

They took the bridge. Edith walked ahead with the flashlight, Anne inching along behind her with the ambulance. Edith bounced the light off the red cross on the ambulance from time to time, in case the Germans were watching. She imagined them laughing at the folly of trying to cross that bridge. The supporting beams were cracked and holes had been shot through several sections, leaving the dark, rushing river visible below. They went slowly, steadily, and finally found solid ground on the other side. They passed silently through a small wood, and then rejoiced when it opened onto a meadow. Edith climbed in the back to explain to the wounded soldiers what was taking so long, while Anne drove on. At the Strasbourg hospital, Edith found the same nun she had met previously and gave her a big hug. They unloaded the wounded. Edith thought a very young man with a simple shoulder wound had dropped off to sleep, but when she touched his face she had to stop herself from screaming. How could he have died? She should have checked him more thoroughly, she should have at least held his hand as he died; she was full of self-reproach, and every bit of it was futile.[10]

Near dawn, another run completed in the city, the nun led them to the kitchen, where the merry chef, creating a world of warmth around his stove, gave them steaming bowls of milk-laced coffee and croissants and Alsatian brioche topped with almonds. Then the nun commandeered the empty contagion ward for the exhausted women, and they slept through what remained of the night.

Further south, at the village of Herbsheim, the artillery was pounding down when Marie-Thérèse turned a corner in her ambulance, and found Raymonde standing in the street, directing Toto in a tight turn of the ambulance. Mortars were falling, wrecks of bombed-out tanks and jeeps littered the road, the soldiers had taken cover in roadside ditches. "And there was Raymonde, imperturbable, making gestures to Toto so she could maneuver to turn the ambulance around," she said, laughing.

Edith and Anne were sent by their Spahi unit to stay a night in a farmhouse near Herbsheim, the Spahis thinking they'd be safer there, behind the front lines. The farm's family, an older couple and their daughter-in-law (the young man having been conscripted by the Germans), welcomed them with hot soup and baked potatoes and plum tart. They offered them a choice of upstairs bedrooms, one with a large double bed and fine mahogany furniture, the other with narrow twin beds. They took the twin beds, and dropped off to sleep happily full and warm, for once.

A terrifyingly loud blast awakened Edith and Anne in the night, and they felt their way to the door in the dark and opened it. A cloud of plaster and dust poured into the room, blinding them. They stood there, waiting for the smoke to clear, and finally saw that they were on the edge of a crater. A heavy mortar had pierced the roof and cut the house in two, smashing the bedroom of fine mahogany furniture into splinters on the floor below. They started wondering how to get down, as the stairs had gone with the explosion. The family came up from the cellar and called out, happy to see them alive. They inched down by the supporting studs for the stairs, hugging the remaining wall. At dawn they left, and thanked the Spahis ironically for their restful night. The soldiers had been worried; they had seen the mortars going over their heads in the direction Edith and Anne had taken. It was the last time the women were sent "to safety" for a night. They stayed with their unit from then on.[11]

Nearby at Erstein, Rosette celebrated her twenty-fourth birthday on December 6. She and Madeleine went rabbit hunting with a couple of officers, she with a carbine and Madeleine with a rifle, and enjoyed the walking. She was stiff from too much sitting, most of it behind the wheel. The women fired off a couple of shots to pretend they were there for the sport, and the officers managed to get a couple of hares. Dinner was in view. Near Erstein, the division requisitioned a stock of rabbit-fur vests that had been made for the German army. Orders called for them to be worn fur side in, for greater warmth, but the officers and Rochambelles like to wear them fur side out, for greater style. Leclerc came through one day and saw an officer wearing his vest fur side out and asked curtly, how was he wearing his vest? The officer saluted and said "Like the rabbits, general!" A glimmer of a smile was detected under the general's mustache.[12]

One afternoon Rosette was walking through the treatment center at Erstein when a wounded artillery lieutenant lying on the floor grabbed her by the ankle. "I'm suffering too much, kill me!" he pleaded. "My revolver is on my hip. Take it and kill me." She went to the doctor and asked him to do something for the man, but the doctor said his leg had been blown off at a point where he could not stop the hemorrhage. The man was going to die. Rosette asked the doctor to give him some morphine so he could go in peace. They were out. The lieutenant died, eventually, in agony. Rosette did not take his gun. "He had his own two hands," she said. "There are services one does not render."

At Kertzfeld, just across the national route from Benfeld, Danièle's unit stopped for the evening with the Germans 150 meters away, rockets at the ready, everyone on edge, mortars slamming down around them precisely every seven minutes. Danièle and Hélène had to evacuate a wounded soldier, and the other soldiers said they would dig a trench for them while they were gone. When they got back, the trench was half-full of rainwater. The soldiers pointed to a shepherd's hut in a field nearby; they could go there. They opened the door and found several officers already occupying the hay on the ground. The officers moved over and made room for the women. The mortars kept falling, and when one hit particularly close, one of the men muttered "Son of a bitch!" The lieutenant snapped that there were Rochambelles in their presence and if he couldn't watch his language he could leave. Afterwards the swearing was muffled in the hay. But no one was sleeping. They could hear footsteps, coming closer and louder, it seemed. Soon they were all lying there listening and waiting for the door to be thrown open and the Germans to start shooting them. Finally the lieutenant got up to check it out. He left quietly, and came back laughing. A gravel quarry behind the hut had filled with rainwater, and the wind had picked up, driving small waves to slap against the gravel. "We laughed out loud, but we had been pretty scared," she said.

In the same area, near Osthouse, an artillery lieutenant they were friendly with asked Danièle and Hélène to accompany him and a friend to dinner at his aunt's house, nearby. They agreed, and the lieutenant drove them in a Jeep, pulling up a long drive to a lovely chateau, classic style, with two wings flanking the central building. "We got there, I wouldn't say with mud-caked boots, but we were dressed like soldiers on campaign. He didn't tell us!" Danièle recalled. They rang the bell, and a uniformed servant led them into the salon. His aunt was there, elegant in an Oriental-style robe and trousers, and they were welcomed to dinner. "The front was five or six kilometers away, no more. And we were in a castle straight out of a fairy tale. We were served on silver trays, with a valet behind us. It was as though the war didn't exist. It was extraordinary." After dinner, they drove back to their ambulances and spent the night on their stretchers, as usual, Danièle wondering if in fact she had dreamed the entire evening.

One day, Danièle went on a reconnaissance mission with a light tank, Jeep, half-track, and ambulance, a dozen soldiers altogether. Danièle said she was always ready to go on missions like that; she enjoyed the edge. They set off at dawn, in a thick early morning fog. At a fork in the road stood a tiny house. The lieutenant called a halt to wait for the fog to lift, as they couldn't see where they were going. They parked on the side of the house and went inside. It was a rustic one-room shack. Suddenly they heard German voices, German conversations, all around. "*Mon Dieu*," Danièle thought, "We're going to be trapped like rats." They stayed quiet and the Germans went on by, apparently never seeing the French vehicles. "That was close. That was throwing oneself into the middle of the wolf-pack."

The Germans had their backs to the Rhine in December, and the fighting there took on the desperation of a last stand. The division battled for every village and many a crossroads in weather that plummeted to - 20°C (- 4°F) and stayed there for a month. Shells striking the snow-covered ground kicked up sprays of black dirt against the white backdrop, like a reverse negative. As the ground froze hard, shells exploded with increasing lethality, instead of sinking partly into the earth before bursting. The Rochambelles started treating cases of frostbite and letting soldiers take turns sleeping in the back of their ambulances. The inside of the ambulances was covered in ice, but the temperature was up to zero (32°F).

At Witternheim, Jacotte found the polar opposite of Edith's warm kitchen, spending the better part of December in a cold cellar. When they arrived, the Germans were trying to take the steeple—a handy observation post—off of the village church, bombarding it with artillery through the day, as Jacotte and Crapette hunkered down as best they could. At nightfall, they made acquaintance with the Katyushka multiple-rocket launcher, commonly known in French as the "*train bleu*," and in English as the "Stalin organ." Incoming rockets had a particular whine that gave a three- to four-second warning before they hit. After a particularly violent night, a home-owner went to complain to the company commander that the ambulance drivers had had a rowdy party the night before and had broken all her windows. She was sent back to her cellar.

The next day a mortar hit the roof of the house and broke some tiles, but didn't explode. The house nonetheless was starting to fall down around them because of percussion damage alone, and that night a nearby blast blew out the candles they were reading by. They checked by flashlight that everyone was okay, and they started looking for a cellar. There was a cellar across the street, and while a soldier accompanied some civilians there, Jacotte went to check on the ambulance. It was intact, but she noticed a fire starting in the barn, and called the others to help put it out—they didn't want it to draw more shelling, or provide more visibility for enemy gunners. It also gave them something to do. There was nothing to be done against mortars and rockets except to get out of the way, but the flames they could try to extinguish. They dug shallow trenches and passed buckets of water, but the fire spread too quickly. They loaded up and left, and as they pulled away, two mortars smashed into the house and destroyed it.

Jacotte and Crapette drove, trying to get out of the line of fire, past several farms in flames, the livestock panicking, farmers leading pigs to safety by their ears. They noticed that an ancient carriage of a fire engine, with a hand pump and a thin canvas hose, was being pulled to a farm by four men. It was hopeless; flames were shooting up into the sky. They found a cellar to sleep in, and the next morning, moving about above ground, they heard the warning screech of the Stalin organ. Crapette dove back into the cellar. Jacotte was too far from the cellar door, so she threw herself against a master wall. Afterwards, brushing off the debris and bubbling with joy at the fact of being alive, Jacotte heard a voice cut through the dust: "The General!"— and ran to put on her helmet, knowing she should have had it on all along. But Leclerc only briefly addressed the officers and did not notice the ambulance crew.

Jacotte realized that the gas tank of their ambulance had a hole in it, most likely having been hit by a piece of shrapnel. A soldier made a quick repair: he measured the hole, and then carved a wine-bottle cork to plug it. It got them to nearby Matzenheim, where they had a more permanent repair done. She and Crapette had a twenty-four-hour break there from the nonstop bombardment of Witternheim, and it was lovely to escape the constant pounding and tension. Upon their return, they were directed to stay in the cellar of the presbytery, the village priest's house, with the tank regiment soldiers. The presbytery was between the church hall and the church tower, which was still being shelled by the Germans. Jacotte noted in her journal her days' work: "Day 1: 17 wounded." "Day 2: 2 wounded." "Day 3: 1 appendicitis." She also noted the temperature. It was −10°C (14°F) inside the presbytery cellar. The tank crews briefly debated whether or not they should dip into the priest's stock of wine. It was resolved in favor of the argument that it would be better if they drank the wine than if the bottles were smashed by a shell. They also made use of the church's large supply of votive candles, which provided their only light. Every few hours, Jacotte

Friends in the snow of Alsace. L-r, Michette de Steinheil, Anne-Marie Davion, Raymond Worms (a nurse) and Crapette Demay.

and Crapette took turns running to the ambulance, head down and doubled over, to start the engine so that it wouldn't freeze.

Jacotte and Crapette were still in the Witternheim presbytery cellar on Christmas Eve. It was clear and cold; the temperature hovered at −14°C (6.8°F). At 5:00 P.M., the shelling stopped, a precious gift of silence against the rolling thunder that had rung in their ears for the past week. They were invited to Christmas dinner, along with several infantry officers, by the *Austerlitz* tank crew. Another tank crew member with a talent for making pastry had worked hard collecting the ingredients for a Christmas cake. Everything was simmering along nicely when a mortar came through the roof, blew out the windows, and left the meal covered in dust and plaster. No one was injured but the goose. Naturally, they cleaned it up and served it: Oie farcie aux miettes de plâtre avec sa sauce poussière (goose stuffed with plaster crumbs in dust sauce). Better than K-rations, just the same.

After dinner Jacotte, Crapette and the soldiers held an impromptu Christmas mass in the church cellar, and found that prayers were more fervent than usual. When they emerged, the moonlight cast a reflective light on the snow that made the house façades look whole again, a ghostly dream that the destruction was not real, that the devastation was an illusion. Sylvain the troubadour came with his guitar and played for them, lifting spirits as he knew how to do so well, and someone delivered a Red Cross gift package to their cellar. And the nurse attached to Jacotte's company, Raymond Worms, had returned from leave in Paris with gifts for everyone. He brought Jacotte a bottle of Guerlain's L'Heure Bleue perfume, and as scent alone can conjure up another place and time, she was instantly transported back to a world of society balls and opera, of innocence and joy. It was a gift from heaven in that damp, dark cellar.

Jacotte considered Worms himself a treasure. He was French, but had been living in Brazil and returned there after the war. "He was very nice, very sensitive, and I had a lot of sympathy for him," she said. "He was afraid. When the artillery fell, that's just the way it was: he was afraid. And he never let it show; he always did what had to be done." Worms overcame his fear, a task far more daunting than not being afraid in the first place. His personality was soothing on the medical group. "It was very difficult to live packed into a group like that," Jacotte said. Conditions were generally terrible, no one was comfortable, and tempers flared. "Personalities also could become difficult. He always knew how to calm irritated tempers. He was a true friend to us all."

Jacotte and Crapette spent another week at Witternheim, and when they left, the church and the presbytery were crumbled stone, but the tower, the target of all that raging firepower, stood tall.

Christmas was also a special occasion for Marie-Thérèse and Marie-Anne, staying in a house with a woman and her daughter at Herbsheim. The woman roasted a goose with potatoes and made an Alsatian cake, and Marie-Thérèse made a quiche lorraine and a chocolate mousse. Three captains and some soldiers joined them, and they rousted the local priest from his cellar and went to the church for midnight mass. The church had been bombed, and as they sang, they could see the stars through the remains of the vaulted ceiling. "It was really nice, very calm, and we felt far from the front, because the Germans respected the Christmas holiday and we weren't bombarded," she wrote in a letter home.

Marie-Thérèse's letters home were full of concern about whether her family in Paris was getting enough to eat. While the women were living in terrible conditions of cold and destruction, they now managed to eat fairly well. At Witternheim, Jacotte said they ate chicken almost every night, free-range fowl abandoned to its fate and snatched up daily by the cook.

Rosette was back in Erstein for Christmas, but her partner Nicole was transferred to a medical company in Paris to be near her fiancé, who had been slightly wounded and was recuperating at Val de Grace Hospital. Rosette met her fourth partner of the war, an eighteen-year-old called Amicie Barnaud. Rosette, feeling like a grizzled veteran next to her rosy-cheeked freshness, agreed to try her out. Along with Amicie, Toto brought Tony Rostand from Paris to join the group. She had worked for the Resistance in Paris, and had lied about being a mother when she signed up to join the ambulance drivers, as Toto wouldn't take anyone with children. Tony became a daring ambulance driver and solid member of the team, and only later admitted, under the influence of a few glasses of wine, that she was the mother of five.

Along with a Red Cross Christmas package of candy and cigarettes, the city of Strasbourg sent the ambulance drivers presents of powder and perfume. Rosette was touched by the gesture. On Christmas Eve she went to midnight mass at the Erstein cathedral. There, amid the choir pews, stood Leclerc and de Gaulle. The local residents and the division members felt blessed by their presence. De Gaulle had come to spend Christmas with the Second Division as partial compensation for placing it under de Lattre's wing. De Gaulle appreciated Leclerc on a personal level, but kept his eye on a broader view of the political horizon. After the war Leclerc remarked that his best operations were precisely when he had not followed orders. This was repeated to de Gaulle, who smiled and said that Leclerc had never disobeyed orders, he simply had carried out some orders that hadn't yet been given.

The Germans, meanwhile, decided to try in December 1944 what had worked so well in May 1940: they attacked through the Ardennes. And, again, the defense was missing just there, where the forest provided thick cover from airborne attack. Four U.S. Army divisions were stretched thinly across a ninety-mile front when the Germans launched their attack on December 16. Leclerc's division was called to come north and lend a hand to what become known as the Battle of the Bulge, named after the bubble in the Allied front line the Germans had managed to create. The Allies had a terrible time, encircled by the Germans and having to fight their way out, but they eventually succeeded and the Germans were pushed back eastward. Part of the Leclerc division stood defense on the Lorraine border of that campaign for nearly a month, but as the fighting was going on further north, they didn't have much to do. Some Second Company tank crewmen found an abandoned German anti-aircraft gun and tried it out on passing flocks of ducks. The men were having a great time, and the ducks were not the least disturbed in their flight. An officer came running from the headquarters nearby to say the flak was exploding beautifully, just over the heads of the unappreciative command staff. Another day, Captain de Witasse took some Rochambelles sledding behind a Jeep. Colonel de Guillebon happened to see them go merrily by, and de Witasse was reprimanded.

The last day of 1944 saw the Rochambelles scattered up and down the eastern border of France. At Kertzfeld, Jacotte and Crapette and three other drivers—Anne-Marie, Michette, and Hélène—had a New Year's Eve dinner at the officers' bivouac. After music and midnight kisses, the officers and the Rochambelles went outside and had a rousing snowball fight. It was the end of a tumultuous year, a time of marvelous highs and tragic lows, and everyone in the division, women and men, had come further and done more than they ever expected. They lived for the moment on the border between beauty and horror, on the edge between now and forever. It was an exhilarating place to be.

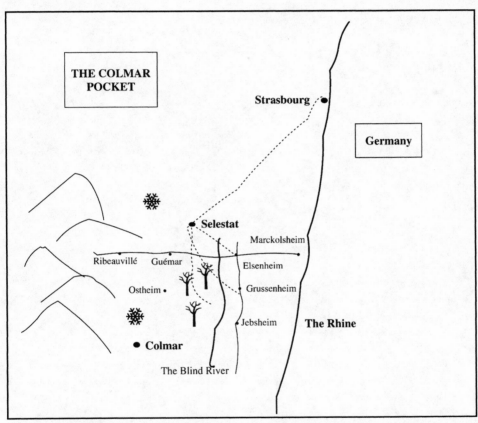

The Rochambelles in the Colmar Pocket, January 20-February 9, 1945

CHAPTER SEVEN

Grussenheim: The End of Winter

The handful of villages sprinkled across the Alsatian plains between the Vosges Mountains and the Rhine River were quiet in peaceful times, some of them little more than a crossroads and a church, connected to one another by narrow country lanes. But this was a time of war, and together, Elsenheim, Grussenheim, Jebsheim, Ohnenheim, Illhauesern, and Ostheim became part of the "Colmar Pocket," where the snow-draped innocence of country villages was stained crimson with the highest casualties since D-Day. Some of the villages had stood for more than a thousand years. When the soldiers left in February 1945, most of them were reduced to rubble and cinder, ashes and dust.

The Rochambelles, and most division veterans as well, counted the battle for Grussenheim as their worst experience of the war. It was bitterly cold, with no shelter and no cover, and the Germans held the villages while the Allies held the flat and bare fields of snow.

It did not help that the assignment to take Grussenheim came from de Lattre and his First Army while Leclerc was away, and that the directions on taking it were close to suicidal. Orders were orders.

The Second Division already had had to fight its way back from Lorraine to Strasbourg, where German troops had retaken positions to drive a wedge between Allied forces to the north and the south. The Allied command, looking at its troops thinly drawn along a wide front, prepared to pull a strategic retreat and let Strasbourg fall back into German hands, but de Lattre and French General Alphonse Juin argued fiercely against it. The price was too high.

It took the French army nearly two weeks to oust the Germans from the Strasbourg area. By January 20, the division was moving south for the final sweep: the Colmar Pocket. The Germans had their backs to the Rhine, and were being squeezed into an ever-shrinking area. The result was some of the fiercest fighting of the war.

The Rochambelles were pleased to be back in Alsace, which, despite harsh conditions, they found to be a more pleasant region than Lorraine. Lorraine had become, in division parlance, "Little Siberia." It was not simply a reference to the weather, but also to their having been sent far from the action by the First Army during the Battle of the Bulge. Now, driving southward into Alsace, the Second Division was one of 12 divisions under de Lattre's command, including two U.S. armored divisions. Their target was a flat triangle of land bordered on the east by the Rhine, on the south by the Colmar Canal, and on the west by National Route 83. Orders were to come down from a northwest-to-southeast angle, aiming at Neuf-Brisach, and push the Germans back across the Rhine. The Third and the Twenty-eighth U.S. Infantry Divisions were to hold the southern flank, and the French Foreign Legion's First Division the northern flank.

Various tactical groups stopped along the way at Sélestat, and several Rochambelles were with them. During a lull in the action, Lucie and her partner Tony Rostand decided to go for a walk. A shell landed nearby when they were bent over to peer in a shop window, and they both were hit with a little shrapnel in the rear end. It was an uncomfortable, slightly embarrassing, but not life-threatening, injury. The incident, naturally, turned into another Rochambelle joke about the division punishment for shopping.

At midnight the night of January 25, Commandant Maurice Sarazac was ordered to take two intersections, numbered 177 North and 177 South, on the Departmental Road 45 between Ostheim and Grussenheim. Both were being blocked by German antitank defenses and the 1st Foreign Legion was unable to push any further. Jacotte and Crapette lined up in the convoy behind their friends in the tank *Uskub* and headed east. Division artillery slammed 500 mortars onto the southern intersection, destroying several German antitank cannons, then took the terrain and moved northward to the next intersection. There, the artillery exchanges were intense, and several French tanks were hit.

Jacotte and Crapette transported wounded soldiers to the Guémar hospital, driving through snowdrifts across rocky fields, each jolt and bump putting the injured soldiers in agony. Twice, in trying to get some wounded soldiers out of there, the ambulance was whipped by the nearby pass of a mortar. In Normandy, the Germans had used ambulances for transporting

Convoy of ambulances in the snow, Alsace, January 1945.

munitions and troops, and apparently figured the Allies would do the same. "It was a very dangerous situation," Jacotte said. "One of the nurses was killed a little further down the road."

They were camped in a small wood, with leafless trees for cover, and the march of mortars followed them no matter how often they moved the ambulance. Snow was falling, the temperature dropping to - 20° C (- 4°F), and the ambulance was full of soldiers trying to warm up. No one slept that night for the artillery and cold. Many soldiers' feet froze: forty-five men from the Colmar Pocket were hospitalized for frostbitten feet in the last week of January alone. "I have to say the shoes were no good. The unlucky ones who got their feet wet in the snow found their feet frozen," Jacotte said. While in Paris, she had picked up her old ski boots, made of water-proofed leather, and wore them with two or three pairs of socks. Her feet stayed dry.

Driving back from Guémar one afternoon, they found the road littered with half-tracks and burned-out tanks, and saw a German antitank gun on the edge of the woods turn and start firing at them, missing three times. A couple of soldiers from their unit poked their heads out of the roadside ditch and told them to get the hell out of the car and into the ditch. They jumped down into the snow, freezing wet, while the shells whistled overhead. One missile landed with a flat thud instead of an explosion, and pastel-colored fumes started spewing out. The soldiers were very afraid of poison gas, a legacy of damaged veterans of World War One. The women's gas masks were in the ambulance: should they risk getting shot to get the mask or risk getting poisoned without it? They decided on the gas and stayed where they were. At dark they managed to slip away and rendezvous with the rest of the group in the wood. Around midnight it started raining mortars again, and two infantrymen from the Ninth Company, known as *La Nueve* because of its many Spanish members, were wounded, one mortally. Captain Raymond Dronne sent a half-track to escort them to the Guémar hospital, but it slid into a ditch, and the women drove on alone. Rather than hazard the route back, they spent the night in a frozen barn on the outskirts of town. They met some American soldiers at Guémar, a couple of guys from Brooklyn and the Bronx, who were shocked to find women on the front lines. The men gave Jacotte cigarettes and chocolate.

The next day the women returned to the wood by the strategic inter-section. At night, mortars from battles for villages eastward, particularly Grussenheim, slammed around their bivouac. The temperature hovered at –17°C (–1.4°F) in the day and plunged to –23°C (–9.4°F) at night; snow was in thigh-deep drifts on the ground, and a biting wind swept across the unbroken plain. Soldiers took turns sitting in the ambulances in order not to freeze, and still, every morning, Jacotte and Crapette drove new frost-bite cases to the hospital. Next to the heater in the front of the ambulance, it was 8°C (46°F), and in the back it was an even zero (32°F), with ice on the inside walls. It was a miserable, aching cold with no relief. The Rochambelles slept with their boots on to avoid having to thaw them in the morning.

At this point, Danièle had to leave. She was suffering from chronic bronchitis and a scurvy-like gingivitis brought on by a lack of fresh fruits and vegetables. She had endured four years of poor nutrition during the oc-cupation, and her bronchitis was instigated and aggravated by the glacial conditions in which they were living. She still had the key to her apartment in her bag. When she unlocked the door in Caen, her mother said, "Who's that?" Denise Colin also fell ill while working in the Colmar Pocket and was hospitalized with severe bronchitis.

The low and leaden sky precluded air support, and the French were fighting village by village to push the Germans back across the Rhine. At Ebermunster, many soldiers were wounded by mines that bounced up out of the snow and exploded a meter off the ground. The stretcher bearers also were being injured by these deadly mines. Anne-Marie was horrified at the number of bleeding, broken faces she found in the infirmary. "She shouted, pointing at the 50 or so German prisoners, with their hands in the air, who were being held not far from there. 'What are you waiting for, make them go get the wounded themselves in their minefield!'" Rosette wrote her mother.

Orders came down the line from de Lattre while Leclerc was in Paris. The Third March of Chad Regiment (RMT) and the 501st Tank Regi-ment were to take Grussenheim in a frontal attack. The Germans held the village with heavy 88mm artillery. The French were two kilometers away, on the other side of the Blind River. There were only a few stands of bare trees on the open, flat terrain between the woods and the village. A light snow was falling, and each side could see the other through their binoculars. Colonel Joseph Putz and his Third RMT fought through the afternoon of January 26 to take control of the river crossing, even though the bridge was long gone. The river was neither large nor deep, but the tanks were having trouble getting across because of ice on the banks. Finally two tanks and a tank destroyer made it, along with the Third Battalion of the Foreign Legion and several RMT companies, which crossed the river in inflatable boats.

Putz was a commander respected for his intelligence and his courage. He had fought in the international brigades in the Spanish Civil War, leading the defense of Bilbao in June 1937. Ernest Hemingway mentioned him by name in *For Whom the Bell Tolls* as a leader to be trusted. But when Putz laid out the plan of attack, de Witasse was not the only captain to question its sanity. Putz shrugged and said orders were orders. He was clearly tense, and the cold was sharpening everyone's nerves. Marie-Thérèse and Marie-Anne let officers and soldiers take ninety-minute naps in the back of their ambulance, and that was the only sleep the men were getting. Marie-Thérèse urged Putz also to get in to warm up, and he confessed a superstition about ambulances. "He said to me, 'Never, Marie-Thérèse, have I gotten in an ambulance. I would only leave it feet first.'"

Engineers arrived at 8:00 P.M. on January 27 and began trying to put up a floating pontoon bridge, working in the dark and freezing cold. German artillery slammed in on them at 10:00 P.M., killing ten and wounding thirty men, and destroying the bridge. Marie-Thérèse and Marie-Anne ran the wounded men west to the Guémar hospital and returned for more. After their last trip, around 2:30 A.M., they saw Putz rolled up in a tarpaulin and sleeping bag in the snow. From time to time through the night they saw him get up and walk, pacing back and forth, wrapped in his tarpaulin. At first light, Marie-Anne made a hot cup of coffee and took it to him. "The Grussenheim attack depended on him. He had a great responsibility. We figured we'd better keep him in good shape," Marie-Thérèse said.

On Sunday morning, January 28, the Grussenheim church bell rang, a mournful summons to the torn and lifeless bodies in the snow, to the soldiers in green huddled in icy tanks, to the soldiers in gray hidden behind broken walls. Putz, exhausted and worried, got in the ambulance. He stayed there all morning, covering the passenger-side folding tabletop with his maps and papers, teasing Marie-Thérèse that the ambulance would thereafter serve as a command center. Not another word about his superstition.

A new corps of engineers arrived and tried again to lay a temporary bridge across the river, but it was too well defended. They couldn't work under the hail of German artillery. Then suddenly, the shelling stopped, and they were able to finish by 10:00 A.M. De Witasse believed the cease-fire was meant to draw them into a trap on the other side of the river. Then the Germans fired a shell at a tank destroyer that had gotten across the river, leaving it crippled and effectively blocking the bridge. At noon, Putz called the company officers together and ordered the attack on Grussenheim for 1:00 P.M. He modified the plan, sending a diversionary group through the southern village of Jebsheim, part of which had been taken the previous day by the Third U.S. Infantry Division. The officers stood in a circle in the snow, conferring amid the bare trees. "I said, Are they nuts? The Germans can see that there's an officers' meeting," Marie-Thérèse said. They were there only ten minutes before a barrage of ar-tillery came crashing down. The men started breaking into different directions, looking for a ditch to roll into, but there was none. Then an-other mortar smashed into them, killing Putz on the spot and fatally in-juring another officer. Putz had fought for the freedom of two nations, and had not lived to see the achievement of either. The bell had tolled, at Grussenheim, for him.

Marie-Thérèse and Marie-Anne loaded up the injured and took them to Guémar. They had to leave Putz because they were not allowed to trans-port the dead. When they returned to the camp, the need to do something for him coalesced into finding one of his feet that had been blown off. They fixated on the foot. They couldn't help him and they couldn't move him, but they could put his body back together. They searched through the snow for a half-hour, and found the foot in a bush. They laid it next to him, said a quiet goodbye, and left.

Marie-Thérèse was later awarded a citation for her work at Grussen-heim: "for bravery, calm and magnificent devotion in carrying out numer-ous evacuations under violent bombardment."

The attack went on as scheduled, with Commandant Regis Debray stepping in to lead the group. De Witasse took his company to Jebsheim, crossing the Blind further south at the Jebsheim mill, and started up the narrow path to Grussenheim, but confused communications led the attacking companies to retreat. They had to start all over again, through drifting snow and under unrelenting artillery. It was continual firing from both sides, with artillerymen packing snow on the guns to keep them from overheating. By nightfall, however, the French had surrounded the village and pounded it mercilessly into surrender. Flames licked the night sky as the village burned to the ground. In the morning, some 300 Germans who had survived the firestorm were taken prisoner. They said they had been told they would be shot if they retreated back across the Rhine.[1]

The wounded could be counted in scarlet patches of blood on the snow. Edith and Anne were driving in a convoy towards Grussenheim, a long black snake of vehicles across a white blanket, on a narrow road with no cover, when German artillery began picking off vehicles from high ground positions. They finally got into the woods, but it offered no shelter from the lethal hail, and they picked up the wounded and left as quickly as possible. They drove west toward Ostheim, on the main Strasbourg-Colmar route, and saw a pink glow on the horizon that, as they approached, turned out to be the entire village burning. No hospital would take their wounded there. They continued westward, crawling through the smoldering wreckage, to Riquewihr, where a field hospital ostensibly had been set up. They found it, but it was empty of any medical supplies and they were reluctant to leave their wounded there. The locals told them that the mountain pass to Ribeauvillé, the nearest hospital, was blocked with snow. More injured soldiers were waiting to be picked up back at Grussenheim; they had no time to spare. They unloaded the soldiers into the bare room, thinking that at least they were out of danger there. Edith looked at one of them, a young man whose hands were drenched with blood from holding his intestines inside, and thought that if she could get him to a hospital, he might be saved.[2]

They had to go back down the treacherous road into the center of the firestorm, and returning to certain danger required purposeful courage. "It was sometimes difficult to think, I've got to go back," Anne said. Back they went, retracing their path through still-burning Ostheim and approaching Grussenheim gingerly, hardly saying a word, watching the flames rise and the mortars fall. Edith, less than ten kilometers from her parents' home in Colmar, kept thinking that it would be too unfair to die on their doorstep. They got through, picked up the wounded, and took them straight to the hospital at Ribeauvillé this time. Ostheim was little more than ashes as they passed.

When chunks of rubble and smoldering beams fallen from the ruins of buildings blocked their path, the two women got out of the ambulance to push them aside. On their second day of bringing wounded soldiers to Ribeauvillé, they learned that an American field hospital had been set up nearby to relieve the overburdened town hospital. They were glad to take the injured men there instead. Edith and Anne worked nonstop for three days, getting no sleep and eating only a few crackers they happened to have in the ambulance. "It was a nightmare," Edith said later.

After Grussenheim was taken, de Witasse collapsed with septicemia and tetanus and was hospitalized. He had been getting worse and worse over the previous week, and the effort of the attack was more than he could stand. De Witasse was one of the lucky ones. The division counted 278 dead and wounded, eighteen of whom were officers. Some 250 Germans were killed, and after the war, Grussenheim's mayor calculated that fifty-two farms were destroyed, and twenty-two civilians and 125 animals killed in the four-day battle.[3] Grussenheim had cost the division more casualties than the entire campaign from Baccarat to Strasbourg, and yet it offered no strategic interest whatsoever. Leclerc, back from Paris, was livid. He sent a blistering report on de Lattre's lack of judgment and leadership to de Gaulle. It was the end of any slightly civil communication the two men had enjoyed.[4]

On January 31 Jacotte and Crapette left their snowy wood and crawled along roads crowded with burnt-out tanks and armored cars through Elsenheim, where they were hit with some shrapnel, to Ohnenheim. Dr. Alexandre Krementchousky was there; he had set up a field hospital in the village café. The women found a jar of milk and started to stoke up the furnace. They hadn't been indoors and they hadn't slept a full night in ten days. The idea of a glass of warm milk was like a vision, a dream. They gathered around the furnace, holding their stiff hands up to its growing bloom of heat, daring to feel the exhaustion in their bones. And the order came: immediate depart for Markolsheim.

They climbed leadenly back into the ambulance. Jacotte asked Crapette to mix her some instant coffee with cold water—anything to stay awake. They sang songs until they got close to the town and the artillery started pounding in, loud and close, and staying awake was no longer difficult. Marckolsheim was the last village west of the Rhine, and apparently its bridge was still intact, and the command staff wanted to push any remaining Germans in the area back across and then seal the access.

They drove into the village at 2:00 A.M., sheltered the ambulance, and were directed to a cellar where a dozen or so other soldiers were waiting out the battle. At morning light, Allied air support destroyed the last German defenses. They emerged from the cellar and realized that they had finished their task: they had pushed the Germans out of the Colmar Pocket and back across the Rhine. "There was an explosion of joy and of satisfaction," Jacotte said. "It was over."

They found a small hotel, abandoned, and everyone crowded in as Crapette struck up some silly songs on the piano. They were running on empty, coming out of two weeks of icy horror, and the happiness that erupted was in equal measure to the depth of their exhaustion and despair.

Edith was denied permission to drive the ambulance to Colmar, but a Spahi friend found a Jeep and took her there. First they stopped at her late husband's parents' house, and she was pleased to see they were well. She missed her husband, killed in an airplane crash before the war began. Then she went to her parents' home and the nostalgia of better times. She had to forego a night in her own bed, as they all slept in the cellar, and the Spahi came to fetch her in the morning. It was a brief respite from the brutal edge of the Alsatian campaign.

A week later, the rest of Alsace was in French hands as well. De Lattre announced on February 9 that the last of the German troops had crossed back over the Rhine. The division celebrated the liberation of Alsace in Geipolsheim, on the southwestern outskirts of Strasbourg, with a parade and review by Leclerc. The division was being split between those sent to extinguish an isolated band of Germans on the Atlantic coast at Royan, and others sent on an extended vacation in the center of France. The U.S. Army and de Lattre's First Army would lead the invasion into Germany, a decision with which Leclerc predictably disagreed. At the same time, the Second Division was broken, battered, and exhausted. They needed a break. "After Alsace, we were shattered," Jacotte said. "We had suffered greatly, from a lack of sleep, from the injuries and loss of friends, from the cold. And the Germans were very punishing in the end. We never had a respite."

Jacotte and Crapette took *Tante Mirabelle* in for some repairs, such as replacing the back windows that had been shot out in Lorraine two months before. They counted the shrapnel holes, some of them not so small, and found thirty-five. That was thirty-five times they had been missed by a paper-thin margin. They considered it irrefutable evidence of their incredible luck.

CHAPTER EIGHT

Expectations and Surrender

From the end of February to the middle of April, the Rochambelles and most of the division were on leave in the Loire Valley. They visited the monumental chateaux, organized numerous picnics, held many a musical evening, and generally tried to recover from the crushing fatigue of the campaign to liberate France. The first few weeks of enforced rest were practically medicinal, but as the men and women found the top of their form again, they were eager to get back to the war.

Leonora Lindsley, one of the young Americans who had signed on with the Rochambelles in New York and had been working since August 1944 at Val de Grace Hospital, rejoined the Rochambelles in the Loire Valley. She hoped to write about the war from the French perspective. Soon after she arrived, the division was ordered to depart for Germany, and she described the tanks draped with wisteria and lilacs, and the men singing their regimental song, "The March of Chad," as the convoy rolled out.

A few days later, writing from Germany, Leonora noted that the victory march into Germany so anticipated by the division soldiers and the Rochambelles was turning out to feel a little hollow. Having known the experience of defeat, it was difficult for them not to recognize the pain and loss on German faces. "The French are unhappy. They arrived a little arrogant and sure of themselves. When they crossed the border, after so many years of waiting, standards flying in the wind, they were truly radiant. But battle has not yet taken place on this side of the Rhine. . . . They became the Conquistadors (for lack of a better term) and are not happy about it," she wrote. Division soldiers talked loudly in the streets about Nazi atrocities and reassured themselves that their punishing attitude was correct, but they felt a little ugly and very unhappy, she wrote. "We have done a lot of driving since April 25, and it resembles more and more 1940, but this time in reverse. Soon, there probably will be no more resistance and my next letter will have a different tone."

Leonora Lindsley, April? 1945.

Resistance largely came from the hands of snipers when the division moved into Germany behind the American offensive sweep. Two motorcycle men were shot, and division vehicles had to be kept under guard whenever they stopped. The civilians they encountered were somber, unsmiling: Nazi Germany had been defeated, even if the white flag had not yet flown. The Rochambelles were coasting on a victory wave, but it was not the joyride they had anticipated.

The Second Division crossed the Danube on a pontoon bridge erected by engineers of the Twelfth U.S. Armored Division, following the American advance through Bavaria toward Munich. There the Second Division was ordered to halt and move off the road to let U.S. troops pass by them: the Americans wanted Munich. The French had taken Paris and Strasbourg, and they were told there were fresh American troops who had not yet engaged in combat.

Jacotte and Crapette pulled the ambulance over to the side of the road with the rest of the convoy and watched the parade of every imaginable type of military vehicle: Jeeps, half-tracks, amphibious vehicles, tow trucks, bridge builders, tank carriers, gas tankers, supply trucks, medical trucks, tanks, armored cars, and on and on. It took them all day to pass. When the French got to Munich, snow was on the ground and the city was in Allied hands.

In countryside villages, white sheets began to appear draped from chalet balconies, reflecting the surrounding blanket of snow, and wrapping the entire nation in a symbolic surrender. The German people knew it was over, even if Hitler and the Nazi command were still huddled in their Berlin bunker to the north. The Second Division encountered light and sporadic fighting, more for show than in any serious attempt to repel the Allied forces. In the south, the landscape was pristine, but the roads were crowded with military traffic. Liberated prisoners seemed to be everywhere. Those from the concentration camps stumbled in the snow, clinging tenaciously to life, indescribably fragile.

Zizon had a new partner, as Denise, recovered from her bronchitis, had returned to Paris to finish medical school. They stayed with German families as they traversed the country, and Zizon wrote that she felt that the Germans were trying to pretend that it was only a small minority who had supported the war. She didn't believe it was true, and said she saw in family albums photographs of Poles hung after being mutilated, and of Germans looting among dead French soldiers. "I was dismayed to see how the people put all the horrible crimes committed by the Germans on the backs of the S.S.," she wrote. "They look plainly to set themselves apart from those who, so they say, were the only perpetrators of atrocities."

Janine Bocquentin, who left her hospital duty to rejoin the Rocham-belles during their Loire Valley stay, was attached to Commandant Dronne's tactical group in Germany. There wasn't much physical fighting, but the psychological battle had yet to be won. She said that they saw German teenagers kicking newly released prisoners, particularly the skeletal concentration camp survivors. She and her partner threw food and clothing out the ambulance window to the ex-prisoners when they passed them in convoy. They also were supposed to find lodging among the German popu-lation, and Janine did not find that easy. One woman chased them off a farm with a pitchfork, shouting that the Americans were coming and would teach them a lesson, as though they were on opposite sides. "I never saw an open door, an extended hand, never," Janine recalled. "I could feel the hatred of that population."

The men soldiers found a different kind of welcome. Marie-Thérèse said the engines on the convoy would still be warm when groups of German women came around their nightly bivouac. "Those who resisted were really strong, because the girls were literally jumping on them. They were real whores."

And, as night follows day, venereal disease followed prostitution. Sol-diers asked the ambulance drivers for treatment. "I yelled at them," Marie-Thérèse said, but they didn't care because penicillin, now available from the Americans, was a quick cure. One soldier had to be hospitalized three times for syphilis, the last time in Bavaria in late April. The Rochambelles had fi-nally gotten clearance for a good night's sleep under deep down covers, and Marie-Thérèse was ill with what was probably an appendicitis attack. She had been driving stretched out straight so that the bumps in the road didn't send her into agony, and her belly was swollen up so that she couldn't but-ton her pants. She was very much looking forward to resting in bed. At 4:00 A.M. there was a knock on the door and a call to evacuate a soldier. "Where was he?" she mumbled. There at the door was the syphilis victim, walking like a duck, his testicles and abdomen swollen up and in severe pain. "We were furious," she said.

Marie-Thérèse Pezet with division member and actor Jean Gabin, Germany, May 1945.

Marie-Thérèse drove behind the celebrated actor Jean Gabin and his tank all through Germany. One morning she woke up and the front half of her hair had fallen out on her pillow. It grew back, but white, while the back half stayed dark brown. The doctor said it was the exhaust from the tanks that had scorched her roots. She had to dye her hair for years afterward.

The French troops also were helping themselves to the material spoils of victory. An anonymous donor left the gift of a fox stole on the seat of Zizon's ambulance, and she threw it out the window on a drive to get rid of it. The next day a soldier came running up, holding the wrap, saying "Look what you lost! I'm so glad I found it for you!" She waited for the cover of night to get rid of presents she did not want.

The division kept moving southward, toward the Austrian border, and engaged in its last fighting on May 4, just northwest of Berchtesgaden. Hitler had committed suicide on April 30 and Berlin had surrendered to the Russians on May 2. Would the remnants of the Nazi army try to defend his Bavarian headquarters at Berchtesgaden? Five army columns, four American and one French, rolled down the *Autobahn*, working together and exchanging supplies along the way.

The division's Twelfth Company was ahead of the rest, and entered Berchtesgaden at 5:00 A.M. on May 5. Toto was with them. She wrote that they waltzed into Hitler's abandoned offices with "the drunkenness of pirates," and began looting and pillaging with a heady enthusiasm. She took Hitler's personal stationery, and over the next few weeks sent notes to her friends on it. She was trying to stop the Spaniards of the Ninth Company from defacing a Rubens portrait, when suddenly a lieutenant came running, shouting for her to come quickly, quickly! Ambulance! She feared it was a car accident, but the lieutenant grabbed two other men and led them to an unmarked door in a hillside on the grounds. It was Hitler's private wine cellar, and it was stocked with the best vintages of every country his troops had ravaged, most particularly France. They were loading cases into the ambulance when two American soldiers from the Third U.S. Infantry Division arrived to investigate. Toto steered them toward the stores of sugar, and the French kept piling up the wine cases until the ambulance would hold no more. Toto wrote that if a mouse had been injured, it wouldn't have fit in the ambulance at that point.[1]

A captain in the room next to Zizon's collected an array of sterling silver, platters, teapots, forks, knives, plates, all with the initials A.H. She saw the treasure when she passed by his open door, and couldn't resist a comment in his direction. He said, "You know my wife's initials are the same. This will make her very happy." Another Rochambelle gave her a plate with Hitler's seal on it, as a soldier had given her two of them. The Third Reich leaders' houses at Berchtesgaden were stocked with the finest of everything: paintings, silver, books, rugs, wines, and division soldiers took what they could.

Marie-Thérèse was surprised by the reaction of some German women to the division's presence. She wrote home from Berchtesgaden on May 6: "Curious impression: we are being received by the civilian population exactly like liberators. I personally have been stopped several times in the street by women thanking me for the end of the war!!! A young woman who lost her husband, her father, her brother-in-law and her brother in the war got down on her knees upon learning of the cease-fire in our sector, saying 'Thank God!'"

Janine and her partner arrived at Berchtesgaden late and tired on May 6. They drank a little champagne to celebrate and then headed off to sleep. The next day they had a look around, and installed the infirmary in an office previously used by Emmy Goering, wife of top Hitler aide Hermann Goering. She picked up and kept some Goering family photos, some letters from Emmy Goering and a Christmas card: "*Weihnachtsgruss des Führers*" (Christmas Greetings from the Führer). An elegantly dressed German man offered to show them the entrance to Hitler's "Eagle's Nest," a lookout 1,834 meters up in the Alps. He said he was the Goering's cook, but Janine didn't believe him for a minute. "He was very distinguished; he was no cook," she said. She found more Goering family photos in his desk later, confirming her suspicions that he was a friend or associate.

A group of soldiers wanted to climb up to the Eagle's Nest, but found that the elevator built into the rock had been disabled. They started to climb, but Janine's captain complained that his feet were frozen and asked her to accompany him back to the Berghof. Another four or five of their group hiked on up to the top. There was a little shooting in their direction, but the German "cook" shouted at the snipers not to shoot, that the war was over. As Janine was returning to the compound, someone from the division delivered some bad news: Leonora Lindsley had been badly injured. She had been riding in a Jeep crowded with soldiers, they hit a bomb crater in the road and she was thrown out onto her head.

Rochambelles at Berchtesgaden, May 1945. Driving: Crapette Demay; passenger front seat, Toto; rear passengers l-r, Amicie Berne, Biquette Ragache; on wheel cover, Yvonne Negre

Janine went to her and held her through the night, sponging blood from her face, but she never regained consciousness. "Leonora loved France," Janine said. "She wanted to show the state of spirit of the French soldiers; that was what interested her."

Leonora was twenty-eight years old when she was buried at the American cemetery at St. Avold, in Lorraine. She is identified there as an American Red Cross worker, a civilian, rather than a Second Division soldier. Her great adventure had ended in a banal accident, and, with painful irony, she died on the day the Germans surrendered.

It was on that day—May 7, 1945—that Jacotte and Crapette pulled into the parking lot of Hitler's favorite lakeside hotel at Dorf-Königsee. A radio car next to them howled out the news: the war was over; the Germans had officially surrendered. Some nearby soldiers went crazy, shooting into the air every bullet and cartridge they could find. Eight of the Rochambelles happened to be there together, and they whooped with joy at the news. The war was over!

And then, in the midst of rejoicing, a pall fell over the women. If the war was over, so were their careers as ambulance drivers. For most of the women, returning to civilian life did not hold much promise. Options for women, in 1945, were limited and predictable: family, home, maybe a low-paying job, but nothing nearly as fulfilling as what they had been doing. As Rochambelles, they had touched the sky, rocked the earth, and defeated death on a daily basis. They were glad the war was over. But what would they do now?

Toto had an idea. She had heard that once the war in Europe was over, Leclerc was going to organize a volunteer division for the Pacific front, French Indochina in particular. Surely he was going to need ambulance drivers. With that prospect of adventure ahead, the women started celebrating again. Their futures seemed marvelously uncertain.

After Berchtesgaden and the surrender, there was still post-war clean-up to be done, and the Rochambelles were figured into the tasks. Part of the division was sent to rural Bavaria, where Marie-Thérèse and Marie-Anne were dispatched to a large and wealthy farm. There, three women proprietors had been fattening up their one billeted French prisoner of war like a favorite goose. "We were shocked to see that he was the king of the farm," Marie-Thérèse said. The women's husbands had been sent to the Russian front, and were not really expected to return alive. The prisoner hoped not, in any case, because he didn't plan to liberate himself. "He said, 'I'm just fine here, I'm not going home.'" He was from Béarn, in the rocky French Pyrénées, and had left his wife and three children on a farm smaller and far less productive than the Bavarian farm. Marie-Thérèse reminded him of the difficult life his wife was most likely living, but he said she would get along fine without him.

His attitude was disappointing to the Rochambelles, but it was intolerable to the French officers who had fought their way to Germany to free the comfortable Béarnais farmer. At the same time, the French Repatriation Commission was sweeping through Germany, picking up nearly 1 million French former prisoners, giving them their back pay, demobilizing them officially, and taking them to Strasbourg. Before the commission arrived in an area, a motorcycle messenger posted announcements of the appointed day, hour, and place the officials would be. Any French prisoners in the area were to report in for repatriation, and the large majority were very happy to do so. But in the area where Marie-Thérèse was stationed, about thirty of them hid in the woods when the commission came through, including the Béarnais farmer.

After this happened three times, Marie-Thérèse's unit commander flew into a fury. The group would be returning to France soon, and he was determined to take the prisoners with him. An officer suggested they throw a party—supplies remained from the sacking of Berchtesgaden—and invite the prisoners and some Rochambelles for dancing. Marie-Thérèse, Marie-Anne, and Raymonde were among the Rochambelles present. "The prisoners came, with no apprehension, to enjoy the party. We let them drink deeply, and when they were ripe, the guards appeared," Marie-Thérèse said. Twice prisoners now, they were put in the cellar of the officers' headquarters. A few days later, the column moved out for France, with one prisoner per vehicle, chained to the tank or half-track, and disguised in as much uniform as they could find. No civilians were allowed on the military vehicles; the men had to look like soldiers. They resisted, they said they were better off in Germany, that people were starving in France. Those who had wives said anything could have happened in their prolonged absence, that it didn't matter anymore. Their protests fell on deaf ears. The French soldiers had fought the war to liberate them and by God, they were taking them home. When they got to Strasbourg, the commanding officer was reprimanded by his superiors, not for bringing the men home against their will, but for violating transport regulations. The prisoners thus were "freed" in Strasbourg, and Marie-Thérèse deeply suspected they returned to Bavaria.

On May 19, the entire Second Division was assembled for the first and only time for de Gaulle to pin the Grand Croix de la Legion d'Honneur on Leclerc near Landsberg, just west of Munich. The oddest group of men the French military had ever seen had pulled off an amazing feat. From New York to North Africa, French soldiers and exiles, Jews and Muslims, Catholics and Communists, aristocrats and workers had come together for a single mission: to help liberate France from the Nazis. One veteran aptly noted: "As with wolves, they tear each other to pieces, but they hunt in a pack."[2]

EPILOGUE

Coming Home Is the Hardest Part

At the end of the European war, Leclerc took the Second Division—and some of its ambulance drivers—to Indochina, where Suzanne Torrès eventually commanded 1,200 medical corps troops. Not all of the women were free to follow the front, and many of those who left the division found themselves staring at the flatline horizon of civilian life with a mixture of dread and relief. They were back home, and home was where they belonged. The problem was that most of them had been changed to a point that they could hardly fit back in their previous roles. They were returning to a society in which women had the same legal status as children. They could not open a bank account, enroll in a university course, or sell property without their husband's permission. They could not vote. Despite their patriotic service, they did not have the rights of full-fledged citizens.

There was a social dimension to their dilemma as well. The Rochambelles had become accustomed to a tremendous amount of personal freedom, even within the confines of a military organization, and an equal amount of responsibility. Returning to civilian life meant scaling back their ambitions and readjusting their sights. It meant, in many small ways, taking a big step backwards. Yet the Rochambelles' experience in the war and the network of friends they made there also became a springboard for new opportunities. Some of the women found jobs through division friends, and others went to work in veterans' services that emerged after the war. All of them said that focusing on work and family helped them adjust.

Jacotte cried for days after returning to Paris, but there was no getting around it. Her father was ill and her mother needed her to come home and help support her two younger sisters. A division officer recommended her to the Ministry of Defense, and she went to work there as a bilingual secretary. She wanted, more than anything, to go to Indochina and continue as a Rochambelle. "We had had an adventurous life, we slept anywhere, ate anything. To return to the fairly rigid framework of office, family, office . . . I thought I was going to be ill having to work in an office," she said. "It was physically difficult."

As partial remedy, Jacotte walked down the Champs-Elysées to the officer's mess for lunch through the grass and weeds rather than on the sidewalk, just to have contact with the natural world. She had been living more or less outdoors for nearly two years, and she felt like an alien next to other civilians. At the same time, she was removed from her friends in the division, from relationships built on daily contact under often terrifying conditions. "Those friendships are totally unique and cannot be understood in civilian life," she said. Her friends were not just the other women drivers, but also the division soldiers. "We represented their family. They had no mothers or sisters around, they had us, Crapette and me," she said. "We went through the same difficulties, we took the same risks. And we took away with us those friendships."

Jacotte worked at the Defense Ministry for eight months, and then transferred to the Organization for Economic Cooperation and Development (OECD), which eventually was assigned to oversee Marshall Plan aid to rebuild Europe. She spent her career there, and rose through the ranks to become secretary to the secretary general. She never married, and neither did her two sisters. She lived with her youngest sister Yvonne, and after Yvonne died, her sister Suzanne moved in with her. In 2005, at the age of ninety-five, Jacotte's health was fragile, and her hearing and vision were fading, but her mind remained as acutely sharp as ever. And she could still do a fine imitation of the sound of an incoming mortar. Whisssstle, thwack!

Danièle Heintz, after recovering from bronchitis, was sent to the First French Army's medical group in Germany in May 1945. There she met her future husband, Jacques Clément, a biologist working as an army pharmacist. They were married in 1952, and went on to have three sons. After returning to France, Danièle earned a degree in nursing, and then worked with her husband in a laboratory. She also studied for and received a law degree, and continued on to doctoral work in law, but did not finish the program. She combined her knowledge in law and medicine by working with biological laboratories, helping them sort out the new postwar rules for analysis and security. She said that the transition to civilian life would have been difficult without her studies to focus on.

Danièle also said she felt that her six months' tour of combat, from the Battle of Caen to the Colmar Pocket, had strengthened her character. "We had to confront fear and exceptional circumstances. That certainly gives a firmness of character and a toughness that one wouldn't have had, otherwise," she said. "It is the kind of experience that if you can do it without falling down, it gives you a resilient character."

At the time, Danièle did not feel her individual existence was of overriding importance. And like many of her generation, she felt her national identity deeply. "Life has no price, no value, without freedom," she said. "It was all the same to me if I died. There was a spirit in that era that does not exist today." Young people have told her she was lucky to have lived during those years, to have experienced the passion and sacrifice of World War II. She responds that they must find their own luck, build their own adventures. She donated her uniform to the World War II Memorial at Caen, where it is displayed with those of British paratroopers and U.S. infantrymen, and titled simply "Uniform of a Rochambelle."

Marie-Thérèse Pezet also left the Rochambelles and went home to Paris to try to return to her normal life. She had been working at the Ministry of Foreign Affairs in 1938 and 1939, and had taken an extended leave of absence when the Vichy government was installed. When she reported back to the ministry's personnel department in January 1946, the personnel director was pleased to inform her that she had just missed the deadline for recouping prewar posts. She told him she had been in the army. "He told me no one had forced me to join," she said. The personnel director had worked under the Vichy regime, and petty revenge was all that was left him. The war was still going on, on certain levels.

Marie-Thérèse joined the Finance Ministry instead, and then, in the ever-shifting sands of the Fourth Republic, worked for various government ministers, finishing her career at the Labor Ministry as chief of staff to the minister. In 1948, she was sent to a meeting at Colmar for the Ministry of Health. General Koenig was there, and placed her at his right to review a military parade of Second Division veterans. Upon learning that she had the citation for the Croix de Guerre, but not the actual medal, he sent for one and pinned it on her himself.

The local prefect noted that if she was with the Leclerc division in the war, then she had been in Alsace. "I said, like all Leclerc's soldiers, I left part of my heart in Alsace," she said. He asked if there was anywhere she would like to visit in the area, and she remembered Ostheim, a village she had driven through many times during the battle for Grussenheim, and had used the same three landmarks to find her way: a church steeple that had been bombed and was half falling off, a tall chimney with a stork's nest, and the body of a dead German in a neighboring field. The prefect took her to Ostheim, and as they rounded the corner, she saw the chimney with the stork's next, and the church steeple being rebuilt, and she suddenly began to cry. The emotion of those intense days only came to the surface long after the fact.

In 1950, Marie-Thérèse married Ivan Tarkoy, a Hungarian diplomat. He had arrived in Paris in 1946 and did not return to his homeland. They managed to get his parents out of Hungary after five years and they also came to Paris and lived with them. They had no children.

One afternoon, Marie-Thérèse was at the Second Division Association House, a restaurant and club for veterans, when a nurse called her over to a table where a group of veterans were sitting. The nurse asked her to speak to one of the veterans. He had been accosting every Rochambelle he met, looking for the one who saved his life. Marie-Thérèse approached the table, facing the soldier in question, and he described how and where he had been wounded. She realized he was the one they had taken to Lunéville against orders, the soldier hemorrhaging so badly they were sure he had died. She was very pleased that he was alive, though she could see that he had lost both arms. He was delighted to find her, thanked her for saving his life, and asked if she would give him a kiss. She came around the table toward him, and as she leaned over, saw that he was sitting in a round buoy-type cushion to hold him up in the wheelchair, as he had no legs. "I almost fainted," she said. "I said to myself, what have I done? Maybe I should have let him die. We disobeyed orders, and who is punished, but him! He was only twenty." The young man seemed happy just to be alive, even in his reduced state. It took her a long time to stop feeling sick at heart over him, and to let go of the guilt. Her job had been to drive an ambulance, not to make judgments on life or death. And she had done her job well enough to earn three citations for bravery, as well as the Military Medal, the Croix de Guerre with palm added for extra valor, and membership in the Legion of Honor.

⊷⊸⊙⊂⊷⊷

Christiane Petit also left the Rochambelles, and worked in social services for veterans for about a year before she married an ex - army officer in 1946. They had three children in four years, and then separated. Christiane and the children moved to the south of France to her parents' home, and she worked at a series of jobs, including that of librarian. With her children grown and her parents gone, she moved back to Paris in the 1960s, and Marie-Thérèse helped her get a job as librarian at the Labor Ministry.

Of her time as a Rochambelle, Christiane kept her Croix de Guerre with palm, her Military Medal, and her pair of brown leather, lace-up army boots. She received the Legion of Honor medal from President François Mitterand at the 1995 ceremony of the fiftieth anniversary of D-Day, the only woman among seven veterans.

"I don't regret anything. It was a marvelous time, it brought me many things," she said. "I prayed a lot for France, and Providence put me on that path. With the things I did with the Second Division, I saw the sign of God. I have always been guided by God." Faith was Christiane's support during the war and has remained so afterward. Faith, along with work, marriage and children, helped her make the transition to civilian life.

⊷⊸⊙⊂⊷⊷

Having a baby also helped Raymonde Brindjonc, who eventually became a mother of three. After the war, she followed her husband around army postings in North Africa, and worked as a secretary for an oil company before returning to France in 1962. She divorced in 1964 and reclaimed her maiden name, Jeanmougin. At a Second Division reunion in Strasbourg, she encountered Rosette Trinquet, now Peschaud, and her husband Philippe, who owned a petroleum transport company. The company offered her a job, and she kept it for twenty years. After retiring, she volunteered to work at the veterans' association headquarters, the Maison de la 2e DB, serving as secretary general since 2003. The veterans' association has been downsized over the years, from a mansion on Rue Grenelle to a two-story building on the Rue de Miromesnil, and most recently to a small office at the Jardin Atlantique, atop the Montparnasse train station. The circle of surviving veterans has been shrinking along with their office space.

Raymonde said that having a baby brought her focus back to the day-to-day existence of civilian life, and that without her role as a mother, she would have found the transition difficult. Among the characteristics she took from her experience as a Rochambelle was a new assertiveness and willingness to take risks. "It allowed me to go full speed ahead. Even if I didn't know what I was doing, I knew I would get by. Maybe I had a little of that in me already, because I signed up [for the division]," she said. "You have to take chances in life."

⊷⊶◉⊷⊶

Zizon Sicco decided not to go on to Indochina because she missed her family. She wanted to go home to Morocco, to her parents. But while waiting for an official discharge from the Army, she was sent to work at the General Staff headquarters in Paris. The Rochambeau Group was officially dissolved in September 1945, but some of its members still were not discharged from the Army.

One day, elegant in her fur coat, Zizon went with two friends to an Army demobilization office in Rambouillet and stood in a long line of men with discharge papers ready to be signed. She and her friends finally arrived in front of a desk where a gaunt young man sat, his clothes too large, one of his hands still and gloved. Zizon asked what happened to him. He said he'd been hit by machine gun fire in both arms and his heart. He had had a lot of nerve damage, among other injuries, and had spent a year in the hospital. One of her friends asked where he'd been wounded, and he said near Badonviller, a village called Fenneviller. The name clicked in Zizon's head, bringing an image of a dying soldier and a doctor telling her she had wasted her time in bringing him to the treatment center. "You didn't die!" she exclaimed.[1] It was the soldier who said that he would never hold the hand of another woman, and he made his claim true by marrying her within the year. Zizon stayed in France after all and became a municipal councilor for the town of Boulogne-Billancourt, a western suburb of Paris, and then assistant to the mayor. She wrote her memoirs on the Ile d'Yeu during the summer of 1956, and her husband, Jacques Bervialle, had them published after she died in 1974. Toto wrote the preface, referring to Zizon as "that intrepid little silhouette."

Like Raymonde, Anne Hastings also declined service in Indochina and instead followed her husband in his work abroad, first to England and then to Saudi Arabia. They had three children, and she was happy to focus on them after the war. She said she didn't think that the war changed her much, but added that her daughters have reminded her that her personal standard for what was a thrill was pretty high.

The Hastings eventually returned to the Cambridge, Massachusetts area and Anne began working with the Harvard University archaeology department, going on digs and writing about the discoveries. She didn't return to her graduate studies after the war because "my heart wasn't in it," she said. She stopped going on excavations when she was about seventy, and her husband fell ill. They moved to Washington, D.C. to be close to one of their daughters, and her husband died in 1999.

Although her war experience was positive, Anne remained unenthusiastic about women in the military. "I was glad we were there, and Leclerc was very nice. We did all right, but I still don't like the idea of women being in the war," she said. "I don't think we did any damage. But I still think it's a little bit complicated to insert women into active combat units. Of course there were people losing their hearts to each other all the time."

Losing their hearts, and committing their lives. The postwar Second Division magazine, *Caravane*, ran an article in January 1949 poking fun at the division as matchmaker. "The Second Division is known all over the world for its qualities and performances that it would be too immodest to list here. But did you know that it also has been a quite brilliant matrimonial agency?" The article went on to list twenty Rochambelle marriages, noting that it was not counting the couples who were already married when they joined the division:[2]

1/ You Courou-Mangin m. Jacques Guerin
2/ Arlette Hautefeuille m. Georges Ratard

3/ Nicole Mangini m. Michel Carage

4/ Michelle "Plumeau" Mirande m. Jean de Rogaisky

5/ Hélène Langé m. Michel Musnier

6/ Michette de Steinheil m. Alain Rodel

7/ Florence Conrad m. Paul Lannusse

8/ Liliane Walter m. Henri Uzan

9/ Anne-Marie Davion m. Jacques Branet

10/ Zizon Sicco m. Jacques Bervialle

Ten marriages resulted from the European campaign. Those who continued on to Indochina carried on the trend. They were:

1/ Edith Schaller m. Lionel Vézy

2/ Jacqueline Lambert de Guise m. Maurice Sarazac

3/ Geneviève Vaudoyer m. Edmund Grail

4/ Yvonne Negre m. Lucien Berne

5/ Sabine de Saint Martin m. François Sanguinetti

6/ Rosette Trinquet m. Philippe Peschaud

7/ Amicie Berne m. Jean Barnaud

8/ Lucette Brochot m. Zonk Brezina

9/ Ghislaine Bechmann m. Alfred Bergamin

10/ Suzanne Torrès m. Jacques Massu

Anne-Marie and Jacques Branet were married in July 1946, three months after her divorce became final. His family became reconciled to the marriage, despite their misgivings. They adopted two children, and their daughter, Marie-Pierre Branet, said in an interview that the Rochambelles were like surrogate aunts to her while growing up. Edith and her daughter, and Michette and her daughter would join Anne-Marie and Marie-Pierre for ski trips in the Alps in winter, and vacations at the Branet's country house in Savoie in the summer. "They were very close and they all loved life," Marie-Pierre said. "I don't know if it was because they had lived through some very tough times. They didn't talk about that, they talked about the good times they had."

Jacques stayed in the army and rose to the rank of general. He died in 1969, and then Anne-Marie died in 1984. It took Marie-Pierre twenty years to finally clean out her clothes and things from their house in Savoie. "I miss them every day," she said.

⊷⇒◉⇐⊷

Rosette went on to Indochina, where she met her husband, Philippe Peschaud. They were married in Rabat in April 1947. Leclerc served as best man at their wedding, and wrote a dedication in a book on the history of the division: "To the cadet Rosette Trinquet, who, after having taken part splendidly in all the operations of the 2e DB in France and in Indochina, wanted to conserve the spirit . . . in choosing a husband!" Rosette said that she had developed such strong arms from driving ambulances that when the seamstress was pinning the sleeves on her wedding gown, she inadvertently flexed her muscle and popped all the pins out.

Seven months later Leclerc was in Algeria, posted to his beloved North Africa again. A plane ride, a sandstorm and a mountain brought his life to an abrupt end. He had already said goodbye to the Second Division, when he left its command at Fontainebleau, on June 22, 1945: "I leave you, but I do not leave behind our division insignia. I will keep it: it will be my finest decoration. I ask you, you also, to keep it. When you find your energy flagging, remind yourselves of Koufra, Alençon, Paris, and Strasbourg. Stay with your comrades, find your leaders, and continue to spread through the country the patriotism which has been our strength." The nation, as well as the division, wept. Leclerc was forty-five years old. Patton preceded him in death, killed in a car accident in Germany in 1945. They were two of a kind, Patton and Leclerc, and neither of them made it to the old soldier fade. If there is an afterlife for stubborn and cantankerous warhorses, they are arguing still.

When the French pulled out of Indochina, the Peschauds returned to Paris. Philippe left the Army and founded his oil transport company. Rosette, after all the years of adventure, was suddenly stranded at home, a wife but not yet a mother, and spent four difficult years trying to find a new footing. Remembering those days of long nothingness wiped the smile off her face. "That was hard," she said. Then came two children, and she got involved in organizing the postwar division's associations and especially the Fondation Maréchal Leclerc de Hauteclocque, formed in 1974, serving as its vice president since 1996. The foundation helped set up a museum about

the Second Division and the Resistance, as well as a research documentation center, and continues to organize seminars and award prizes. For
years, the Rochambelles directed an annual charity sale to benefit veterans' services and a scholarship fund, giving it up only in 2004 when it simply became too much for them to handle. Rosette also has written several
articles for veterans' publications and has spoken regularly at historical
forums about the Rochambelles, keeping the group's reputation alive and
polished.

She noted that a group of army ambulance drivers was formed in 1982
and named itself the Rochambeau Group, after the World War II originals,
making the Rochambelles the first women's unit to begin a tradition in the
French Army. Three of the new Rochambelles served in the Balkans in the
1990s. Rosette said she believed Suzanne Torrès and Florence Conrad
would have been proud to see their project continue in service.

⇢═◉═⇠

Toto and Jacques Massu were married in Paris in 1948. After returning
from Indochina to France, Toto also worked on the postwar organizations,
heading the veterans' association for a year, before following Massu to various army postings abroad. She and Massu had a daughter, and asked Florence Conrad to be her godmother. Conrad, meanwhile, had married
Colonel Paul Lannusse and bought a small chateau at Rouziers-de-
Touraine in the Loire Valley. She died there on July 4, 1966, at the age of
eighty, and was buried in her Rochambelle uniform with full military hon-
ors. For all their shared experiences, Conrad and Toto never had an easy
friendship. Conrad's demands and Toto's temper brought conflict too
quickly to the fore. Still, Toto wrote a laudatory obituary in the veterans'
magazine when Conrad died.

"When I met Florence Conrad in New York in 1945 [sic], she already
had the glow, in many American circles and above all in the French community, of a veritable legend, a legend that, if one looks at the sources, did not
surpass the reality," Toto wrote. "I am certain that tomorrow and long after,
as long as one of our 'young ones' evokes the great moments of her life,
Florence Conrad will dominate the scenario with her unforgettable personality."[3] The young ladies have grown old, and Toto was right: stories about
Florence Conrad are still being told.

In 1969, Toto published her memoir, entitled *Quand j'étais Rocham-belle* (When I was a Rochambelle), the title taken from the song the women used to make up as they went along while peeling vegetables in that desert tent many years before. Toto died in November 1977, and her daughter a year later, both of them struck by different forms of cancer. Massu, retired from the army at the rank of general, remarried and settled in rural village south of Paris. He said in an interview in 2000 that the Rochambelles had earned the devotion of the entire division. "No one ever saw an ambulance driver crack. They were very courageous to the end," he said. "Anyone who had any doubts was quickly reassured." Massu died in October 2002.

Of the fifty-one women who served in the Rochambeau Group in Europe, thirty-six left the group in the summer of 1945, and fifteen went on to Indochina (four new recruits served in Indochina only). In the European campaign, one Rochambelle was killed (Leonora Lindsley), one disappeared (Micheline Grimprel), and six were wounded (Polly Wordsmith, Edith Schaller, Marianne Glaser, Tony Rostand, Lucie Deplancke, and Marie-Thérèse Pezet). Only Polly's injuries were serious enough to end her career as an ambulance driver; the others bandaged themselves up and kept on going.

Among those who went to Indochina, Janine Bocquentin began training as a paratrooper in order to continue as a nurse with her unit there, but when it came time to jump, the army refused to allow women to participate. She went to the Scouts de France, who helped her train, but again, when it came time to jump, the Scouts' insurance company said it had to follow the army's regulations. She and seven other women went to air circuses and exhibitions, and found instructors willing to let them jump without insurance. They got their number of jumps to qualify, and returned to Indochina as paratroopers, working for two months there until the military command discovered that there were women in the unit. Janine was immediately reassigned to a hospital in Saigon. There she met her husband, a Second Division veteran working as a civilian engineer. They were married in 1949 and started on a family that would eventually include eight children. They returned to France from Indochina in 1957.

Janine, a devout Catholic, became involved in helping displaced Algeri-
ans after the war for independence there sent many thousands fleeing to
metropolitan France in the early 1960s. If she had not been a Rochambelle,
she said, she would have gone to Africa as a missionary nurse. She believed
that the war shaped her destiny by putting her in a position to help the Al-
gerians in France. "The war allowed me to reach my dreams," she said.

→→◦⊂→

Edith also went on to Indochina. There, in 1946, she married Lionel Vézy,
a Spahi she had met in France, with Leclerc and Toto as witnesses. Edith
served as director of the Second Division's convalescence center in Saigon
for a year, caring for a ward of sixty to seventy soldiers at a time. Later she
joined her husband on a rubber plantation in Cambodia, where they spent
three years. They adopted a daughter in France and then moved to the
Ivory Coast to run another plantation. Her husband died in 1995.

Edith published her memoir, *"Gargamelle," mon ambulance guerrière 2e
DB* ("Gargamelle," my warrior ambulance of the Second Armored Division), in 1994, because she wanted to record some of the lighter moments
of the war and not dwell on the pain and suffering. In the book, she out-
lined many of Lucie's and her escapades, and noted with pride that she received five citations for bravery and five punishments for disobedience. She
also received the Croix de Guerre with palm, the Military Medal, and is an
officer in the Legion of Honor. At the age of ninety-five, she was working
as a volunteer twice a week in the Documentation Center of the Memorial
de Maréchal Leclerc de Hauteclocque. Age neither slowed her step nor
softened her sass: Edith remained incorrigible through the years.

Did being a Rochambelle change her? She said it cemented her national identity. As a native of Colmar, she was under German rule as a child,
then French as a teenager and young adult, only to watch Alsace become
German again in 1939. "I became very French and very patriotic," she said.

→→◦⊂→

Georges Ratard came to get Arlette in Paris after the liberation of Strasbourg in December 1944, and took her to his mother's house in Brittany,
leaving her with his mother and grandmother, both of whom were con-

vinced that he had married her because she was pregnant. "That annoyed me," she said. The baby (a boy indeed) was born in May, and Georges was posted to Alençon after the war ended. They lived in a wing of a chateau the army had requisitioned, a building with lovely grounds but neither heat nor running water. They took turns washing the baby's diapers in a brook, trading off when their fingers froze up.

Georges went to work for NATO, they had two more sons, and then he retired in 1967 and began teaching Latin in a high school in Les Sables d'Olonne, an Atlantic coast resort town where Arlette had found an apartment. They built their own house on a sand dune, and watched development spring up around them. By the end of the century, there were thirty or so division veterans living in the area and meeting for lunch once a month. Having shared the experience of war was the foundation of solid friendship, Arlette said. "We have good memories, of camaraderie, of having had the courage to do it," she said. "War isn't pretty, when you see the burned-out tanks, the swollen animals in the fields. If I saw it today it would make me sick. But at the time, we didn't think about it." She believed the soldiers were pleased to have women taking care of them if they were suffering or in pain. "They all said the women were more like their mothers, for consoling them, for taking care of them, it's better than a man," she said. "Picked up by a Rochambelle, you had a more maternal hand."

Into her eighties, Arlette traveled every year to visit her youngest son in Brazil, where he ran a small hotel in a coastal village, and bodysurf in the warm south Atlantic waters. She also stayed close to Rosette, who regularly invited several of her old comrades to her vacation home in Corsica, and to Lucie, who came to see her and Georges often at Sables d'Olonne. She frequently found little notes Lucie wrote in books she gave her, all to "Marlette," short for Mon Arlette. "Lucie was the definition of joy. She was radiant," Arlette said. "I miss her the most."

Lucie died in August 1985. The decade of the 1980s took Denise Colin (1980), Marie-Anne Duvernet (1985), Crapette Demay (1987) and Suzanne Evrard (1988) as well. 'You' Guerin died in 2000 and Tony Rostand followed in 2001. As of March 2006, there were sixteen surviving Rochambelles who served in the European campaign, some of them ill, others enjoying good health. The youngest of them was eighty-two, the eldest ninety-five. Each of them had received the Military Medal, an honor reserved for soldiers and not for officers, and most of them had won the Croix de Guerre, with palms added for extra valor. They kept their medals wrapped in tissue paper and tucked away in desk drawers, along with fading photographs and occasional souvenirs of the war.

⊷⊷⊙⊷⊷

France hurried to remember its heroes of the war, and nearly every town or city has an Avenue du Général Leclerc. Two towns have seen fit to honor the Rochambelles. Vendôme, 200 kilometers southwest of Paris and birthplace of the revolutionary era Comte de Rochambeau, named a major traffic circle Carrefour des Rochambelles in May 1984. Then in September 2002, Argentan, the Normandy town that slipped through the division's fingers back into German hands and then finally was liberated by the Americans in August 1944, honored the women with a Square des Rochambelles. Assistant Mayor Marie-Joseph Pierre said that town officials in Argentan thought the Rochambelles' story was fascinating and wanted to do something for them. The officials found a square near the entrance of town that would bear their name, and even if it becomes the inevitable traffic circle in a few years, it will be called the Rond Point des Rochambelles. The town also put up a plaque honoring the memory of Micheline Grimprel, who disappeared forever on the road to Argentan. Edith and Rosette drove out from Paris for the dedication ceremony.

Along the coast of Normandy, officials have organized a Marathon for Liberty around the annual D-Day anniversary celebrations, and in 2001, began a women's race called the Rochambelle. A thousand women ran its 8.6 kilometers in 2004, launched by a starter gun fired by Edith. (Finally, in Normandy, she got to shoot back.)

The sixtieth anniversary of the war was commemorated in 2004 and 2005, the last big celebration for many of the veterans. Six Rochambelles participated in the ceremony on August 25, 2004, the anniversary of the liberation of Paris, where Rosette was promoted to Grand Officer of the National Order of Merit for her work with the Leclerc Foundation. French President Jacques Chirac pinned the Grand Croix on her chest, but she moved it to her lower jacket pocket. There wasn't room for it among the other medals she won for her work during the war. A chill wind swept across the Place de la Concorde that morning, but the veterans—both men and women—stood as straight as they had sixty years before, steeped in the pride and honor of having been there when it counted. The Rochambelles had opened the door to women as integrated members of an army and not simply as auxiliaries, set apart and removed from possible danger. They had worked at the front, under the worst of conditions and through the deadliest of wars. They did so despite initial opposition and hostility, and they earned the admiration and respect of their fellow soldiers. The women also found out about themselves, about how far they could reach and how tall they could stand. The personal limits and social roles they had been born into were stretched out of all imagination.

The passage of time has only heightened their achievements. Today the Rochambelles' youth has been confided to history and their beauty rests in fragile bones, but their hearts remain those of the spirited young women who drove off, so long ago, to help free their country.

Toto's Rules of Rochambelle Order

What one must do, not do, and had better know about

Suzanne Torrès wrote this shortly after the war and left the undated manuscript amongst her papers when she died. Her husband, Jacques Massu, sent it to Rosette and Philippe Peschaud. It gives an idea of the sense of humor and inside jokes that developed amongst the Rochambelles.

1. Never speak of "one's battle."

2. The words "mine" and "my" are unknown. Example: Say "our" toothbrush.

3. The 501st is the only tank regiment in the world.

4. The medical battalion should be mentioned only when absolutely necessary.

5. Never forget that you are not on a cruise and that you are not part of the Russian Ballet.

6. Never receive a male visitor dressed in less than a Serge Lifar [Army-issue long underwear].

7. A salute to officers, when one is without a cap, will be done in turning the head toward the officer and not in the other direction. [Regulations called for headcover when saluting an officer.]

8. The G.T.V. fights three times more than the other tactical groups. [The G.T.V. was the Group Tactique Warabiot, the unit to which the Rochambelles were attached.]

9. Never give a light vehicle to an engineering battalion.

10. Since the Third Regiment of the March of Chad began "romping" around, the Second Regiment of the March of Chad is definitely looking better. Don't lose hope that the Second RMT will soon be attached to the G.T.V. [She used the word "barbotte," which was a play on the commander's name, Barboteu. Her then-boyfriend, Jacques Massu, was the Second RMT commander.]

11. The greatest danger in operations is comparative architecture.

12. Before throwing the furniture out the window, make sure none of your buddies is in the street and that there is enough flame-starter.

13. Do not marry except within the division and with those who joined before Paris.

14. Never ask, when in convoy: "When are we leaving?" Nor in cantonment, "How long are we here for?"

15. The word "Houseboat" is written with a capital 'H.'

16. No candidacies for the Archi-pures will be accepted. The mold has been broken. [The Archi-pures were those who formed the original group in New York.]

17. Any unannounced arrival of more than two Red Berets [Spahis] should be signaled urgently to the brass so that adequate measures may be taken. [The Spahis were notable flirts.]

18. When the commanding colonel of the G.T.V. is present, avoid running into ditches.

19. The helmet is exclusively reserved for foot baths.

20. The song, "To the fields, my companions," is in bad taste; please abstain.

21. If you sleep in the lieutenant's bedroll, take off your shoes.

22. Do not respond to inspectors that a rear chassis needs an oil change every three days.

23. Avoid sticking out your tongue at doctors wearing lots of stripes.

24. Avoid taking General Leclerc for the subordinate of supply.

25. Don't lose more than one clothing kit per week.

26. When leaving the group to get married, take your parasites with you.

27. When going to shower, do not fear the process of de-licing.

28. After getting the tank filled with gas by a prisoner, be sure the lieutenant doesn't see you thanking him with a kick in the ass.

29. When you slap an American, give him a second slap to make sure he understood that you aren't happy.

30. Raising turtles is allowed, but not in the bedroll of your partner.

31. When going out without permission, try not to go to the same restaurant as the captain.

32. When commanding the drill, avoid calling for "Heads left!" when the colonel is on the right.

33. On nights of bombings, if wearing a G-string and bra to run across the field, at least put on the double-helmet. [A reference to Zizon Sicco at Ducey.]

34. Know how to spend a few hours with the Germans without deserving to have your head shaved. [A reference to Edith Schaller at Argentan.]

35. Don't smoke a pipe except in very small groups.

36. Don't drink Schnapps before 8:00 in the morning.

37. In wrestling matches with the G.T.V. officers, don't knock out more than twelve a day, in case of possible operations the next day. [A reference to Madeleine Collomb having accidentally broken a doctor's finger while mock-wrestling with him.]

38. Avoid telling your life story to Captain Renaud. [Captain Renaud was the head mechanic, and every time a Rochambelle came in for a repair on her ambulance, he snapped, "Don't tell me your life story!"]

39. Don't strike a match if certain commanders are within ten meters. [Danger of alcohol-induced flambée.]

40. Take care of your ambulance: try not to destroy it twice in three days, and avoid backing up over mines. [A reference to Edith Schaller and Lucie Deplancke in Lorraine.]

41. When sent temporarily to another unit, do not insist on wearing that regiment's headgear when the lieutenant is patrolling nearby. [Christiane Petit wore the Spahis' red cap a little more often than Toto thought she should.]

42. Avoid hand kissers in general. Avoid them particularly when one has 2 centimeters of truck grease under her nails or has had onion-peeling duty.

43. When six Rochambelles sleep in the same bed, if there is a cadet in the group, it is at her command when one sleeps and the order in which one turns over. In the absence of an officer, seniority rules.

44. When speaking of the eighteenth century, never refer to Madame Pompadour. [A reference to Zizon Sicco and Captain Ceccaldi.]

45. When going on leave in a car requisitioned by the Captain, do not trade it on the black market to pay for his whisky.

46. Volunteers for Indochina will be received within forty-eight hours of their arrival in the Rochambeau Group, and will be accepted only after six months have passed.

47. From the moment a new village is taken, carry out a census on the number of pickle pots hidden in cellars (start with the village priest).

48. Never believe news announced by Captain Delrue. [He was handsome but unreliable.]

49. Do not imagine, when in convoy, that the Traffic Control Unit is only in charge of keeping you furnished with candy and cigarettes and keeping you awake at the wheel. They are also there to direct traffic.

50. When one sees the General nearby, in operations, do your best to warn the lieutenant, so she can get her ass out of the way of his walking stick. [Toto got poked in Normandy for blocking a convoy and whacked at Châtel when she stopped on a bridge to ask directions.]

APPENDIX II

Timeline of Events

Early 1941	Florence Conrad returns to New York
May 1943	Conrad begins recruiting ambulance drivers
July 1943	Rochambeau Group accepted as part of Free French
September 1943	Rochambeau Group leaves New York for Casablanca
October 1943	Rochambeau Group accepted into Second Armored Division
March 2, 1944	"You" Courou-Mangin marries Jacques Guerin
April 11, 1944	Division moves to Assi Ben Okba
May 20, 1944	Division sails for England
July 30, 1944	Division crosses English Channel to France
August 1, 1944	Rochambeau Group lands in Normandy
August 6, 1944	Rochambeau Group bombed at Ducey

August 8–18, 1944	Battle of Normandy: from Avranches to Argentan
August 13, 1944	Micheline Grimprel disappears
August 22–24, 1944	Division rolls toward Paris
August 25, 1944	Liberation of Paris
August 27, 1944	Arlette Hautefeuille marries Georges Ratard
September 8, 1944	Division leaves Paris, eastward bound
September 12, 1944	Fighting at Andelot and Dompaire
September 15, 1944	Taking Châtel-sur-Moselle
September 18, 1944	Division crosses the Moselle River
End of September	Rochambelles bivouac at Roville-aux-Chênes
October 30, 1944	Division takes Baccarat
November 17, 1944	Division attack on Badonviller
November 21, 1944	Division crosses Vosges Mountains
November 23, 1944	Liberation of Strasbourg
November 27–December 6, 1944	Fighting around Erstein and Herbsheim
December 20–31, 1944	Jacotte and Crapette spend Christmas in the Witternheim cellar
January 2, 1945	Division goes to Lorraine as backup for the Battle of the Bulge

January 20, 1945	Division returns to Alsace, fighting begins for Colmar Pocket
January 25, 1945	Attack at Carrefour 177
January 27–28, 1945	Battle for Grussenheim
February 1, 1945	Fighting at Marckolsheim pushes Germans across Rhine
February 9, 1945	Alsace liberated of all German troops
Mid-February to mid-April 1945	Division on rest-and-recovery in the Loire Valley
April 25, 1945	Division deployed to Germany
May 5, 1945	Division enters Berchtesgaden
May 8, 1945	Official surrender of Germany

Notes

Introduction

1. Linda Grant De Pauw, *Battle Cries and Lullabies, Women in War from Prehistory to the Present*, (Norman, University of Oklahoma Press, 1998), p. 151.
2. *Washington Post*, 13 May 2005, "For Female GIs, Combat is a Fact," by Ann Scott Tyson.

Chapter 1

1. Florence Conrad, *Camarades de Combat* (New York, Brentano's, 1942), p. 12.
2. Ibid., pp. 10–13.
3. Ibid., p. 75.
4. Ibid., p. 143.
5. Ibid., pp. 152–53.
6. Ibid., p. 191.
7. Ibid., p. 199.
8. Ibid., pp. 327–28.
9. François Bertin, *Les Véhicules Américaines de la Libèration* (Rennes, Editions Ouest-France, 1989), pp. 41–43.
10. Suzanne Massu, *Quand j'étais Rochambelle* (Paris, Editions Bernard Grasset, 1969, 2000), pp. 11–12.
11. Ibid., p. 20–21.
12. Jacqueline Fournier, *Souvenirs d'une ambulancière de la 2e DB* (Paris, unpublished, 1993), pp. 12–16.
13. Ibid., p. 6.
14. Ibid., p. 6.

Chapter 2

1. Christian Girard, *Journal de Guerre 1939–1945* (Paris, L'Harmattan, 2001), p. 112.
2. Ibid., p. 105.
3. Suzanne Massu, *Quand j'étais Rochambelle* (Paris, Editions Bernard Grasset, 1969), pp. 78–79.
4. Zizon Bervialle, *Au Volant de Madeleine-Bastille* (Paris, Caravane, 1975) p. 11.
5. Marie-Gabrielle Copin-Barrier, *Marguerite ou la vie d'une Rochambelle* (Paris, Editions L'Harmattan, 2001), pp. 109–113.
6. Jacqueline Fournier, *Souvenirs d'une ambulancière de la 2e DB* (Paris, unpublished, 1993), p. 26.
7. Edith Vézy, *"Gargamelle," mon ambulance guerrière de la 2e DB* (Paris, Editions L'Harmattan, 1994), p. 22.
8. Jacques de Witasse, *L'Odysée de la 2ème Compagnie de Chars* (Lyon, Editions Lyonnaises d'Art et d'Histoire, 1990), p. 78.
9. Jacques Branet, *L'Escadron. Carnets d'un Cavalier* (Paris, Flammarion, 1968), p. 167.
10. Copin-Barrier, *Marguerite, ou la vie d'une Rochambelle*, p. 127, 181.
11. Bervialle, *Au Volant de Madeleine-Bastille*, p. 29.
12. Paul de Langlade, *En Suivant Leclerc* (Paris, Au Fil d'Ariane, 1964), p. 110.
13. de Witasse, *L'Odysée de la 2ème Compagnie de Chars*, p. 165.
14. de Langlade, *En Suivant Leclerc*, p. 111.

Chapter 3

1. Jacqueline Fournier, *Souvenirs d'une ambulancière de la 2e DB* (Paris, unpublished, 1993), p. 47.
2. Christian Girard, *Journal de Guerre, 1939–1945* (Paris, Editions L'Harmattan, 2001), p. 249.
3. Zizon Bervialle, *Au Volant de Madeleine-Bastille* (Paris, Caravane, 1975), p. 38.
4. Ibid., p. 40.
5. Martin Blumenson, *The Patton Papers, 1940–1945* (New York, Da Capo Press, 1996), p. 517.

6. Jacques de Witasse, *L'Odysée de la 2ème Compagnie de Chars* (Lyon, Editions Lyonnaises d'Art et d'Histoire, 1990) p. 127.

7. John Keegan, *Six Armies in Normandy. From D-Day to the Liberation of Paris* (New York, Penguin Books, 1983), pp. 257–259.

8. Edith Vézy, *"Gargamelle" Mon ambulance guerrière 2e DB* (Paris, Editions L'Harmattan, 1994), p. 48.

9. Ibid., p. 50.

10. Ibid., p. 51–53.

11. Marie-Madeleine Fourcade, *L'Arche de Noë* (Paris, Fayard, 1968), pp. 559–560.

12. Bervialle, *Au Volant de Madeleine-Bastille*, p. 43.

13. Ibid., pp. 46–47.

14. Ibid., pp. 51–55.

15. Ibid., p. 49.

16. Fournier, *Souvenirs d'une ambulancière de la 2e DB.*

17. Bervialle, *Au Volant de Madeleine-Bastille*, p.73.

18. Ibid., *Au Volant de Madeleine-Bastille*, p. 88.

19. Jean Compagnon, *La bataille de Normandie* (La Guerche-de-Bretagne, Secalib, 1985).

20. Ibid.

21. Suzanne Massu, *Quand j'étais Rochambelle* (Paris, Editions Bernard Grasset, 1969), p. 142.

22. Blumenson, *The Patton Papers, 1940–1945*, p. 511.

23. Girard, *Journal de Guerre, 1939–1945*, p. 275.

24. Bervialle, *Au Volant de Madeleine-Bastille*, p. 74.

Chapter 4

1. Adrien Dansette, *Histoire de la Libération de Paris* (Paris, Perrin, 1994), pp. 135–39.

2. Ibid., p. 22.

3. Jacques de Witasse, *L'Odysée de la 2ème Compagnie de Chars* (Lyon, Editions Lyonnaises d'Art et d'Histoire, 1990), p. 170.

4. Alain Eymard, *Le 2e DB. 1er Août 1944–8 Mai 1945* (La Londe: Editions Heimdal, 1990).

5. Jacqueline Fournier, *Souvenirs d'une ambulancière de la 2e DB* (Paris, unpublished, 1993), p. 67.

6. Dansette, *Histoire de la Libération de Paris*, pp. 392–94.

7. Robert Aron, "L'Heure des Justiciers des Maquis est Arrivée," in *Les Années 40*, no. 70, p. 1933.

8. Adolphe Vezinet, *Le Général Leclerc de Hauteclocque, Maréchal de France* (Paris, Presses de la Cité, 1974), p. 147.

9. Zizon Bervialle, *Au Volant de Madeleine-Bastille* (Paris, Caravane, 1970), p. 81.

10. Ibid., pp. 82–83.

11. Vézy, *"Gargamelle," mon ambulance guerrière 2e DB* (Paris, Editions L'Harmattan, 1994), pp. 70–73.

12. Ibid., pp. 78–79.

13. Rosette Peschaud, "Témoignage" in *Espoir, Revue de la Fondation et de l'Institut Charles de Gaulle*, no. 107, June 1996, p. 98.

14. Dansette, *Histoire de la Libération de Paris;* Willis Thornton, *The Liberation of Paris* (New York, Harcourt Brace & World, 1962).

15. Henri Amouroux, *La grand histoire des français sous l'occupation. Vol. 8, Joies et douleurs du peuple libéré* (Editions Robert Laffont, Paris, 1985), p. 338.

16. John Keegan, *Six Armies in Normandy. From D-Day to the Liberation of Paris* (New York, Penguin Books, 1983), p. 188.

Chapter 5

1. Edith Vézy, *"Gargamelle," mon ambulance guerrière 2e DB* (Paris, Editions L'Harmattan, 1994), pp. 84–85.

2. Christian Girard, *Journal de Guerre, 1939–1945* (Paris, Editions L'Harmattan, 2001), p. 285.

3. Ibid., p. 289.

4. Jacques Branet, *L'Escadron: Carnets d'un Cavalier* (Paris, Flammarion, 1968), p. 197.

5. Sayer, Nancy, *Témoignage dans le Silence: Un Regard sur la Vie de Pierre Sayer* (Paris, self-published, 2000).

6. Vézy, *"Gargamelle," mon ambulance guerrière 2e DB*, p.96.

7. Jacques de Witasse, *L'Odysée de la 2ème Compagnie de Chars* (Lyon, Editions Lyonnaises d'Art et d'Histoire, 1990), pp. 210–11.

8. Ibid., p. 223.

9. Ibid., p. 211.

10. Martin Blumenson, *The Patton Papers, 1940–1945* (New York, Da Capo Press, 1996), pp. 530–31.

11. de Witasse, *L'Odysée de la 2ème Compagnie de Chars*, p. 211.

12. Blumenson, *The Patton Papers, 1940–1945*, pp. 549, 552.

13. Vézy, "*Gargamelle, " mon ambulance guerrière 2e DB*, p. 108.

14. Raymond Fischer, *325 Jours avec les Spahis de Leclerc* (Issy-les-Moulineaux, Muller Edition, 1999), p. 119.

15. Vézy, "*Gargamelle, " mon ambulance guerrière 2e DB*, p. 109.

16. Zizon Bervialle, *Au Volant de Madeleine-Bastille* (Paris, Caravane, 1975), p. 101.

17. de Witasse, *L'Odysée de la 2ème Compagnie de Chars*, p. 262.

18. Blumenson, *The Patton Papers, 1940–1945*, p. 552.

Chapter 6

1. Jacques de Witasse, *L'Odysée de la 2ème Compagnie de Chars* (Lyon: Editions Lyonnaises d'Art et d'Histoire, 1990), p. 290.

2. Edith Vézy, "*Gargamelle," mon ambulance guerrière 2e DB* (Paris, Editions L'Harmattan, 1994), p. 123.

3. Ibid., p.127.

4. Ibid., p. 128.

5. Suzanne Massu, *Quand j'étais Rochambelle* (Paris, Editions Bernard Grasset, 1969), p. 222.

6. Vézy, "*Gargamelle," mon ambulance guerrière 2e DB*, pp. 132–33.

7. Christian Girard, *Journal de Guerre, 1939–1945* (Paris, Editions L'Harmattan, 2001), p. 307.

8. Ibid., p. 326.

9. Vézy, "*Gargamelle," mon ambulance guerrière 2e DB*, p.138.

10. Ibid., pp. 141–43.

11. Ibid., pp. 154–56.

12. de Witasse, *L'Odysée de la 2ème Compagnie de Chars*, p. 226.

Chapter 7

1. Jacques de Witasse, *L'Odysée de la 2ème Compagnie de Chars* (Lyon, Editions Lyonnaises d'Art et d'Histoire, 1990), p. 329.

2. Vézy, "*Gargamelle," mon ambulance guerrière 2e DB* (Paris, Editions L'Harmattan, 1994) p. 171–72.

3. de Witasse, *L'Odysée de la 2ème Compagnie de Chars*, p. 332.

4. Ibid., p. 327.

Chapter 8

1. Suzanne Massu, *Quand j'étais Rochambelle* (Paris, Editions Bernard Grasset, 1969), pp. 252–53.
2. Jacques de Guillebon, "La Legendaire 2e DB sur le Front," in *Les Années 40 no. 65.*

Epilogue

1. Zizon Bervialle, *Au Volant de Madeleine-Bastille* (Paris, Caravane, 1975), p. 125.
2. "Le 2e DB Agence Matrimoniale,"in *Caravane*, January 1949.
3. "Florence Conrad," in *Caravane*, no. 265, August 1966.

Bibliography

Amouroux, Henri. *La grand histoire des français sous l'occupation. Vol. 7, Un printemps de mort et d'espoir, Novembre 1943–6 Juin 1944*. Paris: Editions Robert Laffont, 1985.

___. *Vol. 8, Joies et douleurs du peuple libéré*, Paris: Editions Robert Laffont, 1988.

Annuaire des Anciens Combattants de la 2e D.B. Published 1949 by the Association des Anciens Combattants de la Division Leclerc.

Aron, Robert. *Histoire de la Libération de la France*. Paris: Librairie Arthème Fayard, 1959.

___. "L'Heure des Justiciers des Maquis est Arrivée," in *Les Années 40* magazine, no. 70, directors Henri Amouroux and Christian Melchior-Bonnet, Paris, co-publishers Librairie Jules Tallandier and Hachette.

Bertin, François. *Les Véhicules Américaines de la Libèration*. Rennes: Editions Ouest-France, 1989.

Bervialle, Zizon. *Au Volant de Madeleine-Bastille*. Paris: Caravane, 1975.

Billotte, Pierre. *Le Temps des Armes*. Paris: Plon, 1972.

Blumenson, Martin. *The Patton Papers, 1940–1945*. New York: Da Capo Press, 1996.

Branet, Jacques. *L'Escadron. Carnets d'un Cavalier. Paris:* Flammarion, 1968.

Cardinal, Agnès, Dorothy Goldman, and Judith Hattaway, eds., *Women's Writing on the First World War*, Oxford and New York: Oxford University Press, 1999.

Compagnon, Jean. *La bataille de Normandie*, La Guerche-de-Bretagne: Secalib, 1985.

___. "*Paris en Ligne de Mire*," in *Armées d'Aujourd'hui*, no. 190, May 1994, 50th anniversary edition.

Conrad, Florence. *Camarades de Combat*. New York: Brentano's, 1942.

Copin-Barrier, Marie-Gabrielle. *Marguerite ou la vie d'une Rochambelle*. Paris: Editions L'Harmattan, 2001.

Dansette, Adrien. *Histoire de la Libération de Paris*. Paris: Perrin, 1994.

De Pauw, Linda Grant. *Battle Cries and Lullabies, Women in War from Prehistory to the Present.* Norman: University of Oklahoma Press, 1998.

Le Deuxième DB, Général Leclerc, Combattants et Combats en France. Editions Arts et Métiers Graphiques, Paris, 1945. Published by the division.

Doppfer, Anne. "Under Two Flags, Des volontaires américaines en Picardie," *in Des Américaines en Picardie.* Péronne: Conseil General de la Somme, 2002.

Dronne, Raymond. *Carnets de Route d'un Croisé de la France Libre.* Paris: Editions France-Empire, 1984.

Eymard, Alain. *Le 2e DB (1er Août 1944–8 Mai 1945).* La Londe: Editions Heimdal, 1990.

Fischer, Raymond. *325 Jours avec les Spahis de Leclerc.* Issy-les-Moulineaux: Muller Edition, 1999.

Fenner, Lorry M. and Marie E. deYoung. *Women in Combat. Civic Duty or Military Liability?.* Washington, D.C. : Georgetown University Press, 2001.

Fourcade, Marie-Madeleine. *L'Arche de Noë.* Paris: Fayard, 1968.

Fournier, Jacqueline. *Souvenirs d'une ambulancière de la 2e DB.* Paris: unpublished, 1993.

Francos, Ania. *Il était des femmes dans la Résistance.* Paris: Editions Stock, 1978.

Girard, Christian. *Journal de Guerre, 1939–1945,* Paris: Editions L'Harmattan, 2001.

de Guillebon, Jacques. "La Légendaire 2*e* D.B. sur le Front," in *Les Années 40* magazine, no. 65, directors Henri Amouroux and Christian Melchior-Bonnet, Paris: co-publishers Librairie Jules Tallandier and Hachette.

Heitzler-Gerig, Jeanne. *Souvenirs de Grussenheim. La Défense de Strasbourg et la Libération de la poche de Colmar nord.* Self published, third edition, 1989.

Jacob, François. *La Statue Interieure.* Paris: Editions Corps 16, 1993.

Keegan, John. *Six Armies in Normandy. From D-Day to the Liberation of Paris.* New York: Penguin Books, 1983.

___. *The Second World War.* New York: Viking Penguin, 1990.

de Langlade, Paul. *En Suivant Leclerc.* Paris: Au Fil d'Ariane, 1964.

Lapierre, Dominique and Larry Collins. *Paris brûle-t-il ?* Paris: Editions Robert Laffont, 1964.

Massu, Suzanne, *Quand j'étais Rochambelle,* Paris: Editions Bernard Grasset, 1969, 2000.

Morin-Rotureau, Evelyne, ed., *1939–1945: Combats de femmes, Françaises et Allemandes, les oubliées de la guerre*. Paris: Collections Mémoires, Editions Autrement, 2001.

Nora, Pierre, ed., *Les Lieux de Mémoire, Vol. 1*. Paris: Gallimard, 1997.

Oriol-Maloine, Albert. *Les Femmes en Guerre. Les Oubliées de l'Histoire, 1939–1945*. Amiens: Martelle Editions, 1995.

Parthenay-Charbonnel, Gilberte A. *Où est Scarabée?*, Le Croisic: self published, 1989.

Pittino, Hubert. *La 2ème Division Blindée dans la Poche de Colmar*. Self published, 1984.

Poulos, Paula Nassen, ed. *A Woman's War Too. U.S. Women in the Military in World War II*. Washington, D.C.: National Archives and Records Administration, 1996.

Riff, Georges. *Combats de Libération. Le Sous-Groupement Massu de la 2ᵉ DB dans la charge de Strasbourg, 19–23 novembre 1944*, Saverne: Imprimerie et Edition Savernoise, 1946.

Sayer, Nancy. *Témoignage dans le Silence. Un Regard sur la Vie de Pierre Sayer*. Paris: self published, 2000.

Smith, Paul. *Feminism and the Third Republic, Women's Political and Civil Rights in France, 1918–1945*. Oxford: Clarendon Press, 1996.

Thornton, Willis. *The Liberation of Paris*. New York: Harcourt Brace & World, Inc., 1962.

Vagliano-Eloy, Sonia. *Les Demoiselles de Gaulle 1943–45*. Paris: Plon, 1982.

Vézinet, Adolphe, *Le Général Leclerc de Hauteclocque, Maréchal de France*. Paris: Presses de la Cité, 1974.

Vézy, Edith, *"Gargamelle," mon ambulance guerrière 2e DB*, Paris: Editions L'Harmattan, 1994.

Weitz, Margaret Collins. *Sisters in the Resistance. How Women Fought to Free France, 1940–1945*. New York: John Wiley and Sons, 1995. French edition: *Les Combattantes de l'Ombre. Histoire des femmes dans la Résistance*. Paris: Albin Michel, 1997.

de Witasse, Jacques. *L'Odysée de la 2ème Compagnie de Chars*. Lyon: Editions Lyonnaises d'Art et d'Histoire, 1990.

Index